Searching & ReSearching

on the internet and the world wide web

Fifth Edition

Karen Hartman

Ernest Ackermann

FRANKLIN, BEEDLE & ASSOCIATES
22462 SW WASHINGTON ST.
SHERWOOD, OR 97140
WWW.FBEEDLE.COM

Dedication

To Jack, Tracy, and Hilary

—K. H.

To my family—Lynn, Karl, and Oliver—and to the
memory of my parents,
   Henry Ackermann (1904 – 1977)
   Marie Ackermann (1914 – 1997)
always encouraging, always loving.

—E. A.

Publisher   Jim Leisy (jimleisy@fbeedle.com)
Production Editor   Tom Sumner
Associate   Jaron Ayres

Printed in the United States of America

Library of Congress Cataloging-In-Publication data

Hartman, Karen (Karen P.)
  Searching and researching on the Internet and the World Wide Web / Karen Hartman, Ernest Ackermann. -- 5th ed.
     p. cm.
  Rev. ed. of: Searching & researching on the Internet & the World Wide Web. 4th ed. c2005.
  ISBN 978-1-59028-242-7
  1. Internet searching. 2. Internet searching--Problems, exercises, etc. 3. Web search engines. 4. Web search engines--
Problems, exercises, etc. 5. Internet research. 6. Internet research--Problems, exercises, etc. I. Ackermann, Ernest C. II.
Hartman, Karen (Karen P.). Searching & researching on the Internet & the World Wide Web. III. Title.
  ZA4201.A25 2010
  025.04--dc22
                          2010013950

contents

preface

Searching and Researching on the Internet and the World Wide Web, Fifth Edition provides a straightforward and accessible approach to finding information on the World Wide Web and the Internet. It is primarily designed for students in college-level courses or for self-study. The topics address the research needs of students in a broad range of disciplines, as well as college-level instructors, researchers, prospective and in-service K–12 teachers, librarians, and others interested in tapping the Web and the Internet for information. It also serves as a guide to the appropriate methods to acquire, evaluate, and cite resources. It addresses the needs of people with experience working with the Web and those who are first learning.

Certain assumptions are made about the reader of this book. We expect the reader to be acquainted with the fundamental operations of a personal computer, particularly the ability to launch and use applications software. Access to the Internet is equally important to successfully completing the activities and exercises.

Important Features of the Book

In the course of this book, you'll learn how to find answers to research and reference questions; how to find maps, images, and podcasts; and how to use social media tools. We discuss several different types of information resources, including directories, search engines, and specialized databases. The main topics are formulating search strategies, understanding how to form search expressions, evaluating information, and citing resources. We carry these themes throughout the book. The 10-step search strategy developed in Chapter 6, for example, is applied to activities and exercises in many of the subsequent chapters. This strategy, combined with the numerous activities throughout the book, provides a variety of techniques and concepts that are useful to the beginner and the more advanced researcher alike. As you work through the activities and projects, you'll come to understand that for every research question you ask there is a process of creating the most appropriate search strategy. You also need to decide whether to use a directory, search engine, or other type of resource. You'll see that this search formation process guarantees more precise results and is applicable to any search engine or database.

The step-by-step activities were developed using Mozilla Firefox. You'll find, however, that the essential search skills, the ways to determine which types of resources to use, and the ways to evaluate and cite resources that we cover in the book depend very little on the specific Web browser and computer system you use. After reading the text and working through the activities you'll be better prepared to effectively find what you need, determine the appropriate tools and resources to use, and evaluate what you have found.

Using the World Wide Web for Research

The Internet and the World Wide Web have had a profound effect on the way we find information and do research. Part of this is due to the astounding increase in the amount of information available and the tools we have at our disposal for finding it. The information explosion raises a number of important issues. We need to know how to search the Web *effectively*. Sometimes we may get frustrated with the Internet because there appears to be too much extraneous information, yet we are eager to get as much good information as we can. We need to know how the different search engines are constructed so that as new search engines appear we will have developed the skills to search any database. We also need to know when a search engine isn't the most appropriate resource to use. In some cases, we'll want to use a directory or a specialized database. With all the information making up the Web, we also need to know how to evaluate sources we find. In addition to these issues, we also need to keep in mind the ethical issues surrounding Internet use. This includes understanding copyright and citing Web research properly in a paper or project.

Organization and Content

Throughout the book we emphasize using the resources and tools on the Internet and the Web for searching and researching effectively. We discuss some technical details of how the resources are organized and how the tools do their work, but always within the context of getting more precise results. This emphasis, combined with the numerous step-by-step activities throughout the book, gives what we feel is a good blend of techniques and concepts that are beneficial to learners.

The arrangement of the chapters lays out a specific path through the material. The book is organized as follows:

> **Chapters 1 and 2** Introduction to the Internet and the Web; overview of research skills and tools on the Web
>
> **Chapter 3** Evaluating information found on the Web
>
> **Chapter 4** Managing information found using social bookmarking sites and other citation management tools; how to cite information properly
>
> **Chapters 5, 6, 7 and 8** Search strategies and tools—directories, search engines, meta-search tools, specialized databases, blogs, and library catalogs
>
> **Chapter 9** Searching for multimedia, including images and podcasts
>
> **Chapter 10** Working together by sharing information using social media and other Web 2.0 tools.
>
> **Appendix** Learning about privacy and security on the Internet and Web

We start with an introduction to the Internet and the Web, covering the essentials of using a browser and some other technical details. We then move to using the Web for research, where we introduce a number of fundamental concepts and tactics for finding information on the Web. Evaluating resources is considered next. From there we move to how to manage and cite resources in the context of a research paper or other project. Following this we cover how to find resources in directories, including a topical list of important and useful Web sites, "A Researcher's Toolkit."

Next we cover developing a search strategy, constructing search expressions, and using the common features of various search engines and other searchable databases. This is followed by numerous examples using search engines and how to use specialized databases. A chapter devoted to searching for news includes an overview of blogs, microblogs such as Twitter, Really Simple Syndication (RSS) technology, and more. Finally, we cover how to collaborate and learn from one another using the Web to share our ideas and research with others via social media resources such as wikis, social networking, document sharing, and the open access movement. The appendix addresses some of the privacy and security issues related to using the Internet and the Web.

Each of the chapters contains at least one step-by-step activity that demonstrates fundamental skills and concepts. By following the activities and trying them out, readers gain firsthand, guided experience. Including these activities is a bit of a risk because of the dynamic nature of the Internet and the World Wide Web. Nothing is frozen in place, and it may be that when you work with these you'll see differences in the way information is displayed. Don't let that deter you. Using the World Wide Web and the Internet means adapting to changes. Be persistent, and use your skills to make accommodations to a changing, but important, environment. The dynamic nature of the Web is one of its most exciting features.

New in This Edition

The Fifth Edition builds on the successful features of the earlier editions. Activities and exercises have been updated to make them fresher and to meet the challenge of the evolving Internet and World Wide Web, and to be more relevant to students' needs. The text examples and activities all use Mozilla Firefox as the browser, which is a change from the Fourth Edition. Content rearrangement included moving evaluation techniques and citation closer to the beginning of the book, and moving strategies for finding maps to the chapter on multimedia. New content in this edition includes overviews of social media tools such as wikis, social networking sites, social bookmarking resources—such as Delicious and CiteULike—and other collaboration tools. Also discussed is the open access movement, with an overview of institutional repositories and document sharing. In short, this edition is has been updated to cover the tools that comprise what is known as "Web 2.0."

Supplemental Materials

For those teaching courses with this book, instructor support is available from the publisher's Web site (www.fbeedle.com). The book has an accompanying Web site, "Searching and Researching on the Internet and the WWW," with the URL **http://webliminal.com/search-web.html**. Hyperlinks on that site will take you to individual Web pages for each chapter and appendix. These contain up-to-date links to all the resources mentioned in the book. They are periodically updated to keep the activities current. Furthermore, since the material at Web sites can change, this site gives access to the most recent versions of information on the Web.

About Us

The material in this book is derived directly from our experiences. During the past several years we've been involved in teaching students and others about using the Internet and the Web as resources for research. We lead workshops for librarians, teachers, and other groups of professionals interested in using the resources on the Internet in their work. We also give presentations about finding, evaluating, and citing resources on the Web. As a librarian and a professor of computer science, we work as researchers ourselves.

Acknowledgments

There are many people to thank for the encouragement, friendship, support, and help that carried us through the many months of work on this project. We owe our greatest thanks, as always, to our immediate and extended families. They, more than anyone else, have made it possible for us to complete this work. Karen especially thanks her husband, Jack, and their daughters Tracy and Hilary for their patience and support throughout the many years while she's worked on all the versions of this book. They have never complained that she was unavailable for conversation and companionship on many weekends and evenings. Ernie thanks his wife Lynn for all her help, love, and support—reading drafts and making improvements, being encouraging and supportive always, and (as she says) keeping herself amused. He also thanks his children, Karl and Oliver, for their special encouragement, interest, and advice, and for giving him the most important reasons for writing.

We want to thank all the people who fall into the categories of friends, colleagues, and students in Fredericksburg, Virginia, and at the University of Mary Washington who have given us their support, encouragement, help, and understanding. We'd like to especially thank Jack Bales for allowing us to use a piece of his writing in an example of citing Web pages in Chapter 4.

Franklin, Beedle & Associates has been a very supportive and cooperative publisher and has helped us greatly throughout this project. We especially thank our publisher Jim Leisy, Tom Sumner, and Jaron Ayres.

This book has been through several reviews, and we thank our reviewers—Mimi Will, Kris Chandler, Bill O'Connor, Lois Davis, Kathy Finney, and Dave Bullock—for their helpful, insightful, and frank comments and suggestions.

We hope you like this book and find it useful. Feel free to send us email letting us know your opinions, suggestions, or comments about our work. When you have the time, visit our home pages on the Web.

Karen Hartman
kphartman@gmail.com
http://webliminal.com/khartman

Ernest Ackermann
ernie@umw.edu
Department of Computer Science
University of Mary Washington
http://webliminal.com/ernie

CHAPTER 1

Introduction to the Internet and the World Wide Web

Every day, millions of people around the world use the Internet to search for and retrieve information on all sorts of topics in a wide variety of areas. The information can appear in several types of digital formats, such as text, images, audio, or video. Individuals, companies, research labs, libraries, news organizations, television networks, governments, and other organizations all make resources available. People communicate with each other, sharing information and making commercial and business transactions, using electronic mail. All this activity is possible because tens of thousands of networks are connected to the Internet and exchange information in the same basic ways. Never before has so much information from such a wide variety of sources and in so many formats been available to the public.

The World Wide Web is not the same as the Internet, but the two terms are popularly used as synonyms. The Web is the information connected or linked in a way that is like a spider's web. Using a Web browser—the computer program or software that lets you access the World Wide Web—you can find information on almost any topic with just a few clicks of your mouse button. Several search tools (programs that search the Web for resources) are readily available. When you type a keyword or phrase into a form and click on a button or icon on the screen, a list of items appears. You simply click on the ones you want to retrieve. The amount and variety of information available are astounding, but sometimes it's difficult to find appropriate material.

This chapter covers some of the basic information and concepts you need to begin finding information on the World Wide Web. The sections in this chapter are as follows:

♦ The World Wide Web as an Information Resource
♦ Hypertext and Hypermedia
♦ Key Terms and Concepts
♦ Information Sources Available on the Web

About This Book

This book is designed to help anyone who uses the World Wide Web and the Internet to find information or research a topic. We'll cover the tools and methods with which you search for resources on the Web, and we will explain how to access and use those tools. We'll go over the methods and techniques that will help you be effective and efficient in your searching and researching. We'll also talk about how to evaluate and cite resources within the context of a research project. The text and activities are designed to give you the experience you need to tap the cornucopia of information on the Web, find the resources you want, and—just as important —evaluate the material you've found.

Each of the chapters contains at least one detailed activity or example in which you work with a Web browser to access information on the World Wide Web. These activities demonstrate concepts and techniques. As you read the activities and follow along, you'll receive step-by-step instructions for working with the World Wide Web. Remember, though, that these activities and examples reflect the Web at the time of writing. Because some things change frequently, they may not appear to you on your screen as they do in this book. The Web and the Internet are constantly changing, but don't let that hold you back. Be persistent and use your skills to work in this important environment. Change is one of the things that make the Internet and the World Wide Web exciting, vigorous, and useful.

At the end of each chapter, we provide a chapter summary and a list of terms. The terms are defined in the chapter and also appear in the glossary at the back of the book.

The World Wide Web as an Information Resource

You can think of the *World Wide Web* as a large collection of information that's accessible through the Internet. The *Internet* is a collection of tens of thousands of computer networks that exchange information according to some agreed-upon rules or protocols. Because of this uniformity, a computer connected to one of the Internet's networks can transport text and images to be displayed on a computer connected to another part of the Internet.

Whether you've worked on the Web before or not, you'll be pleased with how easy it is to use. It's also enticing. The World Wide Web gives a uniform means of accessing all the different types of information on the Internet. Since you only need to know one way to get information, you can concentrate on what you want, not on how to obtain it. The Internet is commonly used throughout the world, so there is easy and relatively quick access to information on a global scale. That alone is remarkable, but it gets better. The information on the Web is often in a multimedia format called a *Web page*, which may combine text, images, audio, or video. This format lets us take advantage of a computer's multimedia capabilities. A Web page can also contain links to other resources or information on the World Wide Web. This is why it's called a web: One page contains links to another, and that one contains links to another, and so on. Since the information can be anywhere in the world, the term *World Wide Web* is most appropriate.

Tim Berners-Lee, credited with the concept of the Web, made the following statement in the document "About The World Wide Web": "The World Wide Web (known as 'WWW,' 'Web' or 'W3') is the universe of network-accessible information, the embodiment of human knowledge."

(By the way, you can find that document on the Web by using the URL **http://www.w3.org/www**. We'll say more a little later about how to use URLs.) Berners-Lee has made a strong statement, but it's certainly true. There's a wide range of materials available on such subjects as art, science, humanities, politics, law, business, education, and government information. In each of these areas you can find scientific and technical papers, financial data, stock market reports, government reports, advertisements, and publicity and news about movies and other forms of entertainment. Through the Web, you can find information about many types of products, information about health and environmental issues, government documents, and tips and advice on recreational activities such as camping, cooking, gardening, and travel. You can tour museums, plan a trip, make reservations, visit gardens throughout the world, and so on. Just a little bit of exploring will show you the wide range and types of information available.

To access the Web, you start a program on your computer called a ***Web browser***. The browser makes the connections to a specific Web site, retrieves information from the site, and displays it in a window on your screen. The information in the window is often in multimedia format. From there you can go to other locations on the Internet to search for, browse, and retrieve information. You use a mouse to move a hand or pointer to an icon, menu item, region of a map or image, button, or underlined portion of the window, and click the mouse button (the left one if your mouse has more than one button). These items are called ***hyperlinks***, or ***links*** for short. If you've clicked on a link in the document, the browser follows that link; the current document is replaced or another window pops up. Some Web pages, including those you'll use for searching and researching, have a place for you to type in a word or phrase, fill out a form, or check off options.

Items that are accessible through the Web give hypertext access to the Internet. In order for this to work, there are standard ways of specifying the links and creating documents that can be displayed as part of the Web. Information is exchanged according to a specific set of rules, or ***Hypertext Transfer Protocol (HTTP)***; each link has a particular format, or a ***Uniform Resource Locator (URL)***; and Web pages are written using a language called ***Hypertext Markup Language (HTML)***, which the browser can interpret.

The browser window also has text and icons in the borders, outside the portion of the window containing the Web page. Clicking on text or icons in the upper border of a window pops up a menu or a dialog box from which you can choose an action. Figure 1.1 shows these and other portions of a browser window.

Throughout this book, we'll use Mozilla Firefox as the browser. If you're using a different browser—Internet Explorer, Opera, or Safari—you'll see lots of similarities. While your view might be slightly different, we've tried not to rely on any special features of the browser. That way, the explanations and activities will be meaningful regardless of the browser you're using. Figure 1.1 shows the home page for the Library of Congress. When a site has several Web pages available, as the Library of Congress's Web site does, the one that acts as the first or introductory page is called the ***home page***.

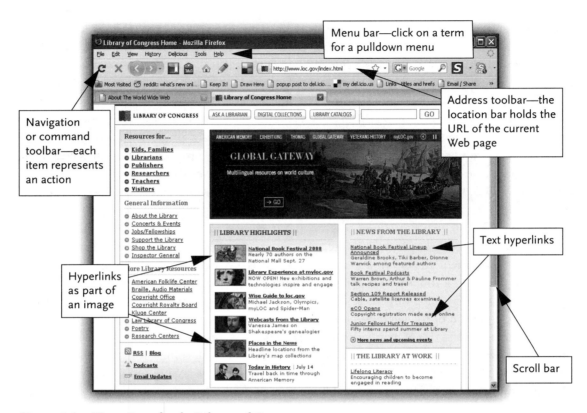

Figure 1.1—Home Page for the Library of Congress

Hypertext and Hypermedia

When you use the Web, you work in a hypertext or hypermedia environment. That means you move from item to item and back again without having to follow a predefined path. You follow hyperlinks according to your needs. Sometimes the items you select are words in other sentences or paragraphs; this way, the links to other Internet resources are presented in context. The links can also be represented by icons or images, or they may be regions in a map or graphic. Working with hyperlinks is fundamental to using the World Wide Web effectively, so we'll go into a little bit of detail on this topic.

The term **hypertext** is used to describe text that contains links to other text. When the hypertext and links are from a variety of media (text, video, audio), as is the case with the Web, we use the term **hypermedia**. On a screen or page certain items will be boldfaced, underlined, or colored differently. Each one represents a link to another part of the current document or other Internet resource. Selecting one of these links allows you to follow or jump to the information the link represents. You can also return to a previous link. There's a definite starting point, but the path you take after that is your choice. You are not constrained by having to go in some sort of straight line; you can think of being able to move up, down, right, or left from any link.

As an example, we'll look at an excerpt from a hypertext glossary. The definitions and explanations in the glossary are connected through hypertext. The excerpt here comes from a glossary of Internet terms that accompanies this book. This glossary is available on the Web in hypertext form. To see it, use the URL **http://webliminal.com/search/glossary.html**. Here is the excerpt:

Web Page The information available and displayed by a **<u>Web browser</u>** as the result of opening a local file or opening a location (**<u>URL</u>**) . The contents and format of the Web page are specified using **<u>HTML</u>**.

If you use your mouse to select one of the underlined words or phrases and click on it, you will retrieve another part of the glossary. For example, choosing (**URL**) takes you to a definition of URL (Uniform Resource Locator). From there, you could browse the glossary by following other links, or you could return to the entry for Web Page. You could always follow the links back to the place you started. The information in the glossary wouldn't change, but the way you accessed it and the order in which you did so would change.

Before we discuss other concepts related to the World Wide Web, let's do an activity that shows what we might see when we start a Web browser and search for some information. We won't focus on the features of a specific browser. We hope that the explanations and activities will be meaningful to you regardless of the browser you use.

ACTIVITY 1.1   USING A SEARCH ENGINE

Overview

We are assuming the browser program is properly set up on your computer and that you have a way of connecting to the Internet. In this activity, we'll search for information on the World Wide Web. We'll use a *search engine*, a collection of software that collects information from the Web, indexes it, and puts it in a database so it can be searched. So a search engine has several parts. Some parts gather information, other parts put the information into a database, and the part that most of us see, which are tools for searching the database.

We type keywords or a phrase into a search form on a Web page, possibly set some options, and then click on a search button on the Web page. In what is usually a short time, we will see matching entries from the database—usually 10 per page. Each of the results contains a hyperlink to the entry, as well as a brief excerpt from the resource. All the results are ranked according to relevance or how closely they match the query.

Search engines have indexed millions of Web pages and put them in their databases. So when you use a search engine, it's likely that you'll get more results than you can check. The key to successful searching is to make your search expression as precise as possible. We'll discuss ways of doing that in much more detail in Chapter 6.

> **About the Activities**
>
> This is the first of many activities in this book. Each activity is divided into two parts: "Overview" and "Details." In the first part, "Overview," we discuss what we'll be doing and enumerate the steps we'll follow. The section "Details" goes through the steps, shows the results we got when we try the activity, and provides some discussion. Your results might be different from what's shown here, but that's part of the dynamic nature of the Web; things are always changing. Don't let those changes confuse you. Follow the steps, use what's here as a guide, and pay attention to what you see. As you work through this and other activities, Do It! indicates something for you to do. These activities demonstrate fundamental skills that don't change, even though the number of results obtained or the actual screens may look very different.

In this activity we'll search for resources related to starting a small business. Imagine that you or someone you know is thinking about starting a business. You will want to find out what experts say you need to know or do. Another scenario for considering this topic is that you are researching a paper or article you are writing that deals with the resources available to those wanting to start a small business. We'll be able to use the topic to demonstrate some ways to use a search engine and move around the Web from page to page. We'll also go over using the online help from the search engine to make our search more precise. As we're searching we'll also want to keep in mind whether the information we find comes from a reliable source.

When you try this activity you're likely to see some differences in the results because new resources are always being added to the search engine's database. Concentrate on the steps to take. You'll use the same techniques for other topics.

The search engine we'll use for this activity is Google. It has a large database of Web pages, and it is the most popular search engine today. We'll go directly to the Web page for Google by typing in its URL, and then we'll read its online help to get some tips on searching and using it. We'll use the search expression **starting "small business"** because that includes the key terms of our search. Then we'll look at some of the results by following some of the hyperlinks. Here are the steps we'll follow:

1. Start the browser.
2. Go to the home page for Google.
3. Read the online help.
4. Type in the search expression and start the search.
5. Follow one of the hyperlinks returned by Google.
6. End the session.

While you're going through the steps in this activity, practice using the **Back** and **Forward** buttons. If you click on **Forward** as many times as you click on **Back**, you won't lose your place.

Details

1   Start the browser.

DO IT!   Double-click on the icon for the browser. We use Firefox, so we look for an icon that looks like the following:

2   Go to the home page for Google.

DO IT!   Click on the location bar, type **http://www.google.com**, and press Enter.

When you start your Web browser, your home page will appear on the screen. We're going to access Google by typing its URL in the location bar, as shown in Figure 1.2.

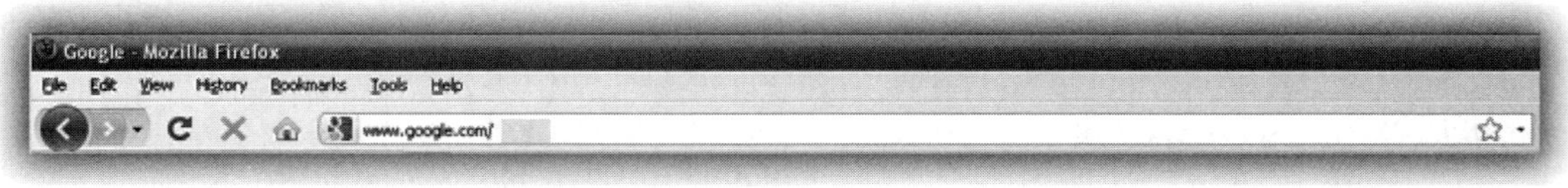

Figure 1.2—Going to Google by Typing Its URL

Soon after you press Enter, the search page for Google ought to appear in the browser window, as shown in Figure 1.3. We've labeled some of the items on the page for future reference.

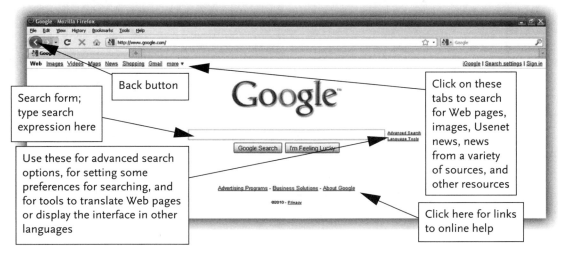

Figure 1.3—Home Page for Google

3   Read the online help.

Remember—it's a very good idea to read the online help before you start using a search tool. The help usually includes a description of the tool's features and what syntax to use for searching. The goal is to obtain more relevant and useful results. Google's home page shown in Figure 1.3 doesn't have a hyperlink labeled **Help** or something similar. It would make accessing the online help easier, but we proceed undaunted!

Checking some of the hyperlinks, we find that **About Google** is the one we need.

DO IT! Click on the hyperlink labeled **About Google**.

You'll retrieve a Web page that has hyperlinks to help topics and answers some questions about Google itself. We're going to take a look at two of the online help pages about searching.

DO IT! Click on the hyperlink labeled **Help**. You'll notice that Google has separate help sections for many of its services, such as its Image Search service, Google Video service, and more. For our purposes, we are interested in general Web searching, so the link we want to access is **Web Search Help**.

DO IT! Click on the hyperlink labeled **Web Search Help**. On the left side of the window you'll see links listed under the heading **Search guides**. Click on the hyperlink **Basic search help**.

Be sure to read this Web page to get the tips you need for making the best use of Google. Figure 1.4 shows a portion of the Basic search help page. You'll want to use the scroll bar to read through the tips on that page.

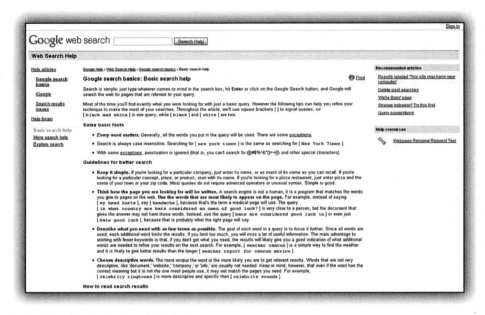

Figure 1.4—Google's Basic Search Help Page

Reading the text, we find several useful pieces of information:

♦ We ought to be specific when describing what we're searching for.

♦ By default, Google returns URLs for Web pages that contain *all* the words or phrases in the search expression. This gives more precise results than retrieving URLs for Web pages that contain *any* of the words.

♦ Google excludes common words so we don't need to include those in our search expression

♦ We can require a match for phrases, not just individual words, by including a phrase in quotes. You can see this and other useful tips by clicking on the link **More search help**.

We're interested in finding out information about starting a small business. After reading this online help, we see that a recommended way to get precise results is to use the search expression: **starting "small business"**.

We also see that there are links to a good deal of other information about using Google. When you have the time, read about using Boolean expressions and using other search features by clicking on **More search help** in this section on help. Clicking on **Advanced Search** on Google's home page gives ready access to some of those features.

4   Type in the search expression and start the search.

We'll go back to the home page for Google so that we can enter our search terms and start the search.

DO IT!   Click on **Google** in the upper left corner of the Web page.

DO IT!   Click on the search field, type the search term **starting "small business"**, and then click on the **Google Search** button.

Typing the search terms is straightforward. If you want to replace or correct what you've typed, you can click on the search field pane to the right of the last word, backspace over the terms, and type new terms. You can also use the left and right arrow keys to add characters or to delete them from the search terms.

Figure 1.5 shows a portion of the previous page with the search expression typed in.

Figure 1.5—Google Search Form with Search Expression

After you click on **Google Search**, the search engine returns a list of hyperlinks to resources that have information containing the words in the search phrase. A portion of that page is shown in Figure 1.6. They are arranged in order so that those that may be most relevant are listed first. There are 10 on this page. We don't show it here, but if you move to the end of the page (use the down arrow key, press **PgDn**, or use the vertical scroll bar), there's a link you can select to go to the next 10 items.

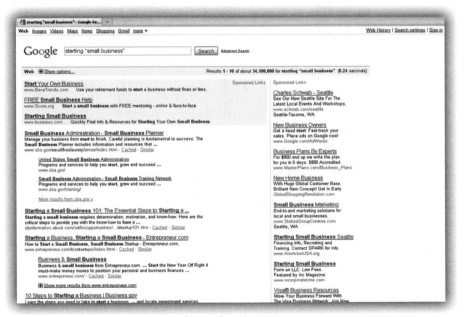

Figure 1.6—Portion of First Page of Search Results

5   Follow one of the hyperlinks returned by Google.

Figure 1.6 shows the first few results of the search. What a popular topic! There are more than 30 million results! This is a lot to consider, but the first few have a good chance of being ones we'd like to see. You can access the items listed by clicking on the hyperlinks. For each item, there's a brief description that you can use as a guide to help you decide whether to follow the link. Before following the hyperlinks take a look at the URLs for the ones listed in Figure 1.6. The URL for the first one starts with **www.sba.gov** and a little farther down the page is a URL that starts with **www. irs.gov**. The **.gov** in the URL means that these sites are published by the U.S. Government. This means they are most likely reliable and contain authoritative information. The URLs for most of the others have **.com** in the start of the URL, for example **sbinformation.about.com**. These are published by commercial sites or other businesses.

For now, we'll follow the first hyperlink in Figure 1.6, **Small Business Administration**, as it looks the most promising. (If that one isn't listed, pick another that you think is appropriate.) When you have time, follow some of the other hyperlinks to help determine which of the results are appropriate to your search.

DO IT!   Click on the hyperlink for **Small Business Administration (SBA)**.

Figure 1.7 shows the SBA Web page. It has links to many topics related to starting a small business. We see it also has links to maintaining a business as well. This looks like a very valuable site. We'll take a look at some of the links about starting a business, but before we do that we'll take the time to add this link to a list of bookmarks we can come back to at any time.

Figure 1.7—SBA Web Page

DO IT!   Click on Bookmarks on the menu bar, and then select **Bookmark This Page.** (If you are using Internet Explorer, you would click on **Favorites.**) Once the link is stored in our collection of bookmarks we can access the link again by clicking on **Bookmarks** in the menu bar, finding it in the list of bookmarks, and then clicking on it.

Before moving on, take a look at the Web page to see if it says who is responsible for the SBA Web site. It helps us to determine the reliability of the information on a Web site when it includes the name of the author or publisher. In this case we see the site is published by the U.S. Small Business Association.

Now on to explore the other hyperlinks.

DO IT! Click on the hyperlink **Write a Business Plan**.

Clicking on the hyperlink **Write a Business Plan** brings up a Web page that contains a collection of links to guides for writing a business plan. Feel free to follow any of them. You can use the **Back** button in the toolbar to return to this Web page.

Figure 1.8—Write a Business Plan Web Page

Now let's take a look at some of the other resources on the SBA Web site.

DO IT! Click on the link **Services** to view some of the services of the SBA.

This takes us to another portion of the site that lists the services offered to all by the SBA. We could easily spend hours exploring this Web site. Browse a little, but don't forget two things: there are other sites listed in the Google search to consider, and you can get lost or forget whatever else you need to do today.

You always need to check more than one source for information, so you'll want to return to the list of links returned by our initial search at Google. Use the **Back** button in the command toolbar to return to the Google page with the search results.

6   End the session.

You knew when we started that this had to end sometime. Now's the time. (You can, however, keep the Web browser open so that you're ready for the next activity.)

DO IT! Click on **File** on the menu bar and select **Close** from the menu.

That's it!

———————————————————————————————**END OF ACTIVITY 1.1**

In this activity, we used a search engine to find hyperlinks to Web pages about starting a small business. After using the online help, we used search terms to make the search more precise. When you look at some of these Web pages, you may want to make the search even more specific. Perhaps you're interested in starting a business that provides a specific service or you are interested in learning about seeking funding in the form of a loan or a grant to start a business. You can do that by modifying the search phrase or coming up with a new one.

A Note About Bookmarks or Favorites

During the activity we also saved a link to the site we were exploring as a ***bookmark*** (or ***favorite***, in Internet Explorer terminology) in the browser. This has the advantage of being accessible whenever you are using a specific computer. An alternative is to use the Web-based service Delicious to store this bookmark. The advantage to using a Web-based service is that you can access your bookmarks from anywhere, whenever you are connected to the Internet. It is also easy to classify the bookmarks, share your bookmarks with others, and search all the bookmarks stored by everyone that uses Delicious. Using Delicious is free but you have to register with a username, password, and email address to use it. The registration process takes several steps, so we won't go through those steps here, but we will cover the registration process in an exercise at the end of this chapter. In later chapters we'll discuss using Delicious in more detail. This type of service, where users contribute information they can use, share that information with others, and all work together to classify the information is typical of what some call Web 2.0.

Now we'll go over some key terms and concepts related to the Web and the way information is presented on it.

Key Terms and Concepts

In this section, we'll discuss some of the terms and concepts that are important to know about as you're working with the Internet and the Web. The topics we'll cover include:

- ◆ Client/Server
- ◆ HTTP (Hypertext Transfer Protocol)
- ◆ HTML (Hypertext Markup Language)
- ◆ URL (Uniform Resource Locator)
- ◆ Error Messages
- ◆ Selected Web-based Guides to the Internet and the World Wide Web

Client/Server

When you start a Web browser or follow a hyperlink, the browser sends a request to a site on the Internet. That site returns a file that the browser then has to display. This sort of interaction in which one system requests information and another provides it is called a ***client/server*** relationship. The browser is the client, and a computer at the site that provides the information is the server.

HTTP (Hypertext Transfer Protocol)

The documents or files are passed from a server to a client according to specific rules for exchanging information. These rules are called *protocols*. The protocol used on the Web is named HTTP, which stands for Hypertext Transfer Protocol, because the documents, pages, or other items passed from one computer to another are in hypertext or hypermedia form.

HTML (Hypertext Markup Language)

Many of the rules for creating or writing a Web page are specified as HTML—Hypertext Markup Language. This language provides formal rules for marking text. The rules govern how text is displayed as part of a Web page. In order for text or an icon to represent a hyperlink, it has to be marked as a link in HTML, and the URL has to be included. The URL doesn't appear, however, unless someone clicks on a hyperlink. Web pages are often stored in files with names that end in **.html** or **.htm**.

As the Web develops, other technologies and specifications are being used to specify the form of the information on a Web page. These include XHTML (eXtensible Hypertext Markup Language) and CSS (Cascading Style Sheets). In the near future we can also expect markup languages that help us specify the meaning or semantic content of a Web page.

URL (Uniform Resource Locator)

The hyperlinks are represented in a specific format called a URL, or Uniform Resource Locator. Each Web page has a URL as its address. For example, the URL for the Library of Congress's home page is **http://www.loc.gov**.

The URLs that point to Web pages typically start with **http://** because they are all transmitted according to HTTP. You may see something different for URLs that access information through other Internet protocols.

You'll find it helpful to think of a URL as having the form:

$$\text{how-to-get-there://where-to-go/what-to-get}$$

When you cite a resource on the World Wide Web, you include the URL for it. You'll also want to include the URL when you're telling someone else about a resource, such as in an email message. It's much more effective to include URLs. Here's an example:

> "A good resource for information about African studies is African Studies Internet Resources, **http://www.columbia.edu/cu/lweb/indiv/africa/cuvl/,**" or "check out the World Wide Web Virtual Library at **http://vlib.org**."

People reading this message can use their browsers to go directly to the items you mention.

We will now show you the different parts of a URL so that you have a better idea about the information a URL conveys:

$$\text{http://paprika.umw.edu/~ernie/glossaries/list.html}$$

Most URLs have this format. By indicating which Internet protocol to use, they tell you how to retrieve the information. By naming both the Web server and the file or directory holding the information, they tell you where the site is located. If only a server name is present and not a file name, as in **http://www.loc.gov**, you still retrieve a file; by default, the server passes along a certain file, usually named **index.html**. Sometimes you'll see URLs written without **http://** in front. You can safely omit **http://** when you open a Web page or location by typing the URL into the browser's location bar.

Error Messages

As amazing as some computer systems are, they generally need very precise instructions, so you have to be careful about spacing (generally there aren't blank spaces in a URL), the symbols used (a slash and a period are not interchangeable), and the case of the letters. Here's an example: The URL for the online glossary that accompanies this book is **http://webliminal.com/search/glossary.html**. Replacing search with SEARCH, as in the URL **http://webliminal.com/SEARCH/glossary.html**, will cause the server to report an error back to the browser The information displayed will include:

```
404 - page not present on our server
The page you requested with URL http://webliminal.com/
SEARCH/glossary.html isn't present on our server. Please
check the URL
```

The error message tells us that part of the URL was correct—the name of the Web server, **webliminal.com**—but that the Web server could not find the file on the server because there was something wrong with the rest of the URL.

A message such as this is called a *404 Error*. You may see this message if the URL is incorrect, if a Web page has been removed from a Web server, or if it is no longer available. If you click on a hyperlink and get a 404 message, you may have come upon what is sometimes called a *dead link*. Here's another message you may see:

```
403 Forbidden
Your client does not have permission to get URL /ernie/
abc.html from this server.
```

That means the URL was correct and the file is on the server, but the file isn't available to the public.

If the URL contains the name of a Web server that your browser can't find, you'll see an error message such as this:

```
Host Name Lookup Problem
Check the spelling and try again.
```

Selected Web-based Guides to the Internet and the World Wide Web

Taking advantage of the resources on the World Wide Web, using a Web browser, and using the Internet aren't difficult, but they require a lot of knowledge. If you're not familiar with the Web or the Internet, you may want to look at some Web-based guides. Here is a list of some of the good ones available on the Web, including the name of the resource and its URL. To access any of these guides, double-click on the location bar (it should turn blue), type the URL, and press **Enter**.

- net.TUTOR: Getting Started on the Web,
  http://liblearn.osu.edu/tutor/les2/pg1.html
- The HelpWeb: A Guide To Getting Started on the Internet,
  http://www.imagescape.com/helpweb/welcome.html
- Learn the Net,
  http://www.learnthenet.com/english/index.html

There's a Web site to accompany this book. The title of the site and its URL are:

♦ Searching and Researching on the Internet and the World Wide Web, **http://webliminal.com/search**

Information Sources Available on the Web

Because there's so much information available on the Web, it has to be organized so that you can find what you need. There must also be tools or programs to help you locate information. Throughout this book, we'll be discussing the major information sources on the Web.

Directories or Subject Catalogs

These are directories, arranged by subject, of selected Internet and Web resources. Several of the directories contain reviews or descriptions of the entries. The Open Directory Project, **http://dmoz.org**, for example, is a directory that is built by volunteers who serve as editors to select and verify resources. The section Internet Subject Directories, **http://www.digital-librarian.com/subject.html**, at the site Digital Librarian, **http://www.digital-librarian.com** contains a list of directories.

Search Engines

Search engines provide keyword searching capability of most of the available Web resources. Google, **http://google.com**, is the most popular and one of the best general-purpose search engines. Google also includes collections of images, videos, news, and other types of resources to be searched. A listing of the most-used search engines is available at Recommended Search Engines, **http://www.lib.berkeley.edu/TeachingLib/Guides/Internet/SearchEngines.html**. The document 100 Useful Niche Search Engines to Focus and Finetune Your Academic Research, **http://www.collegeathome.com/blog/2008/06/19/100-useful-niche-search-engines-youve-never-heard-of**, contains a list of specialized search engines.

Meta-search Tools

A meta-search tool usually allows you to search several search engines or directories simultaneously. Many meta-search tools take your query, do the search, and then integrate the results. Examples of meta-search tools are Clusty, **http://www.clusty.com**, and Dogpile, **http://www.dogpile.com**. A list of meta-search engines is available at Meta-Search Engines, **http://www.lib.berkeley.edu/TeachingLib/Guides/Internet/MetaSearch.html**.

Specialized Databases

Specialized databases are self-contained indexes that are searchable and available on the Web. Two examples are MedlinePlus, **http://medlineplus.gov**, a special databases focusing on medical and health information, and EDGAR Online, **http://www.edgar-online.com**, a specialized database of information about businesses. Directories such as ipl2: Information You Can Trust (**http://www.ipl2.org**), are good places to find these tools.

The types of resources we've mentioned above are those where the information in each collection is gathered automatically by software that prowls the Web or is selected by individuals who act as editors. Now we're going to describe information sources that are built by the people who use them. The information in each collection isn't added or deleted, except for checks to see that the information meets the criteria for acceptability set by the law and community decency standards.

Online Group Discussions

Email discussion groups are sometimes called *interest groups*, *listservs*, or *mailing lists*. Internet users join, contribute to, and read messages to the entire group through email. There are other types of groups where people communicate with the group by posting messages or articles online. In many cases, it's more appropriate to think of the group's members rather than the group's archives as good sources of information. Google Groups, **http://groups.google.com**, is a good place to start to see what groups are available.

Blogs

The term blog is derived form the words "Web log." The information in a blog is written by one or more people and is arranged in chronological order with the most recent information first. Blogs have become very popular in the last few years, with well over 100 million in existence as of the writing of this book, though the exact number is impossible to calculate. There are several sources of easy-to-use blog software, so almost anyone can create and maintain a blog. Many blogs contain substantial and authoritative information. Many more contain very opinionated views. Blogs are now a worldwide phenomena and can be rich sources of information. You can search for information in blogs using Google Blog Search, **http://blogsearch.google.com**, or Technorati, **http://technorati.com**.

RSS and News Aggregators

RSS is a collection of formats implemented in software to allow for sharing information from blogs, Web sites, news sources, and almost any digital collection of information. The information is called an RSS feed. Whenever you check the feed, you'll see a link to new information that has been added. A news aggregator is software that allows you to display the results of RSS feeds in some orderly way. News aggregators such as Google Reader, **http://www.google.com/reader**, and Bloglines, **http://www.bloglines.com**, are Web-based. Using these makes it convenient to keep up with several blogs or other sources.

Tagged Collections

A number of sites have been very successful in providing easy ways to store information and then classifying it by assigning tags, such as words or phrases, to the items stored. One example of this type of service is the way Flickr, **http://www.flickr.com**, allows you to store, classify, and share photographs. If you are, let's say, looking for a picture of a pine snake, you can search for images that have those words in the tags, titles or description. You can discover items that can be useful to you. The site or service gets more valuable as more people participate. Making it easy for someone to add information, tag it, and search for their own and information added by others is a hallmark of what some call *Web 2.0*, an affirmation of the participatory nature of the Internet and the Web. Delicious, **http://delicious.com**, is an online bookmarking service that we mentioned after Activity 1.1. You can search for bookmarks others have saved with assigned tags. Searching for bookmarks with the tag "small business," for example, returns a collection of URLs, each with a count of how many other people have used the tag "small business" for these links. It's a great way to discover resources others have found valuable. When you register for the service you can start saving your own bookmarks, accessing them from anywhere on the Web, and sharing them with others.

Wikis

A wiki is software that one or more people use to write and edit documents on the Web. The software is designed to be easy to use, and easy for people to cooperate in preparing materials. A public wiki is likely to be indexed by one of the major search engines, so results from wikis often come up in searches using a general-purpose search engine. The collection of information put together with this type of software is also called a wiki. One of the most famous wikis is Wikipedia, **http://wikipedia.org**, a collaborative encyclopedia with millions of entries on a wide variety of topics. Thousands of people throughout the world create and edit its content. Wikipedia is easy to search, and the information in articles with references or citations can be checked for accuracy.

Images & Videos

There are several collections of images on the Web. Some are specialized collections, such as the Prints & Photographs Online Catalog, **http://www.loc.gov/rr/print/catalog.html**, an example of a specialized database. On the other hand, the images accessible through Google, **http://images.google.com**, and Yahoo!, **http://images.search.yahoo.com**, are searchable collections gathered from public locations on the Web. A third type is collections of images that individuals have posted to save and share them. Flickr, mentioned above, is one such service. Likewise there are similar specialized and general collections of videos. A service similar to Flickr is YouTube, **http://youtube.com**, storing several hundred million videos, though it's impossible to know exactly how many. Anyone can place a video in the collection, and when they do they provide a title, a description, and a location. They then put it into one or more categories, and supply tags in the same way that information is tagged in Flickr. This allows anyone to browse the collection and also to search by location or by terms in the title or description. At the time of this writing searching video and image collections is based on accompanying text including title, description, category, tags, location, and other accompanying attributes.

Summary

Millions of people around the world use the Internet for communication, research, business, information, and recreation. One of the most popular and effective ways to tap into its resources is through the World Wide Web, a vast collection of information connected like a web.

There is no beginning or end; the information is accessible in a nonlinear fashion through connections called hyperlinks. You view the resources on the Web by using a program called a Web browser. You navigate through the Web by pointing to hyperlinks (underlined or boldfaced words or phrases, icons, or images) and clicking. To use the Web and the Internet effectively, you need to know how to find and use the services, tools, and programs that give you access to their resources.

It's possible to link information in almost any digital form on the World Wide Web. Text files, programs, charts, images, graphics files, digitized video, and sound files are all available. Not only can you find things from a variety of media, but you also get a great deal of information in many categories or topics.

When using the Web, you work in a hypertext or hypermedia environment. A Uniform Resource Locator, or URL, specifies items, services, and resources. Web browsers use these URLs to specify the type of Internet service or protocol needed and the location of the item. For example, the URL for the Web page General Collections Library of Congress is **http://www.loc.gov/rr/**

coll-general.html. The protocol or service in this case is HTTP, or Hypertext Transfer Protocol, and a Web browser using that URL would contact the Internet site **www.loc.gov** and access the file **coll-general.html** in the directory or folder named **rr**. The documents on the Web are called Web pages.

A number of different types of information sources are available on the World Wide Web. They include:

◆ Directories of selected collections of Internet and Web resources, arranged by subject

◆ Search engines, which are tools that provide keyword searching capability

◆ Meta-search tools, which allow you to access databases from one place

◆ Specialized databases, which contain comprehensive collections of hyperlinks in a particular subject area, or which are self-contained, searchable indexes made available on the Web

◆ Discussion groups, of which several thousand groups exist to share opinions and experiences, ask and answer questions, or post information about a specific topic

◆ Blogs, wikis, and tagged collections, enabling individuals to easily classify and put information on the Web.

Selected Terms Used in This Chapter

bookmark	Hypertext Markup Language	Uniform Resource Locator
client/server	(HTML)	(URL)
favorite	Hypertext Transfer Protocol	Web 2.0
home page	(HTTP)	Web browser
hyperlink	Internet	Web page
hypermedia	link	World Wide Web
hypertext	search engine	

Review Questions

Multiple Choice

1. The computer network comprising thousands of networks that exchange information is known as the
   a. Wide Area Network.
   b. Client/Server Network.
   c. Internet.
   d. Arpanet.

2. You may get an error message accessing a site if
   a. there is a space in the address.
   b. you use the wrong case letters.
   c. you use a comma (,) instead of a dot (.).
   d. a and c
   e. all of the above

3. A computer that provides information to your browser is called a
   a. server.
   b. client.
   c. backup.
   d. bookmark.
4. Text that provides links to other text is called
   a. multimedia.
   b. http.
   c. hypertext.
   d. a browser.
5. Each Web page has an address known as a(n)
   a. server.
   b. URL.
   c. WWW.
   d. hypertext.
6. Web pages are written using a language called
   a. HTTP.
   b. HURL.
   c. HPLM.
   d. HTML.
7. Which of the following can work as a hyperlink?
   a. underlined words
   b. an image
   c. a button
   d. a and b
   e. all of the above

True or False

8. T F All URLs start with **http://**.
9. T F A search engine allows you to search the Web by keyword.
10. T F A favorite or bookmark is a way to save a link to a site on the Web you'd like to visit again.
11. T F To navigate using a hyperlink, you click on the link with your left mouse button.
12. T F Usenet newsgroup archives cannot be searched for information contained in them.
13. T F You can copy text on a Web page by using your left mouse button.
14. T F A Web page may include multimedia, such as audio or video formats.

Completion

15. A subject listing of Web resources is known as a(n) _____.
16. To access a Web site, you type its URL into your browser's _____.
17. A directory of Web pages selected and evaluated by an information professional or librarian is called a(n) _____.

18. Before the World Wide Web, a protocol used to share information through the Internet was _____.

19. A software program that allows you to access information on the World Wide Web is known as a(n) _____.

20. _____ is an open-source alternative to Internet Explorer.

Exercises and Projects

1. Let's go back to Google, as we did in the chapter. Did you save the site as a favorite or bookmark? If so, click on **Bookmarks** and then on **Google**. If not, type the URL **http://www.google.com** into your location bar and press **Enter**.
    a. Let's look for information about NASCAR. Type **NASCAR** into the search box. What happens if you click the button that says "I'm Feeling Lucky?" What is the URL of the site that you arrive at?
    b. Click your Back button to return to Google. **NASCAR** should still be showing in the search box. Click on the **Google Search** button. How many Web pages are found for that topic?
    c. Google used to say how many sites it knew about on its home page. Check to see if that information is there now. If it isn't there, how can you find the answer to the question "How many sites does Google know about?" *Hint:* Look for the article whose title is "We knew the Web was big" on the official Google blog.

2. This chapter talked about other kinds of search tools available on the Web. Try using the meta-search engine Clusty. It's available by typing in **http://clusty.com** in your location bar. You may want to set this site as a bookmark as well. We'll put a different twist on our NASCAR search this time. Try putting in the words **NASCAR ballet** into Clusty's search box. Click the **Search** button. We'll try to find out what company created this dance.
    a. How many results does Clusty return? Click on the first result. Does it tell you what dance company created this ballet? What is the name of the company? If that result doesn't give you the information, click your Back button to go back to your results list. Sometimes you need to click on more than one search result to find what you want to know! Click on some of the links till you find the answer.
    b. Notice that Clusty clusters its results into **Categories**. What are the first five categories you find on the left hand side of your browser window? Click on the first category. Does this help you to narrow down your search? How?

3. Do you know the meaning of the words *mendacious* and *singultus*? What would you do if someone called you mendacious? If you were diagnosed with singultus? Let's look them up before deciding what to do! Go to the Open Directory Project that was mentioned in the chapter at **http://dmoz.org**. Notice that besides the search box, there is also a directory of information that you can browse. Click on **Reference**.
    How many dictionaries does this directory include? Click on **Dictionaries**. From that page of results, click on **English Language**.
    a. Scroll down the page. Click on **Merriam-Webster OnLine**. Look up the word *mendacious*. Type the word in the search box, then click the **Go** button or press **Enter**. What is the meaning of the word?

    b. Notice that you can type in a new search from this screen. Try a search for the word *singultus*. Do you find a definition?

    c. Go back to the list of dictionaries by clicking on your **Back** button till you return to the Open Directory Dictionaries page. Click on **OneLook Dictionaries.** Can you find the word *singultus* in one of the links listed here? What meaning is given for the word?

4. There are some other very different dictionaries listed at the Open Directory Project. (We were particularly taken by the Skeptic's Dictionary.) Go back to the Dictionaries page and click on the words **By Subject.** Click on **Computers.** Click on **Computer Dictionary**.

    a. Look up the word **Fortran** here. What is the definition of the word?

    b. Go back to the **Open Directory Dictionaries** listing. Click on the category **Rhyming.**

       Choose one of the dictionaries listed and click on it. Type the word **flower** into the search box and search for it. What do you see? List three words that rhyme with it.

5. Now we can look at one of the directories mentioned in the chapter. Type the URL **http://www.ipl2.org** into your location bar and press **Enter**. This site is the home of ipl2: Information You Can Trust, a merger of the Internet Public Library and The Librarians' Internet Index.

    a. What collections are available here?

    b. Click on **Resources by Subject** and then click on **Reference** Genealogy has become a very popular topic on the Web, so scroll down the page and click on **Genealogy**. Try clicking on the **Beginner's Guide to Family History Research, http://www. arkansasresearch.com/guideindex.htm**. What are the first two chapters listed? How many other resources are listed on the **Genealogy** page?

    c. Go back to the main page of ipl2. Look through the site by clicking on some other links. Do you find it easy to use? Why or why not?

6. Let's stay at ipl2. Go back to the home page, **http://www.ipl2.org**.

    a. Click on **Special Collections Created by ipl2**. Then click on **Associations on the Net**. On that page click on **Business and Economics**. Give the names of three associations for accountants. Visit at least one and describe what you find.

    b. Click on your **Back** button to return to the Special Collections page. Click on **Pathfinders**. What is a "Pathfinder"? Describe how it can be useful.

    c. Click on your **Back** button to return to the home page for ipl2. Note that you can search the site using the search box at the top of the page. Try typing a search for film history. Describe what you find.

    d. One more search. This time search ipl2 for podcasts. Again, describe what you find.

7. The World Wide Web is just the latest invention in a long history of communication breakthroughs. Let's go back to Google and look back in time at the beginnings of communication. Go to **http://www.google.com**. In the search box, type in **cuneiform writing**. Click **Google Search**.

    a. Look at the first three sites that appear in the results list. What are they? Give the titles and URLs of the first three sites.

    b. What is cuneiform writing? When and where was it invented? Do you get this information at one of those first three sites listed?

    c. Just for fun, there's a site that's called Write Like a Babylonian at **http://www.penn. museum/cgi/cuneiform.cgi**. Take a look and see what your name looks like in cuneiform! You can go back to the museum's main pages, and find even more fun cuneiform information and projects at **http://www.museum.upenn.edu**.

8. Google provides a toolbar that you can add to your browser to give you easier access to Google's features and some additional tools like a tool to block pop-up windows. Try to install it. You can uninstall it if doesn't suit you.

    a. Go to the Web site for Google toolbar by typing the URL **http://toolbar.google. com** into the location bar and pressing **⌈Enter⌋**. Read information about the toolbar by clicking on the link **Help.** This takes you to the page with the URL **http://www. google.com/support/toolbar**. You'll want to read this to learn what you can do after the toolbar is installed. Write about three features that you think would be useful to you. What feature to do you think you would not find useful? Explain.

    b. When you are ready to install the toolbar go back to the home page for the toolbar (the one with URL **http://toolbar.google.com**) and click on the button labeled **Install Google Toolbar**. When you click on that button, depending on your security settings a dialog box may pop up that warns you about downloading information from the Internet and asks you what you'd like to do with the downloaded file. Since this is coming from a trusted source (Google), it is all right save and open the file. If we weren't sure of the source of the file, then we might download it and check it with anti-virus software before opening and installing it. Once the program is downloaded and installation begins, you'll be asked to read and agree to the conditions of use from Google. The agreement is typical. Install the toolbar. Restart your browser and write a description of how things have changed.

    c. Try using the Google toolbar. Find two features that you think will be especially useful to you when you need to research a subject. Explain what they are and why they will be useful.

9. Using Delicious can be very helpful to store bookmarks that will be accessible whenever you use the Internet and to find what bookmarks others have saved on a topic. This exercise takes you through the steps of registering for the service.

    a. Start at the home page for Delicious, **http://delicious.com**, and click on the link **Join Now**. That takes you to the page with to a secure page to sign up through Yahoo!, which operates Delicous. Click on the link **Sign Up** to get an account. Enter the necessary information, noting that Yahoo! Will sign you up for a free e-mail account. The registration page asks you to enter a certain piece of information at the bottom of the page. Describe what it is and why it is there. If you can't come up with an answer at Delicious, open another browser window and look up the term CAPTCHA in Wikipedia.

    b. Click on the button labeled **Create My Account** to take you to the next step. Verify your information on the next page and click **Continue**. Choose a link for your Delicious account (Step 1), then install three buttons in your browser to make it easier to use Delicious. Click on the link labeled **Add a Bookmarklet** to install the buttons. Read the description on the next page and describe what each of the buttons is supposed to do.

If you are using Firefox your browser will restart.

If you are using Internet Explorer, the buttons will be installed without restarting the browser. Now go through Activity 1.1 again and add bookmarks and appropriate tags to at least three different sites you can find using the search term expression starting "small business." Print out a copy of your first page of bookmarks in Delicious.

CHAPTER 2

Using the Web for Research

The Internet and the World Wide Web have revolutionized the way we do research. Instead of spending hours combing library indexes and catalogs, making endless telephone calls, or traveling to far-off places, with a few clicks you can find an enormous amount of information on virtually any subject: government statistics, fast-breaking news stories, up-to-the-minute weather reports, sales catalogs and business information, radio programs, movies, music, and virtual art galleries and museums.

Searching the Web for this information can be a challenging and possibly frustrating task. The Web will not always have everything you're looking for, and sometimes the information you want is on the Web, but difficult to find. Keep in mind that even though the Web has billions of pages, most published literature is not Web-based, but rather exists in books and periodicals that are in paper form, or are located in fee-based databases. Librarians can help you determine the best sources to consult for the subject you are researching. Once you've decided the Web is the place to look, how do you proceed? Several major search tools are available; which one do you start with? This chapter will help you decide.

The sections in this chapter are as follows:
- The First Step: Evaluating Your Information Needs
- Searching the World Wide Web: Using Search Engines
- Browsing the World Wide Web: Using Directories
- The Impact of Web 2.0 on Searching

In the course of this chapter, we'll provide you with an introduction to research skills on the World Wide Web so that you can start finding whatever interests you. You will learn the difference between **browsing** and **keyword searching** the Web, and you will see examples that focus on each method. You'll discover when it is better to use a **directory** or **subject catalog** (topical lists of selected Web resources, hierarchically arranged) and when it makes sense to start with a **search engine** (a tool that provides keyword searching ability of Web resources).

If you know different tactics for finding information on the Web, your searches will be more successful. We'll provide activities in this chapter that will give you practice in browsing and keyword searching. Once you learn how to use the Web to its fullest potential, you will be amazed at what you can locate in a short period of time. Let's start researching!

The First Step: Evaluating Your Information Needs

Before you get online and start your search for information, think about what types of material you're looking for. Are you interested in finding facts to support an argument, authoritative opinions, statistics, research reports, descriptions of events, images, or movie reviews? Do you need current information or facts about an event that occurred 20 years ago? When is the Web a smart place to start? Keep in mind that a lot of information is on the Web, but much of it is part of proprietary or commercial services that are subscription-based. Your local library may subscribe to a database that will be useful for the subject you are searching for.

Types of Information Most Likely Found on the Internet and the World Wide Web

- **Current information.** Many major newspapers, broadcasting networks, and popular magazines have Web sites that provide news updates throughout the day. Current financial and weather information also is easily accessible.
- **Government information.** Most federal, state, and local government agencies provide statistics and other information freely and in a timely manner. Most foreign governments provide official information as well.
- **Popular culture.** It's easy to find information on the latest movie or best-selling book.
- **Open access literature.** Works such as Shakespeare's plays, the Bible, *Canterbury Tales*, and thousands of other full-text literary resources are available. More and more academic journals are being published on the Internet in all subjects. Read more about the open access movement here: **http://www.earlham.edu/~peters/fos/overview.htm**
- **Business and company information.** Not only do many companies provide their Web pages and annual reports, but several Internet-based databases also provide in-depth financial and other information about companies.
- **Consumer information.** The Internet is a virtual gold mine of information for people interested in buying a particular item and who want opinions from other people about it. With access to everything from automobile reviews on the Web to Google Groups and other forums, consumers can find out about almost any item before they buy it.
- **Medical information.** In addition to the hospitals, pharmaceutical companies, and nonprofit organizations that publish excellent sources of medical information, the National Library of Medicine freely provides the MEDLINE database to the public.
- **Entertainment.** The Web is the first place many people go to find games, audio files, and video clips.
- **Software.** The Web hosts software archives in which you can search for and download software to your computer without cost.
- **Unique archival sites.** To take one example, the Library of Congress archives Americana in its American Memory collection.

Some Reasons the World Wide Web Won't Have Everything You Are Looking For

- Publishing companies and authors who make money by creating and providing information usually choose to use the traditional publishing marketplace rather than to make their information available for free via the Internet.
- Scholars most often choose to publish their research in reputable scholarly journals and university presses rather than freely on the Web, although there are some scholars that are publishing their research in open access journals.
- Several organizations and institutions would like to publish valuable information on the Web, but don't because of a lack of staff or funding.
- The Web tends to include information that is in demand to a large portion of the public.

The Web can't be relied on consistently for historical information, which is often not in high demand. For example, if you need today's weather data for Minneapolis, the Web will certainly have it. But if you want Minneapolis climatic data for November of 1976, you might not find it on the Web.

By evaluating your goals before starting a research project, you may find that you don't need to use the Internet. You may find out that your library has access to an excellent commercial database that provides exactly what you need. Perhaps your library will have a better source in paper form. Don't be shy about asking a reference librarian to help you determine whether the Internet or some other resource will have the most appropriate material to choose from on the topic you are researching.

Choosing the Best Search Tool to Start With

Once you've decided that the Web is likely to have the information you're seeking, you'll need to choose an appropriate *search tool*. Table 2.1 shows the major types of search tools available on the World Wide Web and their major characteristics.

Search engines	Meta-search tools	Directories
- These attempt to index as much of the Web as possible. - Most are full-text databases. - Many require knowledge of search techniques to guarantee good results. - They are most often used for multifaceted or obscure subjects. - They search very large databases that are created by computer programs and are updated regularly.	- Some allow you to search several search engines simultaneously. - Some supply lists of databases that can be searched directly from their pages. - They provide a good way to keep up with new search engines. - They may not fully exploit the features of individual search engines, so keep your search simple.	- These contain topic lists of selected resources, usually hierarchically arranged. - Most resources in these tools have been evaluated carefully. - They can be browsed or searched by keyword. - They contain links to specialized databases and subject guides.

Table 2.1—Major Search Tools and Their Characteristics

A Checklist to Help You Choose the Right Tool

Search engines and meta-search tools should be consulted when looking for the following:

♦ Obscure information

♦ Multifaceted topics

♦ A large amount of information on a particular topic from different perspectives

Search engines and meta-search tools should not be used to find the following:

♦ News that happened yesterday or even last week. You'd be better off going to a specialized database that is updated daily or weekly.

♦ Information in a particular form, such as journal or newspaper articles. You'd be better off searching a specialized database that focuses on the format

♦ Someone's telephone number or email address. Certain services focus specifically on this type of information.

♦ Maps. There are special databases for maps, too.

Directories are most useful for finding the following:

♦ An overview of a topic.

♦ Evaluated resources.

♦ Facts such as population statistics or country information.

♦ A specialized database for specific or very recent information.

Searching the World Wide Web: Using Search Engines

Search engines are tools that use computer programs called **spiders** or **robots** that traverse the Internet and locate hyperlinks available to the public. These spiders or robots load these resources in a database, which you can then search by using a search engine. Each of the major search engines attempts to do the same thing—namely, index as much of the entire Web as possible—so they handle a huge amount of data.

There are advantages to computer-generated databases. They are frequently updated, give access to very large collections, and provide the most comprehensive search results. If you are looking for a specific concept or phrase, a search engine is the best place to start. And you would be smart to look in more than one, because each engine gives different results.

Here are the major search engines:

♦ Google, **http://www.google.com**

♦ Ask, **http://ask.com**

♦ Yahoo!, **http://www.yahoo.com**

♦ Bing, **http://www.bing.com**

Search Engine Similarities

All major search engines are similar in that you enter keywords, phrases, or proper names in a **search form**. After you click on **Search**, **Submit**, **Seek**, or some other similar command button, the database returns a collection of hyperlinks to your screen. The database usually lists them according to their **relevance** to the keyword(s) you typed in, from most to least relevant. Search engines determine relevance in different ways. Generally, they base this determination on how many times the search terms appear in the document. Other search tools (Google, for example) rank results by the number of other Web pages that link to them, or by the most popular sites that others have chosen in the past (for example, Ask.com).

All search engines have online help to acquaint you with their search options. Two common search options that most search engines support are ***Boolean logic*** and ***phrase searching***. We will briefly discuss these two options below. Then, in Chapter 6, "Search Strategies for Search Engines," we will cover these and other search options, which are available on many (but not all) search engines, including *relevancy ranking, field searching, truncation searching,* and *proximity searching*.

Boolean Logic
The Boolean operators are AND, OR, and NOT.

hiking AND camping
♦ The use of AND placed between keywords in your ***search expression*** will narrow the search results.

For example, *hiking AND camping* would narrow your search so that you would receive only those sites that have both the words *hiking* and *camping* in them. The major search engines assume an AND between two words, so there is no need to type AND.

hiking OR camping
♦ Placing an OR between keywords broadens your search results. For example, *hiking OR camping* would retrieve those sites that have either the word *hiking* or the word *camping* in them. The major search engines support the OR operator—but it must be capitalized.

> **F Y I**
> **Finding search engines and other databases on the World Wide Web.**
>
> If you want to look for other search tools on the World Wide Web, or want to keep up to date with the new ones that have been added, there are two excellent places to go:
>
> **FIND NEW ONES HERE**
> ✎ Proteus Internet Search
> **http://www.thrall. org/ proteus.html**
> ✎ Search Engine Watch
> **http://www. searchenginewatch.com**

hiking NOT camping
♦ The NOT operator will also narrow the search. Many search engines allow you to use a minus sign (-) before the word or phrase that is not wanted.

For example, *hiking NOT camping,* or *hiking –camping* would narrow your search so you would get all hiking that did not include camping.

Phrase Searching
Searching by phrase guarantees that the words you type in will appear adjacent to each other, in the order you typed them. Let's say you are searching for information on global warming. If you typed in the two words *global warming* separated by a space, the search engine you're using will assume that you are in effect saying *global AND warming*. In the last case, your search results would not be very precise because the words *global* and *warming* could appear separately from each other throughout the document.

Most search engines support phrase searching, requiring the use of double quotation marks around the phrase, like this:

"global warming"

As search engines have improved their relevancy ranking algorithms, using the phrase searching feature has become less important. Usually search engines will automatically put words together that are often searched as a phrase. It becomes more important when you need to have two words together in a particular order and it may not be readily apparent that they belong together; for example, a person's name, quotation, or a line of poetry containing several words.

Search Engine Differences

The major search engines differ in the following ways:

- Size of the index
- Search options (many search engines support the same options but require you to use different *syntax* in order to initiate them)
- Update frequency
- Ranking of the search results
- Special features such as the ability to search for news, newsgroups, images, and so forth. It is important to know these differences because in order to do an exhaustive search of the World Wide Web, you must be familiar with the different search tools. You cannot rely on a single search engine to satisfy every query. While Google is often cited as the best search engine currently available, it is always a good idea to try your search in Yahoo! or Ask.com to make sure you retrieve the most relevant results possible.

Note about Boolean Logic

Even if you have never typed in AND, OR, or NOT in a search expression, you have used Boolean logic. This is because most search engines incorporate Boolean logic automatically. For example, whenever you type two words in a search form without quotation marks around them, the search engine searches for the two words with an AND between them. It's easier to see Boolean logic at work when you use the advanced search option in most search engines. In forms and pull-down menus asking you to find "any of the words" or "should have" you are essentially ORing words together. In a form asking for "all of the words" or "must have" you are ANDing words together. And in those forms that ask you to "exclude words" or "must not have" you are essentially using the NOT operator.

Now we will do an activity that uses Google to find information on how a specific small business will do in the near future.

◆ACTIVITY◆
2.1 USING GOOGLE'S ADVANCED SEARCH FOR BOOLEAN LOGIC QUERIES

Overview

In this activity we are going to search for information on the current trends and opportunities inherent in the pet grooming business. We have read some articles in the newspaper about mobile pet grooming companies, and that is of some interest to us because we would like to work out of the home. We are intrigued with the idea of going to people's homes and grooming animals in a vehicle that is equipped with the equipment and supplies we need. We have also heard of several franchise opportunities in this field, but we don't want to buy a franchise. With Boolean logic we can exclude that term, and we can OR keywords together. Google supports Boolean logic in the general search mode, but it's much easier to go to its Advanced Search mode and do the search there. Let's see how it works. We'll start by accessing Google at **http://www.google.com**, and then follow these steps:

1. Use Google's Advanced Search mode.
2. Type in keywords and start the search.
3. Examine the search results.

Details

1   Use Google's Advanced Search mode. First, we need to access the Advanced Search page.

DO IT! Click on **Advanced Search** on Google's home page.

2   Type in keywords and start the search.

DO IT! Type **mobile** in the **all these words** box

DO IT! Type **pet grooming business** in the **this exact wording or phrase** box.

DO IT! Type **trends** and then **opportunity** in the **one or more of these words** box.

DO IT! Type **franchise** in the **any of these unwanted words** box.

Your screen should look like the one featured in Figure 2.1.

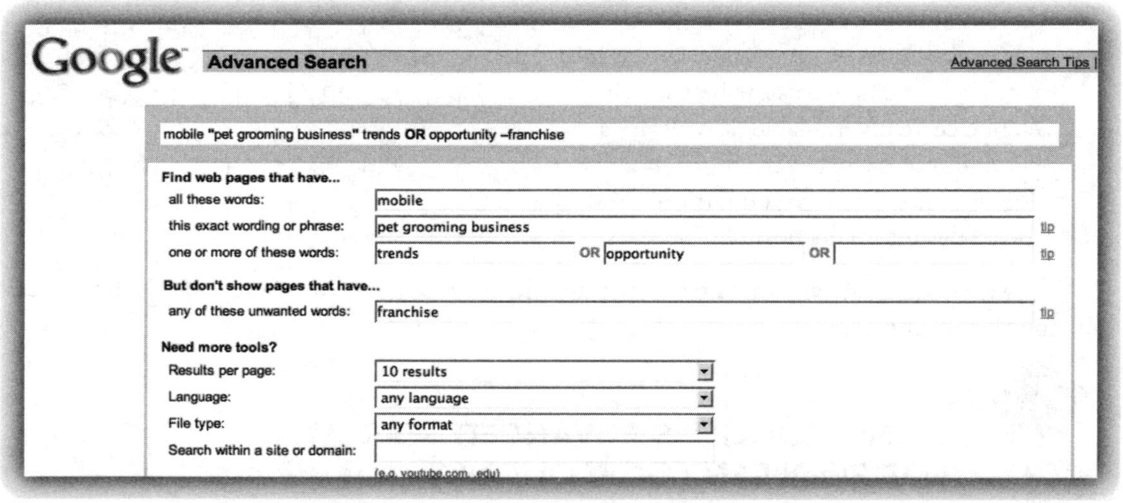

Figure 2.1 —Google's Advanced Search Mode with Keywords Typed In

DO IT! Click on **Advanced Search**.

Figure 2.2 shows the search results. Note that the keywords you typed in the Advanced Search mode appear in the search form at the top of the page. This is the search expression you would have typed in using the general search mode. The links on the right side of the page are "sponsored links"—this means that they have been put there by companies that have paid Google to have their Web sites come up in a search with these keywords.

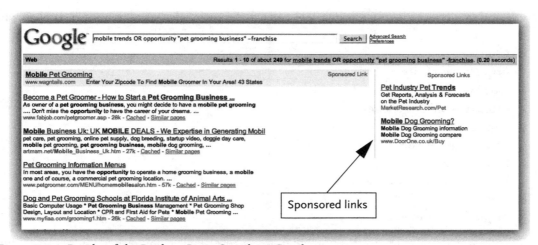

Figure 2.2—Results of the Boolean Logic Search in Google

3   Examine the search results.

Open a few of the Web sites that appear on the first page. Do any of them look useful? If you like any of them, you can bookmark them or add them to your favorites. You could also add them to your Delicious account, if you have registered for it. Note that you can also try other options in Google's Advanced Search mode, such as limiting by domain. Perhaps you'd like to retrieve only those sites that have been produced by U.S. government agencies. To do this, you would type **.gov** in the box next to **Search within a site or domain**. You could also limit your results to a particular file type, for example, **.pdf** (portable document files) or PowerPoint presentations (**.ppt**) in the box next to **File type**.

END OF ACTIVITY 2.1

In this activity, we focused on using Boolean logic in Google's Advanced Search mode. We saw how the Advanced Search mode made using Boolean logic quite easy. Most search engines have advanced search features. It's a good idea to get in the habit of using them because they can help you obtain more precise results. In Chapter 6, we'll discuss this and other search features in more detail.

In the next section, we'll talk about using meta-search tools. These resources allow you to use several search engine databases simultaneously.

Using Several Search Engines Simultaneously: Meta-search Tools

We have mentioned the importance of looking in more than one search engine when trying to find relevant Web pages. Each search engine varies in size, indexing structure, update frequency, and search options. It can be confusing and time-consuming to do your search in several databases, especially if you have to keep track of all of their differences.

To solve some of these problems, database providers have come up with *meta-search tools*. If meta-search tools allow you to use several search engines simultaneously, they are often called *parallel search tools* or *unified search interfaces*. Instead of building their own databases, meta-search tools use the major search engines and directories that already exist on the Internet and provide the user with search forms or interfaces for submitting queries to these search tools. Simply by submitting a query, the meta-search tool collects the most relevant sites in each database and sends them to the screen. Here are the most popular meta-search tools:

- ◆ Clusty,
  http://www.clusty.com
- ◆ Dogpile,
  http://www.dogpile.com
- ◆ Ixquick,
  http://ixquick.com
- ◆ MetaCrawler,
  http://www.metacrawler.com
- ◆ Search.com,
  http://www.search.com

Dogpile is a popular service that provides access to several major search engines, including Google and Yahoo! Dogpile automatically removes duplicate results, and employs an algorithm that ensures that the most useful sites are at the top of the "pile." See an example of a Dogpile search in Figure 2.3.

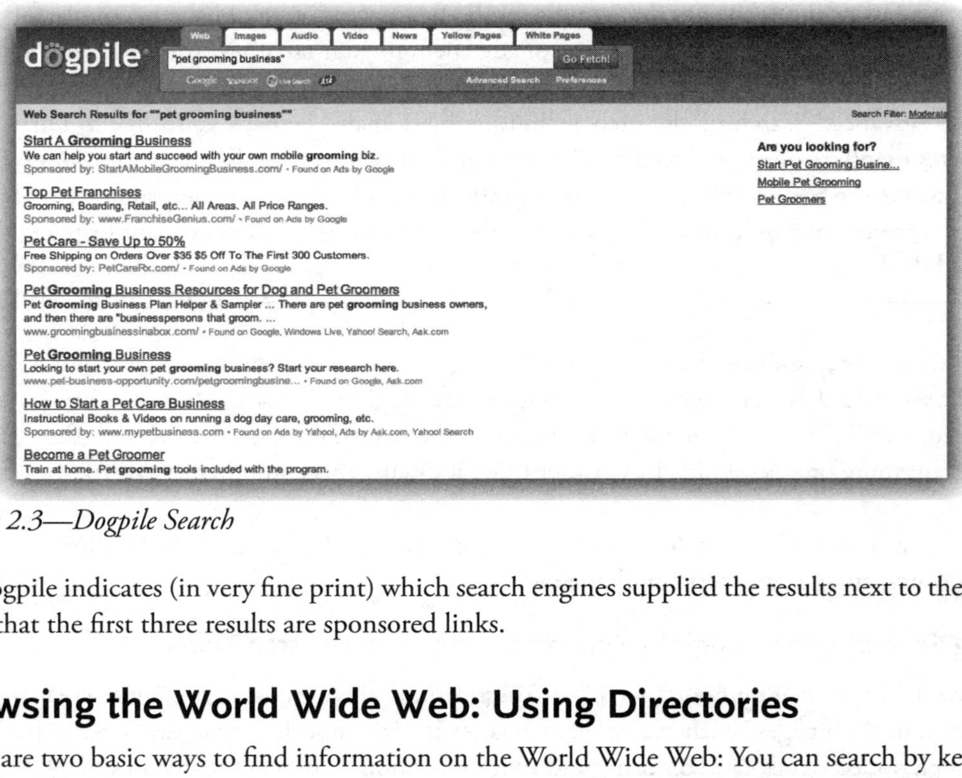

Figure 2.3—Dogpile Search

Dogpile indicates (in very fine print) which search engines supplied the results next to the URL. Note that the first three results are sponsored links.

Browsing the World Wide Web: Using Directories

There are two basic ways to find information on the World Wide Web: You can search by keyword in search engines, or you can browse by subject or search directories by keyword. In this section, we'll focus on browsing and searching directories. While search engine databases are created by computer programs, directories are created and maintained by people. Directories don't cover the entire Web. In fact, directories are very small collections of resources, compared with the huge databases that search engines employ.

Browsing and searching directories can be a very effective way to find the resources you need, especially if you need general information on a broad subject. Some directories contain collections of resources that librarians or other information specialists have carefully chosen and organized in a logical way. The resources you find in these have been selected and placed there because of their excellence and usefulness. In directories, subject experts usually evaluate the included Web sites. Typically, directories provide an organizational *hierarchy* with subject categories to facilitate browsing. Most include query interfaces in order to perform simple searches. If you are at the beginning of your research, or if you are searching for an overview of the topic at hand, it may be helpful to use a directory.

Here are the most well-known directories on the World Wide Web:

- Academic Info: Educational Resources and Subject Guides,
  http://www.academicinfo.net
- ipl2: Information You Can Trust,
  http://www.ipl2.org
- Infomine,
  http://infomine.ucr.edu
- Intute,
  http://www.intute.ac.uk
- LibrarySpot,
  http://libraryspot.com
- Open Directory Project,
  http://dmoz.org
- Yahoo! Directory,
  http://dir.yahoo.com

Browsing Versus Searching a Directory

If you don't want to take the time to browse categories in a directory, you may want to search the directory by keyword. Or you can do both. It is a good idea to use different tactics when looking for something on the Web. Keep in mind, however, that when you search most directories by keyword, you will find Web pages that have the word or words that you are searching for in their titles, annotations, or URLs, not in the Web pages themselves. In the next activity we'll browse a directory by subject, then search by using keywords.

ACTIVITY
2.2   FINDING RESOURCES IN A DIRECTORY

Overview

Let's say you want to find some basic Web sites on entrepreneurship. A good place to find an overview of a subject like this would be a directory like ipl2: Information You Can Trust, **http://www.ipl2.org**. The ipl2 is a merger of two well-known directories created in the 1990s: the Internet Public Library and the Librarians' Internet Index. The ipl2 is currently hosted by Drexel University's College of Information Science & Technology, and is maintained by Drexel and a consortium of universities that have graduate programs in information science. The ipl2 is organized much like a traditional library. It has a reference section, a children's section, a collection of resources for teens, and many others. If you can't find what you're looking for, you can submit your question to a real librarian who will email the answer back to you. You can browse the ipl2 or search its contents. Browsing is sometimes the easiest way to find information; however, because the search tool doesn't search the contents of the resources, only the titles of the resources and annotations attached to them are searched. In this activity, we'll first browse the ipl2 by subject, then we'll search it using a keyword. We'll follow these steps:

1. Browse the ipl2.
2. Search the ipl2.
3. Browse the results of the search.

> **TIP!**
> Remember that the Web is always changing and that your results may differ from those shown here. Don't let this confuse you. The activities demonstrate fundamental skills. These skills don't change, even though what you see when you do this activity may look different.

Details

1   Browse the ipl2.

DO IT!   Type **http://www.ipl2.org** in the location bar and press **Enter**.

ipl2's home page is shown in Figure 2.4.

Figure 2.4—ipl2 Home Page

DO IT!   Click on **Resources by Subject**, as shown in Figure 2.4.

DO IT!   From the list of categories, click on the **Business & Economics** category.

Figure 2.5 shows the resources in Business and Economics. Because we are looking for information about entrepreneurship, the best thing to do would be to click on **Entrepreneurship**, located on the left side of the window, as shown in Figure 2.5.

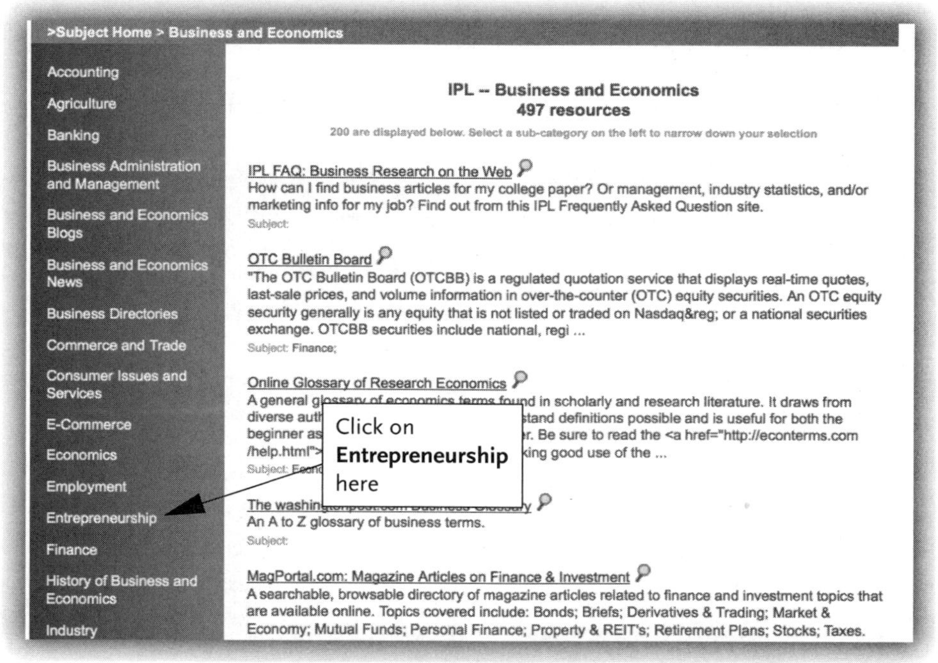

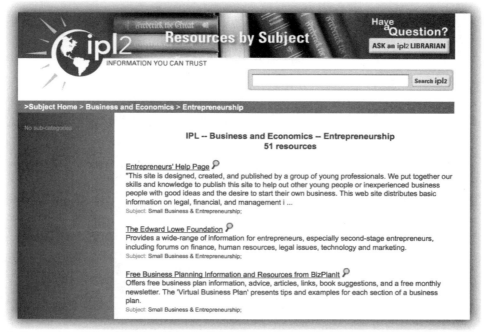

Figure 2.5—Business and Economics Resources in ipl2

DO IT! Click on **Entrepreneurship**, as shown in Figure 2.5.

Figure 2.6 shows some of the resources that are listed in the subcategory **Entrepreneurship**.

Figure 2.6—Entrepreneurship Resources in ipl2

The ipl2 gives us several evaluated Web sites dealing with entrepreneurship. For illustration purposes, let's now search the ipl2 by keyword.

2   Search the ipl2 by keyword.

DO IT!   Type **entrepreneurship** in the form that appears at the top of the page, and click on **Search ipl2**, as shown in Figure 2.7.

Figure 2.7—ipl2's Search Form

3   Browse the results of the search.

Figure 2.8 shows the results of the search. Note that the number of results retrieved from searching yielded over double the amount obtained by browsing. This is because the word **entrepreneurship** shows up in resource annotations and titles located in other categories.

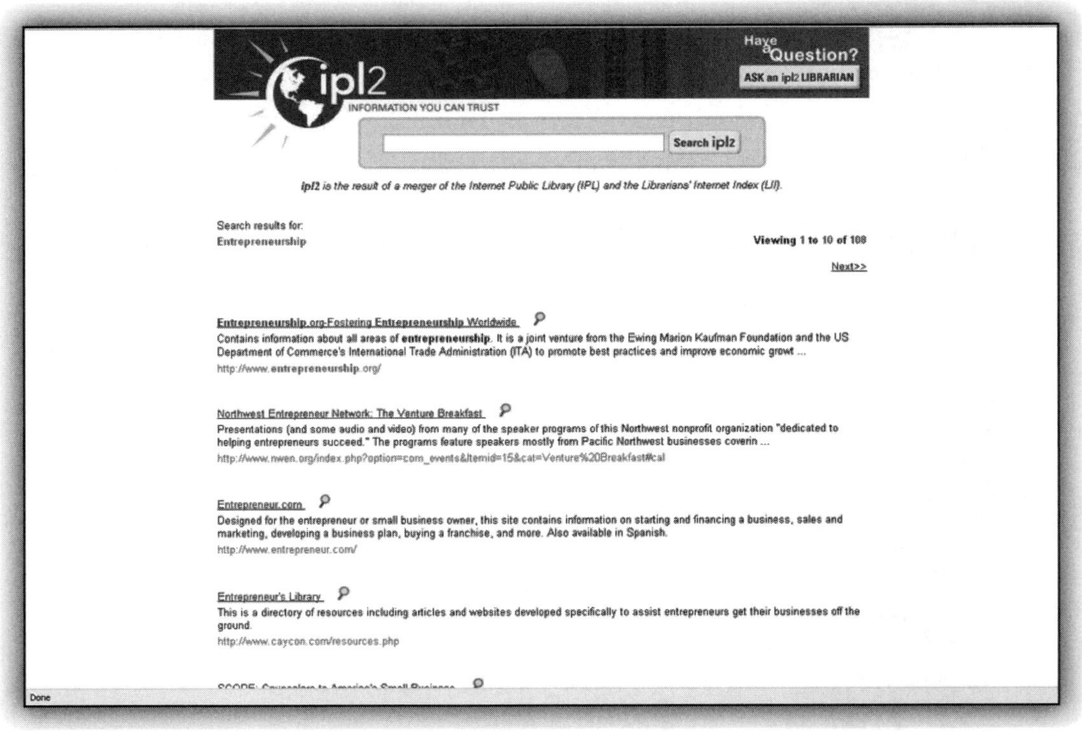

Figure 2.8—Results of Searching ipl2 for Entrepreneurship Resources

---**END OF ACTIVITY 2.2**

You can see from the preceding example that sometimes it is better to search a directory, because you may miss some useful resources if you browse by category only. In this example, entrepreneurship resources were found in more than one subject category. There are other times when browsing yields better results, because the search tool in the ipl2 doesn't find words that are in the body of the Web pages. The words indexed are in the Web pages' titles, their URLs, category titles, and their annotations. Directories can be useful if you have a broad subject and aren't sure how to narrow down the search. They are also helpful if you want to get a general idea about existing resources that will help you focus your topic, and are especially useful as starting points for research and evaluated information on a particular topic.

The Impact of Web 2.0 on Searching

According to the online encyclopedia Wikipedia, **http://www.wikipedia.com**, Web 2.0 is "a term describing the trend in the use of World Wide Web technology and Web design that aims to enhance creativity, information sharing, and, most notably, collaboration among users." Examples of Web 2.0 are blogs, wikis, social bookmarking sites, and others. There are several new search tools that use aspects of Web 2.0 technology; for example, incorporating visual searching, finding results that others have found useful, leading users to particular types of information, such as blogs and wikis, and allowing the user to share and tag useful Web sites that others can tap into. You can see a list of them at Top 25 Web 2.0 Search Engines for College Students, **http://oedb.org/library/ features/top-25-web20-search-engines** and The Top 100 Alternative Search Engines, **http:// www.readwriteweb.com/archives/top_100_alternative_search_engines.php**.

We will show you a couple of search engines that are incorporating some Web 2.0 features: Quintura and Google's SearchWiki.

Quintura (http://www.quintura.com)

Quintura is a visual search engine that gives users a search experience by providing related terms in "clouds" that you then click on to narrow results. For example if you searched for the phrase "organic pet food," as shown in Figure 2.9, Quintura suggests several different terms that are related to your keywords.

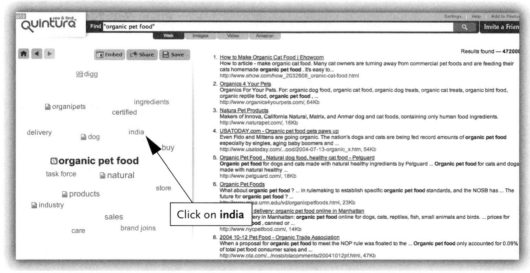

Figure 2.9—Results of Searching for **organic pet food** *in Quintura*

If you clicked on **india**, your search results would be narrowed immediately to those results that contain the word *India*. Note that Quintura automatically added the word India to the original search expression in the search form, as shown in Figure 2.10.

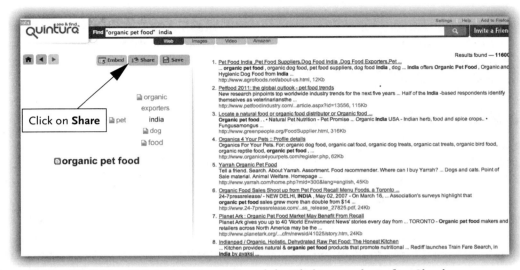

*Figure 2.10—Modifying Original Quintura Search by Clicking on the **india** Cloud*

Quintura makes it easy for users to embed searches into Web pages, to share search results, and to save them using social bookmarking sites, such as Delicious. In Figure 2.11 you can see how easy it is to send your search results or your "organic pet food" cloud to someone else. Simply click on **Share** and a box pops up where you can put in your friend's email address and send a message with the link inserted into the message automatically.

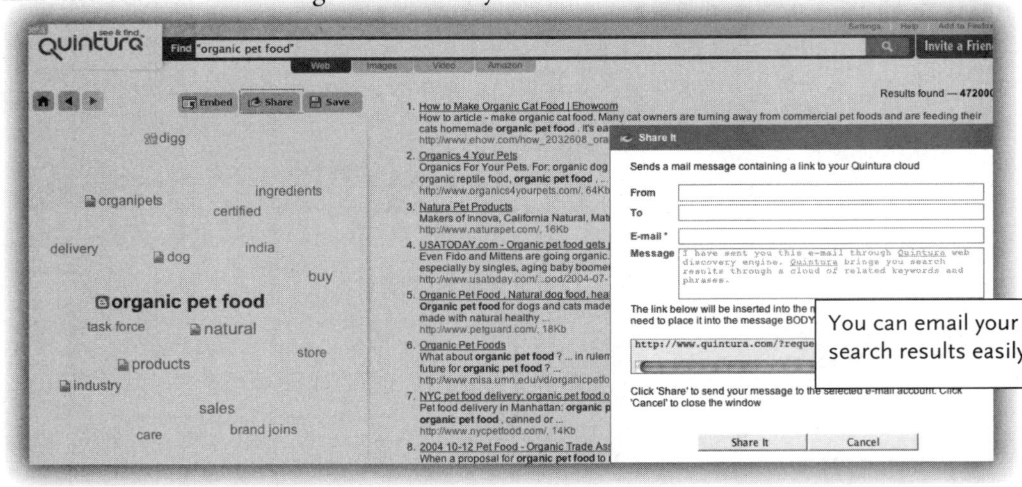

Figure 2.11—Sharing Search Results in Quintura

Google's SearchWiki

If you have a Google account, you can use its SearchWiki function. SearchWiki allows you to customize your search experience by commenting, deleting, and re-ranking search results. You can move results to the top of your list or even add a new site. You can also write notes attached to a particular site or remove results that you feel aren't relevant. If you make modifications using the SearchWiki, the changes will be shown to you every time you do the same search in the future. But you must be signed in to your Google account in order to use it. The changes you make affect only your own searches. You can, however, make your notes public. In that case, others can see the notes you've made by clicking on the link at the bottom of the page, **See all notes for this SearchWiki**.

We'll show you how it works. Remember, in order to try this feature, you must be signed in to your personal Google account.

Let's say you are interested in the COP15, the December 2009 United Nations Climate Change Conference in Copenhagen. Simply type in **cop15**, as shown in Figure 2.12. Under each result, you will see three icons. One is a dialog cloud, another an arrow pointed up, and another with an X. If you click on the first one, a dialog box will open into which you can insert notes. These comments can be kept private, only viewable to you when you are signed in to Google, or you can make them public so that others can see them. The next icon, the upward-pointing arrow, is for pushing the resource up in your results list. For example, if this is a search that you perform often, and this particular resource is one that is particularly useful to you, and you want it to appear at the top of your results list, then clicking on the arrow would put it first. The third icon, the X, is to delete the resource from your results list.

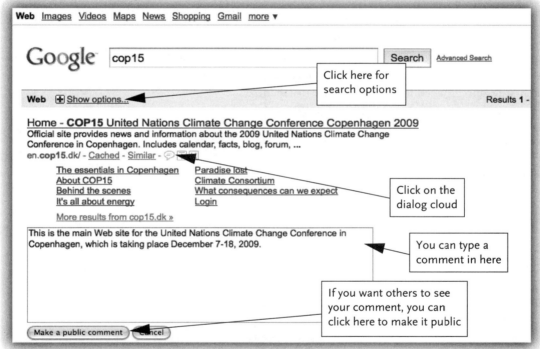

Figure 2.12—The SearchWiki in Google

Another feature of Google is Search Options. Note in Figure 2.12 the link with the plus (+) sign next to it: **Show options**. To use Search Options, you don't need to be signed in to your Google account. If you click on this link, many options will appear on the left side of your window, as shown in Figure 2.13. One of the options is the "Wonder Wheel." If we click on **Wonder Wheel**, a screen like the one shown in Figure 2.13 will appear. The Wonder Wheel gives you a visual representation of related keywords and key phrases related to COP15, much like the visual representation we saw with Quintera.

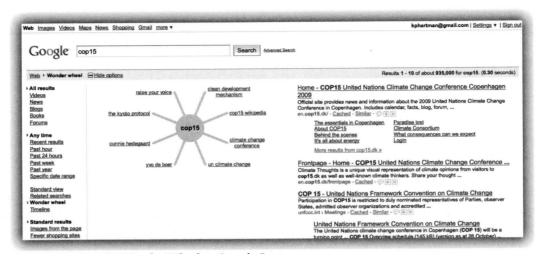

Figure 2.13—Google's Wonder Wheel in Search Options

Another useful search feature is the Timeline. Figure 2.14 gives you a snapshot of this service. The timeline gives you a historical overview of the results on this topic. It provides a graphical representation of information appearing on the Web, broken down by month. If you click on a month, Google will list the resources that have been indexed by Google during that time. Note that the first resources listed in Figure 2.14 are in Japanese.

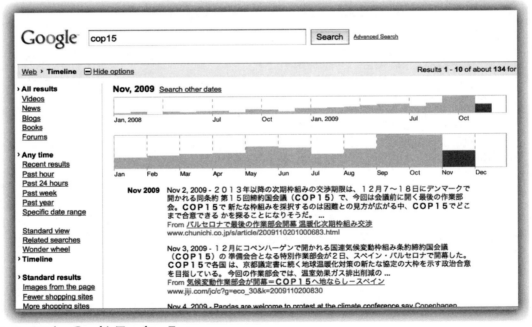

Figure 2.14—Google's Timeline Feature

These are just a few of the interesting search features that Google offers. If you'd like to see other experimental projects that Google is working on, check out Google Labs at **http://www. googlelabs.com**.

Summary

The World Wide Web is an immense collection of valuable information generated by such organizations as universities, corporations, hospitals, associations, and government agencies. Most countries and several languages are represented on the Web. In addition to this, hundreds of thousands of individuals, such as scholars, students, doctors, librarians, teachers, and virtually anyone who wants to contribute to this vast accumulation of resources, are adding their pages to the Web every day, all over the world.

Finding information on the World Wide Web is becoming easier all the time. There are two basic ways to accomplish it: You can either browse or search directories, or you can search by keyword in search engines. Browsing directories can be a very effective way to find the resources you need, especially if you're sure of the general information you're seeking. Directories index neither all of the pages in the World Wide Web nor all of the words that appear in the Web pages they catalog, however, so if you need specific information, a search engine is the tool you'll want to use. Search engine databases aim to cover as much of the Web as possible, and most of them index every word in each Web page.

A directory would be more likely used if we were looking for general information; for example, resources on the AIDS virus. Directories depend on human beings to create and maintain their collections. Directories are the best place to go to for subject guides, reference works, and specialized databases. Some directories are similar to traditional libraries, in that the information specialists who manage them select and catalog the Web pages that are included in their directories, much as librarians select and catalog materials that are included in their libraries.

Search tools are beginning to offer new ways of finding and sharing information using Web 2.0 technologies. For example, some search engines are using visuals and making it easy for the user to share useful Web sites with others.

Selected Terms Used in This Chapter

Boolean logic	parallel search tools	search form
browsing	phrase searching	search tool
directory	relevance	spider
hierarchy	robot	subject catalog
keyword searching	search engine	syntax
meta-search tool	search expression	unified search interface

Review Questions

Multiple Choice

1. A directory
   a. is a subject listing of Web resources.
   b. may be searchable by keyword.
   c. is also called a search engine.
   d. a and b
   e. a and c

2. To browse means to
   a. use phrase searching.
   b. create a search expression.
   c. move from broad to specific subjects in a directory.
   d. move to a top-level directory category.
3. Search engines use _____ to gather information from the Web.
   a. computer programs
   b. information professionals
   c. a and b
   d. none of the above
4. Search engine results are usually arranged
   a. alphabetically.
   b. by subject.
   c. hierarchically.
   d. by relevance or popularity.
5. A meta-search tool is one that
   a. allows you to search a specialized database.
   b. may use several search engines and directories at once.
   c. may give access to many search engine search forms from one page.
   d. a and c
   e. b and c

True or False

6. T F A meta-search tool lets you search different search engines at one time.
7. T F To find information on a very specialized topic, it's best to browse a directory.
8. T F Spiders and robots are software programs associated with search engines.
9. T F Many directories can be searched by keyword.
10. T F Directories are usually larger than search engines since they try to include all resources on a topic.
11. T F A hierarchical directory is one where the subjects are arranged from broadest to most specific.
12. T F One advantage of a search engine is that results have been screened by real people.

Completion

13. The two basic ways to find information on the Web are to _____ a directory or to use _____.
14. Quintura is an example of a search engine that uses aspects of _____ technology.
15. If we type the words **lakes OR oceans** into a search engine, we are performing a(n) _____ search.
16. If we type **"genetically engineered crops"** into a search engine, we are engaging in _____ searching.
17. _____ refers to how closely a database entry matches a search request.
18. Web 2.0 emphasizes _____ information and _____ among users.

19. To find general or background information on a subject, a _____ might be the best place to start your search on the Web.

Exercises and Projects

1. Go to Google at **http://www.google.com** and search for information about Nilo Cruz, the Pulitzer Prize winning playwright. How many results did you obtain? What play of his won the Pulitzer Prize? Give the URL of a site that includes this information.

2. Using Ask.com at **http://ask.com**, look for Dadaism. Find a page that gives a definition of the term. Give both the definition and the URL of the site where you found it.

3. Here's a little exercise on the importance of phrase searching:

   a. Go to Google at **http://www.google.com**. Type the words **bats in your belfry** into the search box. How many results did you find? Look at the first page of results. Are they relevant to your search for that phrase? Now go back and add quotation marks around the phrase. How many results did you obtain this time?

   b. Now suppose you are looking for historical information about the medieval Norsemen and their battles. Go to Yahoo! at **http://www.yahoo.com**. You are looking for a place called the Kirk of Skulls. Type the words **Kirk of Skulls** in at Yahoo! How many results do you find? Now add the quotation marks around the phrase. How many results did you find? Did you find your answer? Where is the site located?

4. Our look at how communication has changed over the years has brought us to the era of illuminated manuscripts. Go to Google at **http://www.google.com** and look for information about them. Will you use a phrase search? How many results do you obtain? Click on some of the results and give the title and URL of a site that gives good information about the history and making of these manuscripts.

5. Using the Open Directory Project, **http://dmoz.org**, find a list of resources available on children's nutrition by browsing the directory. Give the title, URL, and a brief description of each of the three most relevant sites you find. (You may find some interesting recipes here as well!)

6. Using Yahoo!'s directory, **http://directory.yahoo.com** look for information about Great Depression. Choose four sites to visit and compare the range of information you find at each one. Would you, too, recommend these sites? Give the title and URL of the site you think is the best, and explain why you like it.

7. Suppose you collect comic books as a hobby and are interested in finding Web sites about them.

   a. Try browsing through Library Spot's directory at **http://www.libraryspot.com**. How do you like the way this directory is set up? What categories did you browse to find your topic? Is this directory searchable by keyword?

   b. Look for the same subject in the Yahoo! Directory at **http://directory.yahoo. com**. In what category was your topic found here? Is this directory searchable by keyword?

   c. Did you prefer one directory over the other for this topic? Why?

8. Go to the ipl2 at **http://www.ipl2.org** and browse the categories to find resources about the performing arts. Under what category did you find the topic? What other subtopics are listed under Performing Arts?

9. Go back to the ipl2 at **http://www.ipl2.org** and, using the Search feature, look for sites about the following topics. How many do you find? Go to one site for each topic and describe what is available there.
    a. Motorcycles
    b. RSS
    c. Cosmology

CHAPTER 3

Evaluating Information Found on the World Wide Web

Critical thinking skills have always been important to the process of searching for and using information from media such as books, journals, radio broadcasts, television reports, and so forth. With the advent of the Internet and the World Wide Web, these skills have become even more crucial. Traditional books and journal articles need to pass some kind of editorial scrutiny before being published. Web pages, however, can appear without a single person ever reading them through to check for accuracy. Libraries have collection development policies that govern what material they will and will not buy; the Internet and the Web, having no such policies, collect anything. This isn't to say that there isn't information of high quality on the Internet. There are thousands of high-caliber Web sites and well-regarded databases. It is your responsibility to decide whether a page or site is worth selecting and then determine, using well-established guidelines, whether the information is worth using in your research paper, project, or presentation. In this chapter, we'll look at some issues related to evaluating resources on the World Wide Web. The chapter will include these sections:

- ◆ Reasons to Evaluate
- ◆ Guidelines for Evaluation
- ◆ Information About Evaluating Resources on the World Wide Web

Reasons to Evaluate

We use the information found on the Web for a variety of purposes. Sometimes we use it for entertainment, recreation, or casual conversation. When we use it for research, to bolster a belief, or to choose a particular course of action, we have to be sure the information is reliable and authoritative. That puts us in the position of having to verify the information and make judgments about its appropriateness. Reliable information is one of the most important things in life. In order to make decisions and understand our world, we need the most truthful information that we can find.

The nature of the Internet and the World Wide Web makes it easy for almost anyone to create and disperse information. People also have the freedom to design their pages to advertise products or disseminate propaganda unnoticeable within the context of a research report. To think critically about information and its sources means being able to separate fact from opinion. We have to be able to verify information and know its source, we have to determine whether the facts are current, and we need to know why someone offered the information at all. In some situations, we don't have to do all the work ourselves. Some librarians and other information specialists have established directories on the Web in which the listed sources have been reviewed and evaluated. The following are the best directories for evaluated resources:

- Infomine,
  http://infomine.ucr.edu
- ipl2: Information You Can Trust,
  http://www.ipl2.org
- Intute,
  http://www.intute.ac.uk/
- Library Spot,
  http://libraryspot.com
- Refdesk.com,
  http://www.refdesk.com

It's useful to visit these sites to find information that's been reviewed by someone else. Still, when you deal with any information you find on the Web or in a library, it is up to you to be skeptical about it and to assess whether it's appropriate for your purposes. For example, if you want information before buying a new computer, then product announcements from manufacturers will give you some data, but the announcements will probably not be the right source for impartial brand comparisons. If you're researching techniques for advertising electronic consumer products, then the advertisements might be good resource material; if you are writing about the physics involved in producing sound on a MacBook, however, these ads may not be authoritative sources.

Once you find some information, regardless of whether the resource is a book, journal article, Web page, or data from a commercial database, a librarian can help you evaluate its usefulness and quality. Librarians, particularly reference librarians, are trained professionals who have lots of experience with evaluating resources. They can usually tell you within seconds if information is relevant, authoritative, and appropriate for your research needs.

Guidelines for Evaluation

After typing an appropriate search expression in a search tool, scan the results. Open a document, and if it isn't readily apparent why that resource has come up in your hit list, activate the Find operation by clicking on **Edit**, choosing **Find**, and typing one of your keywords in the search form. **Find** will take you to the part of the Web page where the word or phrase appears. Sometimes the Find operation won't locate the keyword or phrase in the page. This may mean that an earlier version of the page contained the keyword. You'll often discover that the keyword is used in a context that is irrelevant to your research needs. Once you've found a page that appears to be fairly applicable to your topic, you can begin to use the following guidelines for evaluation.

The determination of information quality is not a cut-and-dried process. You can infer quality by clues that will either support or negate your research. Sometimes you need to rely on your intuition or your own previous knowledge about a particular piece of information. Noting this, the following guidelines are just that: guidelines. They are not meant to be absolute rules for evaluating documents found on the Internet and the Web. They are questions that you should ask yourself when looking at Web pages and other Internet sources. After briefly explaining the guidelines, we will indicate how you can apply them to documents and other information that you retrieve from the Web or the Internet.

Who Is the Author or Institution?

♦ If an individual has written the resource, does it offer or give links to biographical information about the author? For example, does it mention educational or other credentials, an occupation, or an institutional affiliation?

♦ What clues does the URL give you about the source's authority? A tilde (~) in the Web page's URL usually indicates that it is a personal page rather than part of an institutional Web site. Also, make a mental note of the domain section of the URL, as follows:

  ♦ **.edu**, educational—can be anything from serious research to zany student pages
  ♦ **.gov**, governmental—government resources
  ♦ **.com**, commercial—may be trying to sell a product
  ♦ **.net**, network—may provide services to commercial or individual customers
  ♦ **.org**, organization—is a nonprofit institution; may be biased
  ♦ **.mil**, military—U.S. military sites, agencies, and some academies
  ♦ Countries other than the United States use two-letter codes as the final part of their domain names. The United States uses **.us** in the domain name when designating state and local government hosts, as well as public schools (**.k12** is often used).

Who Is the Audience?

♦ Is the Web page intended for the general public, or is it meant for scholars, practitioners, children, and so forth? Is the audience clearly stated?

♦ Does the Web page meet the needs of its stated audience?

Is the Content Accurate and Objective?

♦ Are there political, ideological, cultural, religious, or institutional biases?

♦ Is the content intended to be a brief overview of the topic or an in-depth analysis?

♦ If the information is opinion, is this clearly stated?

♦ If there are facts and statistics included, are they properly cited?

♦ Is it clear how the data was collected, and is it presented in a logical, organized way?

♦ Is there a bibliography at the end of the document?

♦ If the page is part of a larger institution's Web site, does the institution appear to filter the information that appears at its site? Was the information screened somehow before it was put on the Web?

What Is the Purpose of the Information?

♦ Is the purpose of the information to inform, explain, convince, market a product, or advocate a cause?

♦ Is the purpose clearly stated?

♦ Does the resource fulfill the stated purpose?

How Current Is the Information?

♦ Does the Web page have a date that indicates when it was placed on the Web?

♦ Is it clear when the page was last updated?

♦ Is some of the information obviously out of date?

♦ Does the page creator mention how frequently the material is updated?

♦ Are there any hyperlinks that don't work?

Discussion and Tips

We will now discuss the each of these guidelines in detail, giving you some concrete examples for each question you should ask yourself when evaluating a Web site.

Who Is the Author or Institution?

If you're not familiar with the author or institution responsible for producing the information, you'll need to do some checking to determine whether the source is reliable and authoritative. You can't consider a resource reliable if you don't know who wrote it or what institution published it. If a Web page doesn't give information about the author or the institution, and if there are no hyperlinks to Web pages that give that information, then you should be suspicious of its content.

> **TIP!**
> Cut off, or "truncate back" the URL to find out who sponsored the Web site. Simply delete the end of the URL stopping just before the first slash (/). This is the page's server name and might provide you with some information on who is responsible for the information.

Being suspicious doesn't always mean that you must disqualify the information. For example, the article "A Study of the Effect of Global Warming on the Spread of Vector-Borne Diseases," **http://www.davidzimet.com/words/w99project/index.html**, doesn't give information about the authors and doesn't give a link to the organization that sponsored the information, but with some sleuthing we can find out more about the document and possibly use it to support our research. By truncating the URL—in other words, cutting off the end of it back to the domain name—we can find out who sponsors the Web page. By doing searches on the authors' names in a search engine we can find out more about them. In this case, we find out that this article was written in 1999 by students at the University of Michigan. If you were researching this topic and wanted to use this paper as a documenting source in your research, you would want to clarify that this was an unpublished undergraduate student paper. This shouldn't automatically disqualify the usefulness of the paper if you bolster your list of references with articles from published academic journals.

> **TIP!**
> To find further information about the institution or author, use a search engine to see what related information is available on the Web.

> **TIP!**
> To find out about the sponsor, go to the home page for the site that hosts the information.

Regardless of whether the Web page contains the sponsor's name, we can investigate further by looking for more information about the author or institution. For example, consider the document "Free Expression," **http://www.cdt. org/issue/free-expression**. Looking at that Web page, we

> **TIP!**
> Look for the name of the author or institution at the top or bottom of a Web page.

can see that the Center for Democracy and Technology (CDT) has made it available. There are hyperlinks from that Web page to the home page for CDT. You can follow the hyperlinks to find out more about the CDT, or you can go to the home page by typing the URL **http://www.cdt.org** in the location bar and pressing **Enter**.

When you can't find your way to a home page or to other information, try using a search engine, directory, or other service to search the Web.

> **T I P !**
> Use Google Groups, **http://groups.google. com**, to search for information about the author or institution that produced the Web site.

Who Is the Audience?

Web pages are sometimes written to give information to a specific group: the general public, researchers and scholars, professionals in a specific field, children, potential customers, or others.

Try to determine the intended audience, as that may have an impact on whether the information is relevant or appropriate for your purpose. Suppose you are preparing a report on sustainable forest management. An appropriate information resource, whether in print or on the Web, is one that is written for your level of expertise and for the expertise of your audience. The Web page Strategic Planning and Resource Assessment, **http://www.fs.fed.us/plan**, by the United States Department of Agriculture, Forest Service, might be useful for a general overview of the issues and principles involved in forest management. On the other hand, the Web page Alternatives to Methyl Bromide: Research Needs for California, **http://www.cdpr.ca.gov/docs/dprdocs/methbrom/mb4chg.htm**, is more appropriate for a specialized audience.

Knowing the intended audience can alert you to possible bias. For example, let's say you are looking for information on the anti-acne drug Accutane. You find an in-depth article called "Should Your Teenager Use Accutane?" and learn about both the negatives and positives of this drug, complete with explanations of the possible side effects. By examining the URL and accessing hyperlinks within the document, you find out that the page was published by a well-known pharmaceutical company. Immediately you should realize that the likely intended audience for this page is potential customers. This doesn't mean that you couldn't use the information. But it is important to be aware of bias and hidden persuasion in Web pages.

What Is the Purpose of the Information?

When you are evaluating information that you have found on the World Wide Web or in print, you need to consider its purpose. You need to ask yourself, is this information meant to convince, inform, teach, or entertain? Information on the Web can be produced in a variety of formats and styles, and the appearance sometimes gives a clue to its intent. Web pages aimed to market something are often designed in a clever way to catch our attention and emphasize a product. Some Web pages that are primarily oriented toward marketing a product do not clearly distinguish between the informational content of the page and the advertising. It may appear to be an informational page but actually be an advertisement. It's your job, then, to concentrate on the content and to determine the purpose of the information so you'll feel comfortable using it for research or other purposes.

Is the Content Accurate and Objective?

One of the first things to look for in a Web page is spelling errors. Spelling and grammatical errors not only indicate a lack of editorial control but also undermine the accuracy of the information.

It is also extremely important that statistics, research findings, and other claims are documented and cited very carefully. Otherwise, the author could be distorting information or using unreliable data. In the best situations, claims or statistics on Web pages are supported by original research or by hyperlinks or footnotes to the primary sources of the information.

Sometimes, however, you will have to verify the accuracy and objectivity of published information on your own. A good way to do this is by checking to see if the information can be corroborated by other sources. Some researchers promote triangulation: finding at least three sources that agree with the opinions or statistics that the author expounds as fact. If the sources don't agree, you'll need to do more work before you conclude your research. Remember that traditional resources such as books, journal articles, and other material available in libraries may contain more comprehensive information than what is on the Web. You can use those resources as part of the corroboration process as well.

How Current Is the Information?

In some cases, it's important to know whether the information you're using is up to date. Take, for example, the student research paper we looked at earlier. The fact that it was written in 1999 is important because the data and other research are most probably out of date. If you cited this paper you'd most definitely need to update the research with more recent information. This is particularly true when you're using information that contains statistics. If the information is of the type that is frequently updated—for example, a news report, then try to be sure you have the most recent information. Check the date on the Web page, and if it's more than a month old, search for a more recent version.

A well-designed Web page indicates when the information was last updated, often at the top or bottom of the page. That will tell you the date of the last modification to the file.

ACTIVITY
3.1   APPLYING GUIDELINES TO EVALUATE RESOURCES

Overview

In this activity, we'll apply the guidelines for evaluating information on the Web. If we were researching a topic related to the nutritional advantages of organic food, we might come across the following two articles: one is titled "Unearthing the Truth About Organic Food," **http://www.cgfi.org/2001/09/05/unearthing-the-truth-about-organic-food**, and the other is titled "Is Organically Grown Food More Nutritious?" **http://www.mindfully.org/Food/Organic-More-Nutritious-WorthingtonNov01.htm.** The first article is quite negative about the nutritional advantages of organic food, and the second one claims that organic food is much better for us than food grown in more conventional ways. We'll evaluate each of these two articles by going through the guidelines, asking the following questions:

1. Who is the author or institution?
2. Who is the audience?

3. What is the purpose of the information?
4. Is the content accurate and objective?
5. How current is the information?

In this activity, we'll be able to obtain answers in a rather direct way. It's not always so straightforward, but this is meant to be a demonstration. In your own work, you may have to be more persistent and discerning.

Remember that the Web is always changing and that your results may differ from those shown here. Don't let this confuse you. The activities demonstrate fundamental skills. These skills don't change, even though the number of results obtained or the actual screens may look very different.

Details

DO IT! Go to the first article discussed in this activity by typing in its URL, **http://www. cgfi.org/2001/09/05/unearthing-the-truth-about-organic-food**.

1 Who is the author or institution?

Figure 3.1 shows the beginning of the Web page we're considering. The article is written by Dennis T. and Alex A. Avery, and it's posted on a Web site produced by the Center for Global Food Issues (CGFI). There is a link entitled **About CGFI** on this page. Let's find out about this organization.

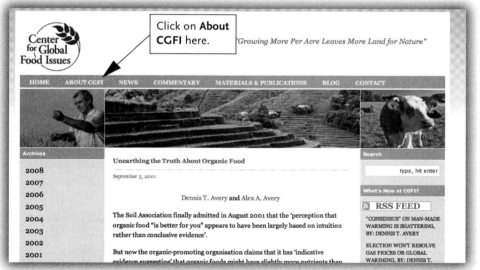

Figure 3.1—"Unearthing the Truth About Organic Food," on the Center for Global Food Issues Web Site

DO IT! Click on the link **About CGFI** as shown in Figure 3.1 Figure 3.2 shows part of the information about the CGFI.

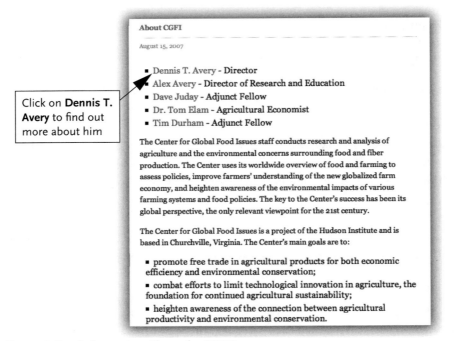

Figure 3.2—Information About the CGFI

We find out that Dennis Avery, one of the authors, is director of the Center for Global Food Issues. We can find out more about him by clicking on the link **Dennis T. Avery** on the About CGFI page, as pictured in Figure 3.2. We find out that Mr. Avery studied agricultural economics and has worked as an agricultural analyst for the U.S. government. We could also find out more about Dennis Avery by doing a search in a major search engine, or going to Google Groups to see what others are saying about him. Google Groups is a service that indexes group discussions.

DO IT! Go to Google Groups, at **http://groups.google.com**. Type in the name **Dennis Avery** in the search form.

Figure 3.3 shows part of the results of this search. There are several discussions that mention his name. They appear to be about the Douglas Avery we are interested in because the discussions center on food issues.

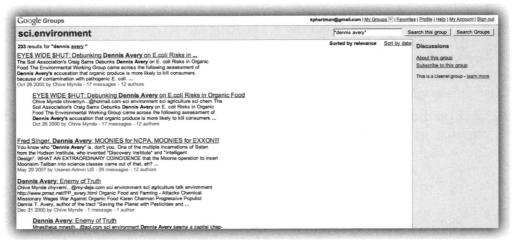

Figure 3.3—Results of the Google Groups Search on Dennis Avery

We also find out that the CGFI is a project of the Hudson Institute. We can do a search in a search engine to learn about the Hudson Institute.

DO IT! Go to Yahoo! at **http://www.yahoo.com** and search for **Hudson Institute**. The first result is a link to the institute's home page at **http://www.hudson.org**. From the home page, there is a prominent link titled **About Hudson**. Click on it and a drop-down menu appears. The first link is to the Hudson Institute's Mission Statement. Go ahead and click on this link. Figure 3.4 shows the beginning of the Hudson Institute's mission statement.

Figure 3.4—The Hudson Institute's Mission Statement

The Hudson Institute is a private, non-profit policy research organization that makes recommendations to government and business leaders on several issues, including global food and the environment.

2   Who is the audience?

While the site doesn't specifically say what audience the information presented is geared towards, we infer that is written for adults who are probably already cynical about the nutritional advantages of organic food. It assumes that the people reading the article have similar views as the authors.

3   What is the purpose of the information?

To answer this question we should return to the Center for Global Food Issues and read more about this institution, and its parent organization, the Hudson Institute. We can read about what these institutions say about themselves, and also what others say about them. At this point, it might be useful to go back to the Yahoo! results and see if there's other information about the Hudson Institute.

DO IT! Click the Back icon in your browser until you return to the Yahoo! results.

One of the sites listed is a Wikipedia article at **http://en.wikipedia.org/wiki/Hudson_Institute**. Let's click on it and see what Wikipedia, the online encyclopedia, has to say about the Hudson Institute. Figure 3.5 shows the beginning the entry. In this article, a footnoted piece of information states which companies fund the organization. This information can help us determine what the information's purpose is—to possibly publish information that fits with these companies' products and concerns.

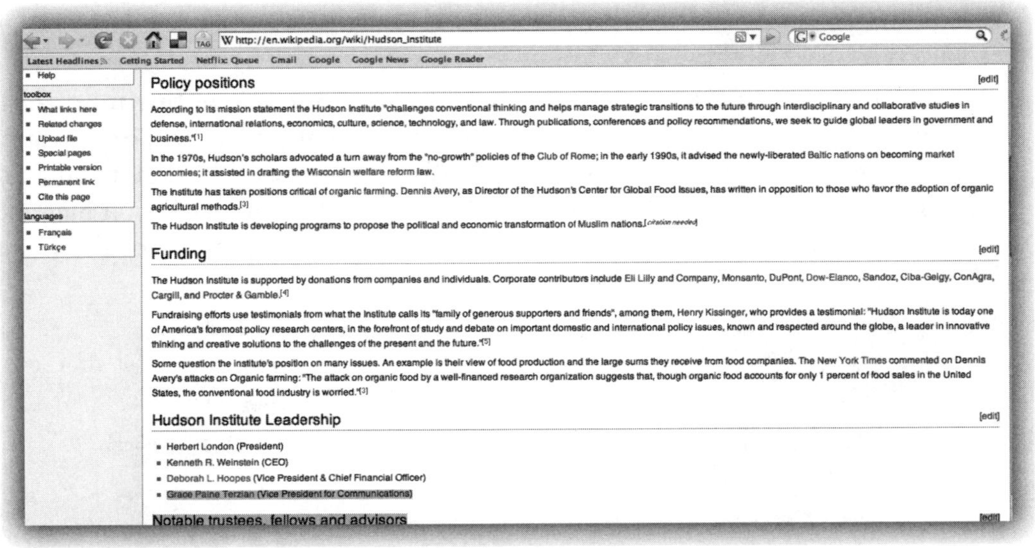
http://en.wikipedia.org/wiki/Hudson_Institute

Latest Headlines Getting Started Netflix Queue Gmail Google Google News Google Reader

- Help

toolbox

- What links here
- Related changes
- Upload file
- Special pages
- Printable version
- Permanent link
- Cite this page

languages

- Français
- Türkçe

Policy positions [edit]

According to its mission statement the Hudson Institute "challenges conventional thinking and helps manage strategic transitions to the future through interdisciplinary and collaborative studies in defense, international relations, economics, culture, science, technology, and law. Through publications, conferences and policy recommendations, we seek to guide global leaders in government and business."[1]

In the 1970s, Hudson's scholars advocated a turn away from the "no-growth" policies of the Club of Rome; in the early 1990s, it advised the newly-liberated Baltic nations on becoming market economies; it assisted in drafting the Wisconsin welfare reform law.

The Institute has taken positions critical of organic farming. Dennis Avery, as Director of the Hudson's Center for Global Food Issues, has written in opposition to those who favor the adoption of organic agricultural methods.[3]

The Hudson Institute is developing programs to propose the political and economic transformation of Muslim nations.[citation needed]

Funding [edit]

The Hudson Institute is supported by donations from companies and individuals. Corporate contributors include Eli Lilly and Company, Monsanto, DuPont, Dow-Elanco, Sandoz, Ciba-Geigy, ConAgra, Cargill, and Procter & Gamble.[4]

Fundraising efforts use testimonials from what the Institute calls its "family of generous supporters and friends", among them, Henry Kissinger, who provides a testimonial: "Hudson Institute is today one of America's foremost policy research centers, in the forefront of study and debate on important domestic and international policy issues, known and respected around the globe, a leader in innovative thinking and creative solutions to the challenges of the present and the future."[5]

Some question the institute's position on many issues. An example is their view of food production and the large sums they receive from food companies. The New York Times commented on Dennis Avery's attacks on Organic farming: "The attack on organic food by a well-financed research organization suggests that, though organic food accounts for only 1 percent of food sales in the United States, the conventional food industry is worried."[3]

Hudson Institute Leadership [edit]

- Herbert London (President)
- Kenneth R. Weinstein (CEO)
- Deborah L. Hoopes (Vice President & Chief Financial Officer)
- Grace Paine Terzian (Vice President for Communications)

Notable trustees, fellows and advisors [edit]

Figure 3.5—Wikipedia article about the Hudson Institute

4 Is the content accurate and objective?

The article discusses a report written by Shane Heaton and published by the United Kingdom's Soil Association, and criticizes its findings that organic food is nutritionally better than food grown with pesticides. The article doesn't provide a link to the Soil Association's report. It doesn't have a list of references supporting its opinion. Therefore, it is quite safe to say that this article is not objective. The tone of the article is dismissive of the Soil Association's perspective. If we do a search for Soil Association in a search engine, however, we discover that it is a proponent of organic farming and makes the claim on its Web site that organic food is nutritionally better for people.

5 How current is the information?

The date of the article, September 5, 2001, is clearly stated at the beginning of the report. At the time of the writing of this book, this information is about eight years old. There could be a lot of contradictory evidence that has been published since this date.

The next article we will examine takes the opposite view from the one on the CGFI site. To begin, you'll want to access the article at **http://www.mindfully.org/Food/Organic-More-Nutritious-WorthingtonNov01.htm.**

1 Who is the author? In Figure 3.6 we see the beginning of the article "Is Organically Grown Food More Nutritious?" It is authored by Virginia Worthington and is published on a Web site called mindfully.org.

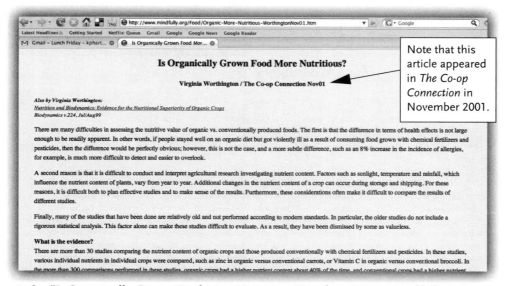

Figure 3.6—"Is Organically Grown Food More Nutritious?" on http://www.mindfully.org

To find out something about Virginia Worthington, we can search for her name in a search engine.

DO IT! Go to Google at **http://www.google.com** and type **"Virginia Worthington"**.

A recent posting tells us that Ms. Worthington died in 2006. Her biography in the *Washington Post* mentions that she was a huge proponent of organic food. Her academic credentials in the subject are noteworthy—a Master's degree in nutrition and a PhD in international health.

By truncating the URL back to the domain name, **mindfully.org**, we can find out something about the organization that published this article.

DO IT! Highlight the URL back to **.org/** and press the ⎡Delete⎤ key. Then press ⎡Enter⎤. Figure 3.7 shows the home page of **http://www.mindfully.org**.

Figure 3.7—Home Page of Mindfully.org, **http://www.mindfully.org**

DO IT! To find out about this organization, click on the link titled **About Mindfully.org**, as shown in Figure 3.7.

Figure 3.8 shows part of this page. The page doesn't give any information about the people who run this organization. There is no telephone number or street address.

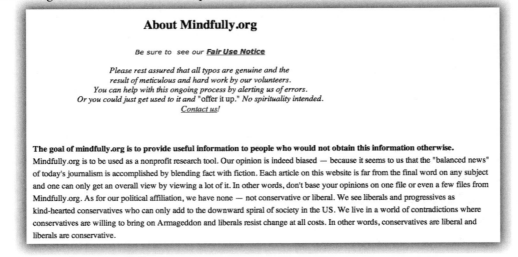

About Mindfully.org

Be sure to see our **Fair Use Notice**

*Please rest assured that all typos are genuine and the
result of meticulous and hard work by our volunteers.
You can help with this ongoing process by alerting us of errors.
Or you could just get used to it and "offer it up." No spirituality intended.*
Contact us!

The goal of mindfully.org is to provide useful information to people who would not obtain this information otherwise.
Mindfully.org is to be used as a nonprofit research tool. Our opinion is indeed biased — because it seems to us that the "balanced news"
of today's journalism is accomplished by blending fact with fiction. Each article on this website is far from the final word on any subject
and one can only get an overall view by viewing a lot of it. In other words, don't base your opinions on one file or even a few files from
Mindfully.org. As for our political affiliation, we have none — not conservative or liberal. We see liberals and progressives as
kind-hearted conservatives who can only add to the downward spiral of society in the US. We live in a world of contradictions where
conservatives are willing to bring on Armageddon and liberals resist change at all costs. In other words, conservatives are liberal and
liberals are conservative.

Figure 3.8—About Mindfully.org

2   Who is the Audience?

We can make some assumptions about the type of audience by going back to the About Mindfully.org Web page. The authors state that they are not liberal or conservative and urge readers to not base their opinions on one or two articles of the site. The audience of the actual article by Virginia Worthington is people who are wondering about the nutritional benefits of organic food.

3   What is the purpose of the information?

The scientific approach and explanation that the author uses would seem to suggest that Dr. Worthington wanted to prove to her audience that organic food is more nutritious.

4   Is the content accurate and objective?

This particular article doesn't have any references. At the bottom of the report, you'll find the following:

> A complete version of this article entitled, "Effect of Agricultural Methods on
> Nutritional Quality: A Comparison of Organic with Conventional Crops" by
> Dr. Virginia Worthington, appeared in *Alternative Therapies*, Volume 4, 1998,
> pages 58–69.

If you want to read the full paper, you could check to see if your local library subscribes to the journal Alternative Therapies. You could also do a search in a search engine on the title of the article to see if it has been published in full text at another Web site. The authors of this book tried this at the time of this writing and could not find the full text on the open Web.

Another bit of information that we can glean from this report on its accuracy and objectivity is the fact that this article appeared in the *Co-op Connection* (see Figure 3.5). At the bottom of the Web page we read:

> The Co-op Connection is published by La Montanita Co-op Supermarket.
> www.lamontanita.org

If we go to the URL **http://www.lamontanita.org**, we find out that the La Montanita Co-op Supermarket is a store in California that sells organic foods. This leads us to think that perhaps the information may be biased.

There is a link to another article the author wrote, which is also on the mindfully.org Web site. You will find that link at the beginning of the article, as shown in Figure 3.5.

DO IT! Click on **Nutrition and Biodynamics: Evidence for the Nutritional Superiority of Organic Crops**, shown in Figure 3.6.

This 1999 article was published in the journal *Biodynamics*. This article includes several references to studies related to this topic.

5   How current is the information?

The date of the article is November 2001. Because this information is more than eight years old, it would be a good idea to do more research on this topic for information published since that date.

Conclusion

After researching the authors and the institutions responsible for posting these two articles, we come to the conclusion that the coverage of this topic is fraught with political biases. We recommend that if you were searching for information on the nutritional aspects of organic food that you should search an academic database such as PubMed, **http://www.ncbi.nlm.nih.gov/pubmed**. PubMed indexes thousands of academic medical journals from all around the world. The database indexes the articles but doesn't usually contain the full text of these articles. If you found an article you wanted to read, you may have to contact your local library to see if it subscribes to the journal, or pay for the article from the publisher's Web site.

Figure 3.9 shows the search we could run in PubMed on this topic, with some of the results listed.

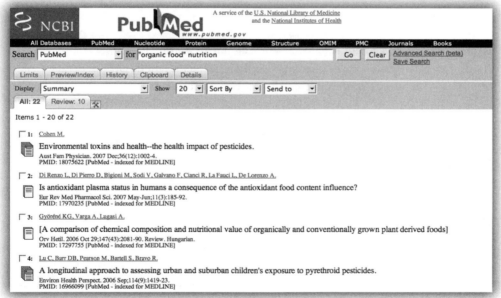

Figure 3.9—A Search in PubMed on Organic Food and Nutrition

END OF ACTIVITY 3.1

In Activity 3.1, we used the guidelines in this chapter to evaluate two Web pages. We used a variety of Web and Internet resources to establish the identity and suitability of the authors, and we considered other issues related to whether the information was reliable and appropriate.

Information About Evaluating Resources on the World Wide Web

There are several good resources on the World Wide Web to help you evaluate information. They give in-depth information about critically examining documents that appear on the Web or in print, and they offer other guidelines and suggestions for assessing Internet and Web resources.

Guides to Evaluating Library Resources

♦ "How to Critically Analyze Information Sources," Reference Services
  Division of the Cornell University Library,
  http://www.library.cornell.edu/okuref/research/skill26.htm

♦ "Evaluating Information Found on the Internet," Elizabeth Kirk,
  Sheridan Libraries, Johns Hopkins University,
  http://www.library.jhu.edu/researchhelp/general/evaluating/

♦ "Thinking Critically about World Wide Web Resources,"
  Esther Grassian, UCLA College Library,
  http://www2.library.ucla.edu/libraries/college/11605_12337.cfm
  http://www.vuw.ac.nz/~agsmith/evaln/index.htm

♦ "Evaluating Web Pages: Techniques to Apply and Questions to Ask," University of California,
  Berkeley, Teaching Library Internet Workshops,
  http://www.lib.berkeley.edu/TeachingLib/Guides/Internet/Evaluate.html

♦ "Kathy Schrock's Guide for Educators—Critical
  Evaluation Information," Kathleen Schrock,
  http://school.discoveryeducation.com/schrockguide/eval.html

♦ "Evaluating Information on the Internet," by D. Scott Brandt, Purdue University Libraries,
  http://www.lib.purdue.edu/research/techman/evaluate.html

Bibliographies for Evaluating Web Resources

♦ "Evaluating Internet Resources: An Annotated Guide to Selected Resources," Business
  Reference Services, Library of Congress, **http://www.loc.gov/rr/business/beonline/**
  selectbib.html

Summary

The World Wide Web gives us access to a great variety of information on many different topics. When we want to use the resources we find on the Web for information or research purposes, we need to exercise some care to be sure it's authentic, reliable, and authoritative. We need to be equally cautious when we use other sources.

Print sources that are available to us through a research or academic library have often been put through a screening process by professional librarians. There are several directories that contain evaluated resources on the Web, and it's useful to consult some of these libraries when doing research. Information in many directories tends to be evaluated before it's listed. Plus, by consulting these directories, we can also observe how librarians and other information specialists evaluate resources.

It pays to be skeptical or critical of information we want to use. It's relatively easy to publish information on the Web, and it can be presented in such a way as to hide its intent or purpose. Generally, as we evaluate documents, we also learn more about the topic we're considering. Assessing resources makes us more confident of the information and helps us become better versed in the topic.

We need to use some general guidelines or criteria when evaluating information or resources. In this vein, we should ask the following questions about whatever information we find:

- Who is the author or institution?
- How current is the information?
- Who is the audience?
- Is the content accurate and objective?
- What is the purpose of the information?

Various strategies will help us find answers to the questions. Here are some of those tips:

- Look for the name of the author or institution at the top or bottom of a Web page.
- Go to the home page for the site hosting the information to find out about the organization.
- To find further information about the institution or author, use a search engine to see what related information is available on the Web.
- Use Google Groups to search archives of discussion group articles. This way, you can find other information about the author or institution. You can also find out if the author has posted anything to a group.
- Check the top and bottom of a Web page for the date on which the information was last modified or updated.

There are a number of Web resources that can help us evaluate information and that discuss issues related to assessing documents, and we have included many of the best in this chapter.

Review Questions

Multiple Choice

1. You might be suspicious of a Web page that
   a. has an author's name only at the bottom of the page.
   b. does not give the date it was last updated.
   c. uses animations.
   d. all of the above

2. When looking for research information, you'd be safest using a page
   a. that ends in **.org**.
   b. that ends in **.edu**.
   c. that ends in **.com**.
   d. that provides information about its author or sponsor and that has references to sources..

3. You can look for information about a Web page's author
   a. by using a search engine to look on the Web.
   b. by looking in Google Groups.
   c. by looking him or her up in a print resource.
   d. a and c
   e. all of the above

4. Information in Web pages
   a. is screened by a Web committee.
   b. can be put on the Web by anybody.
   c. must be clearly and accurately stated.
   d. is easily verifiable.

5. In evaluating a Web page, you need to look at
   a. the author of the page.
   b. the currency of the information.
   c. the attractiveness of the page.
   d. a and b
   e. all of the above

6. Looking at the objectivity of a Web page means
   a. to see if the material on a Web page is objectionable.
   b. to see if there are political, cultural, or other biases on the page.
   c. to see if the material is accurate.
   d. to see if the material on the page is up to date.
   e. all of the above

True or False

7. T F Information on a Web page is screened by experts before being posted.

8. T F A ~ (tilde) in a URL means that the page is a personal Web page.

9. T F You should look both at the top and bottom of a Web page to try to find its author.

10. T F A URL ending in **.org** means that the information is usually reliable.

11. T F Some directories lead you to sites that have been evaluated by information professionals.

12. T F Thinking critically means to separate facts from opinion.

13. T F A Web page whose author isn't listed is a good source of information for a research paper.

Completion

14. A date on a page is an indication of the _____ of a Web page.

15. It's important to verify information in another source to determine how _____ a Web page is.

16. When you look to see if a Web site is designed to inform or persuade its audience, or to advocate a cause, you are looking for the _____ of the page.

17. A Web site with a domain name ending in **.com** is a(n) _____ Web page.

18. One way to find out about the sponsoring institution of a Web page is to go to the institution's _____.

19. A government Web page has a domain name that ends in _____.

20. Web pages with domain names ending in _____ may include pages ranging from serious scholarly research to silly personal pages.

Exercises and Projects

1. These sites have to do with immigration. Use the methods discussed in the chapter to evaluate the accuracy and objectivity of each site. Mention the sponsoring organization.
   a. Texans for Fair Immigration, Inc.: Immigration Facts and Statistics, **http://www.texansforimmigrationreform.com**
   b. Migration Dialog, **http://migration.ucdavis.edu**
   c. Health Reform Legislation and Immigration, **http://www.cis.org/IllegalHealthcareReform**

2. The following resources provide information on alternative medicine. Using the criteria listed in the chapter, evaluate each of these sites for authorship, currency, accuracy, and bias.
   a. Alternative Medicine Health Updates, **http://heall.com/body/healthupdates/index.html**
   b. HerbMed, **http://www.herbmed.org**
   c. The National Center for Complementary and Alternative Medicine, **http://nccam.nih.gov**

3. These Web pages all have to do with the issue of sustainable forest management. Write a brief evaluation of each, focusing on whether the information is objective or is advocating a cause.
   a. TimberTrek, **http://www.nafi.com.au/timbertrek.html**
   b. Sustainable Hardwoods: AHEC Europe, **http://www.sustainablehardwoods.info**
   c. Forest Protection and Watershed Restoration, **http://www.northcascades.org/programs/forest_watershed.html**

4. Now take a look at the topic of smoking. Which of these two sites do you think gives more accurate, reliable information? Would you use any of them as a source for a research paper? All of them? None of them? Why?
   a. Action on Smoking and Health, **http://ash.org**
   b. Virginia Smokers Alliance, **http://www.virginiasmokersalliance.com/**
   c. Quitting Smoking: Why to Quit and How to Get Help,
      http://www.cancer.gov/cancertopics/factsheet/Tobacco/cessation

5. Let's look at some commercial sites. Explore the following sites. What is the audience and what is the purpose of each of these commercial sites? Is the main purpose informational or to sell a product? Is the information given reliable? What do you think of the mix?
   a. Better Homes and Gardens Online, **http://www.bhg.com/**
   b. Michael Flatley's Lord of the Dance, **http://www.lordofthedance.com**
   c. DeBeers, **http://www.debeers.com**
   d. Edmunds.com, **http://www.edmunds.com**

6. Look at these resources about home schooling and compare the information. Evaluate each site based on the criteria given in the chapter.
   a. A Personal Opinion About Home Schooling,
      http://www.adprima.com/homeschooling.htm
   b. Is Homeschool for You?,
      http://homeschooling.about.com/od/gettingstarted/a/homeschool4you.htm
   c. Post-secondary Decisions of Public School and Homeschool Graduates,
      http://www.uwstout.edu/lib/thesis/2001/2001lueckeh.pdf

7. Compare Web site evaluation criteria offered by two of the resources listed on page 58. How are they the same and how do they differ? Which one do you think is the most complete and useful?

CHAPTER
4

Managing and Citing
Search Results

We've covered the basics of searching for resources and evaluating them. Now comes the important step of managing what we've found in a way that makes it easy for us to organize the resources for ourselves and perhaps share them with others. There are several Web-based services that help us do just that. We will cover a few of these reference management tools in this chapter. If we are writing an academic paper or even an article for public consumption, it is also important to cite these resources properly. That way, others who read your work may check the resources you've used.

Sources can be checked for accuracy, to see excerpts or ideas in the original context, or to obtain more information on the topic. You'll also want to cite Internet resources to let people know where they can find this information you've used, whether you're preparing a formal research paper or writing email to a friend. Properly acknowledging your sources gives credit to others whose ideas or expressions you have used in your writing. It is very easy to copy and paste information from the Web, but if you copy material from a source without using quotation marks and present the information as your own work, you are committing an unethical act—plagiarism—and it may have grave consequences. You should also be careful when paraphrasing an author's work—use your own words, don't just rearrange the author's words to make it appear as if it were your own writing. In this chapter, we'll discuss the formats for different resource types and suggest citation styles for them.

Specifically, this chapter will contain the following sections:
♦ Managing Search Results
♦ Guidelines for Citing Internet and Web Resources
♦ Citation Examples
♦ Information on the Web About Citing Electronic Resources

Managing Search Results

There are several ways you can manage your search results. You can create bookmarks or favorites using your browser's toolbar. While this may work just fine for you, it has one major limitation: these bookmarks, or links to Web sites, are kept on the computer you are using. You aren't able to access them when you are at a different computer (unless you export them and download them to a different computer). In the past couple of years, innovative Web-based services have been developed that make it easy for you to save, tag, organize, share, and search saved Web sites. Some call these **social bookmarking services.** The reason they are referred to as a *social* is because you have the option to tag the resources with subject headings and share them with others. We will be discussing sharing information on the Web in more detail in Chapter 10. In this chapter, we will focus on using these resources for organizing your work in a private way.

The words and phrases that users attach to resources are referred to as a **folksonomy.** This means that users freely choose their own keywords rather than using a controlled vocabulary invented by someone else. Thomas Vander Wal, the individual credited with the term, refers to this as a "bottom up social classification." In social bookmarking services the tags that are collected within the service often create what is called a **tag cloud.**

A tag cloud is a visual depiction of user-generated tags, with the tags that have been used most often shown in a larger font or different color. The tags are sometimes arranged in alphabetical order. This makes it possible for the user to find a subject by alphabet or by popularity. These tags are hyperlinks to collections of Web sites that are associated with that tag. Figure 4.1 shows a tag cloud that is included in Wikipedia's entry for "tag cloud" at **http://en.wikipedia.org/wiki/ Tag_cloud**.

Figure 4.1—An Example of a Tag Cloud

With that introduction to tagging and social bookmarking, let's explore a couple of services to get you started using them.

Delicious (http://www.delicious.com)

Delicious is a social bookmarking site that allows you to organize Web sites and tag them with subjects that you choose so that you can easily locate them later. You have the option to share your resources with others so that others can find them using the tags that you have assigned, or you can keep your collection private. Delicious is also a site that you can search, much like a regular search engine. Searching resources that others have already decided are useful can be a good way to find obscure resources that may not come up highly placed in a Google search. In order to save Web resources to Delicious, you must sign up for a free account first. You created a Delicious account in one of the exercises at the end of Chapter 1.

CiteULike (http://www.citeulike.org)

CiteULike is similar to Delicious, but its primary purpose is to allow users to cite scholarly, peer-reviewed articles. CiteULike helps you manage and share scholarly papers that you have read or plan to read. When you bookmark an article you want to save, CiteULike automatically extracts the citation details so you don't have to do it yourself. This makes it nice for preparing bibliographies. CiteULike works with several scholarly journal databases such as Cambridge University Press, JSTOR, Wiley InterScience, WorldCat, and more.

Now we will do a brief activity using both of these services.

ACTIVITY
4.1   USING SOCIAL BOOKMARKING TOOLS: DELICIOUS AND CITEULIKE

Details

1. Go to Delicious
2. Sign in to your account.
3. Bookmark some resources and tag them in Delicious.
4. Sign up for CiteULike and add some resources to it.

1 Go to Delicious.

DO IT! Type **http://delicious.com** in your browser's location bar and press Enter.

2 Sign in to your account.

DO IT! Click on the hyperlink **Sign In** in the upper right corner. Type in your user name and password. Note that Delicious has the option to keep you signed in for two weeks, which is a nice feature. This way you don't need to constantly sign in every time you're researching. Now that you are signed in, Delicious is active. You can now start searching from this browser window or you can minimize the window and open a new one. For the purposes of this activity, let's minimize the window.

DO IT! Minimize the browser window by clicking on the left-most icon on the upper right corner of your browser window (or, for Macintosh users, double-click on the title bar).

3 Bookmark some resources and tag them in Delicious.

DO IT! Open a new browser window and go to a search engine of your choice, such as Google.

In this activity, we will search for the latest edition of the "Human Development Report," published by the United Nations Development Programme.

DO IT!   Search on **Human Development Report** and press Enter. Click on the first link the Google search returns.

After the Web site loads, you will want to add this site to your Delicious account. When you created your Delicious account, you should have added a Delicious button to your browser toolbar. The icon looks like this:

You need to click on this button now.

DO IT!   Click on the Tag button.

Delicious will insert a "Save a Bookmark" window with the name of the URL of the site you're saving and the title of the site. You can insert your own notes and create tags that mean something to you. Delicious includes tags others have used to site this resource and that you are free to also use. Figure 4.2 shows how we have chosen to tag this resource. Note that we have opted not to share this resource, because we want our Delicious account to be private. If you had set up your Delicious account as a public account, then you would be free to either share or not share this resource—it's up to you. Also note that Delicious has given guidance on how to create tags. Each tag should be separated by a space. If your tag has more than one word, then the words must be entered as one word, such as **humandevelopment**.

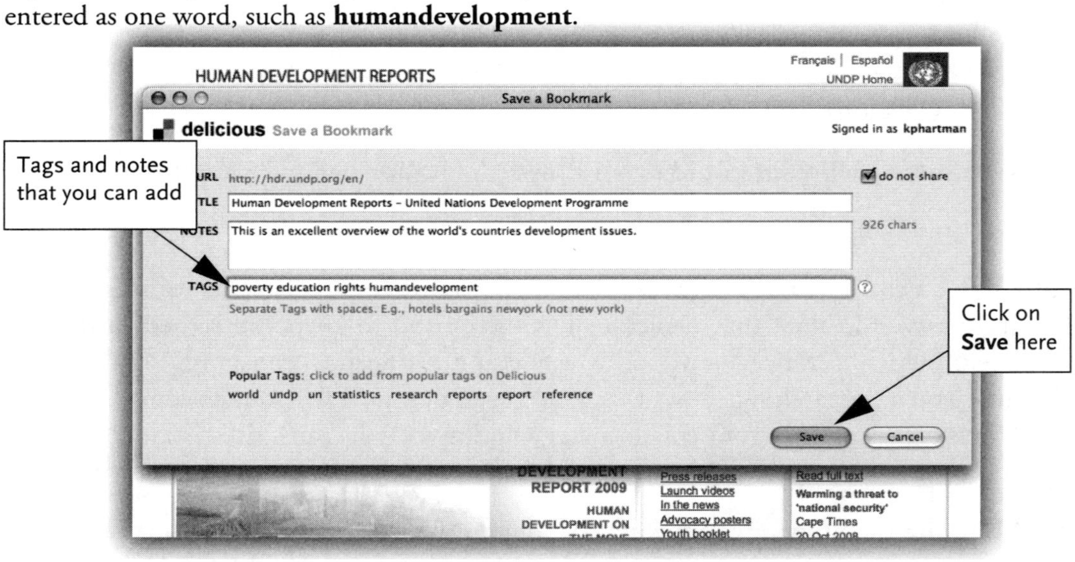

Figure 4.2—Tagging a Web site in Delicious

DO IT!   When you've entered the information you want and you're ready to save this site to your Delicious account, click on **Save**.

DO IT!   Return to your Delicious account by opening the minimized window.

Figure 4.3 shows the site you've just added.

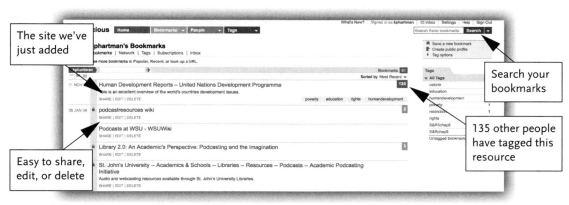

Figure 4.3—Managing Resources Added to Delicious

Note that you can easily delete resources that are in your account. You can decide to share them, or edit the tags or notes that you have made. You can search your bookmarks too. And remember, your Delicious account is available to you wherever you are—from any computer that's connected to the Internet!

4 Sign up for CiteULike and add some resources to it.

DO IT! Go to CiteULike at **http://www.citeulike.org**.

DO IT! Click on **Join Now**.

You will sign up for CiteULike much like you did for Delicious. Once you're a member, you can sign in.

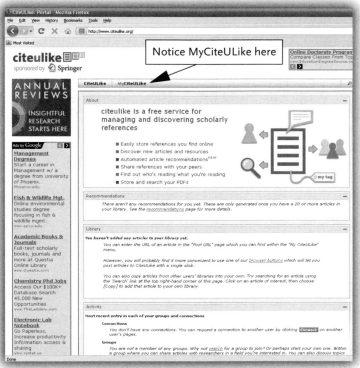

Figure 4.4—The CiteULike Home Page

Once you sign in, you'll see the tab at the top of the page for **MyCiteULike**. If you move the cursor over this tab, you will see a drop-down menu with several choices on it. From here you can choose to Post a URL.

DO IT! Hold the mouse cursor over **MyCiteULike**, then click on **Post URL**.

A window will pop up that looks like the one in Figure 4.5.

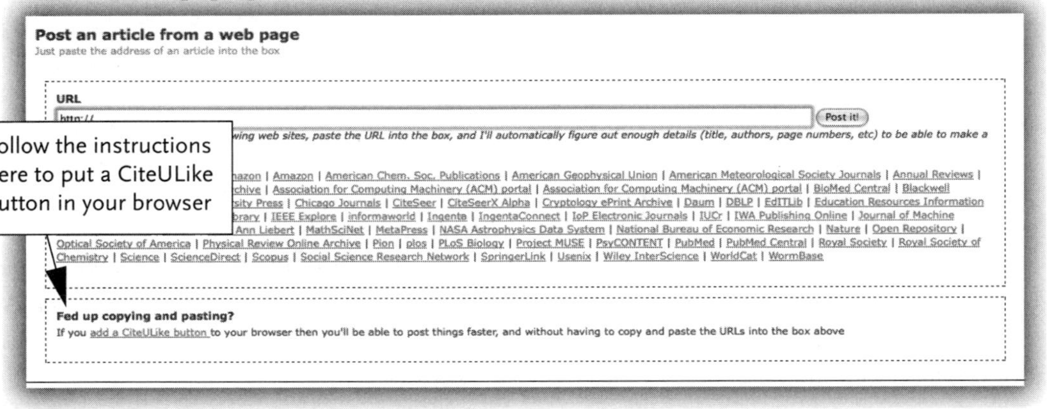

Figure 4.5—Posting an Article to CiteULike

Note that you can add a CiteULike button in your browser toolbar so that you can easily add sites to CiteULike. We suggest that you do this to make it easier.

DO IT! Click on **add a CiteULike button** and follow the steps to add the button to your toolbar.

Before you go any further, scroll down to the bottom of the page. You'll see the sites that support CiteULike. Pick one of these sites that CiteULike supports. In this activity, we picked WorldCat. Click on **WorldCat** and do a search. We searched for the book *Searching and Researching on the Internet and World Wide Web*. Open the record and click on the **Post to CiteULike** link in your browser toolbar, as shown in Figure 4.6.

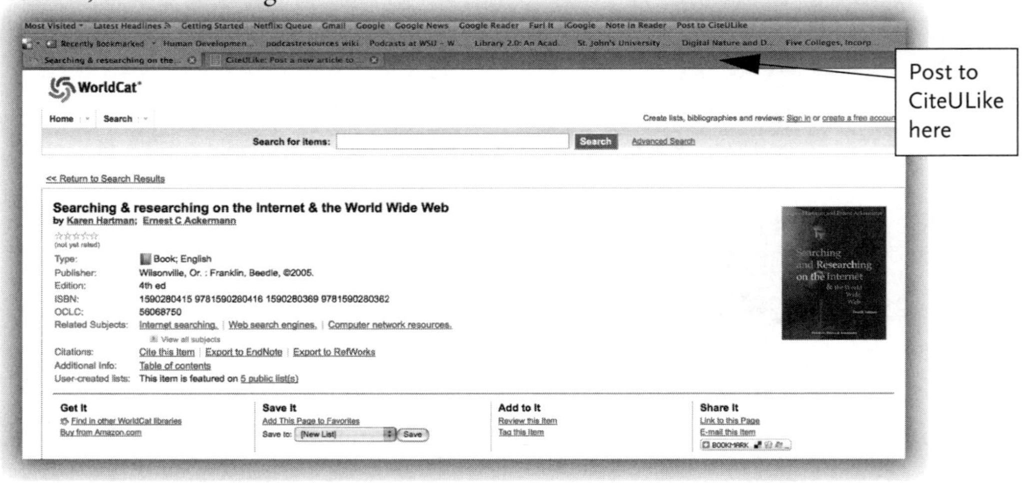

Figure 4.6—Searching WorldCat for a Book Citation to Add to CiteULike

Figure 4.7 shows the CiteULike window that appears next. This is where you can add your subject headings, or tags. We've added the two words **searching internet**. You can also select from the Priority categories choices such as **I will read this article** or **I might read this article**. We've chosen **I've already read it**. You can also indicate if you'd like to keep your resource private or share it with others. After you've finished with this window, you simply click on the **Post Article** link and you're done.

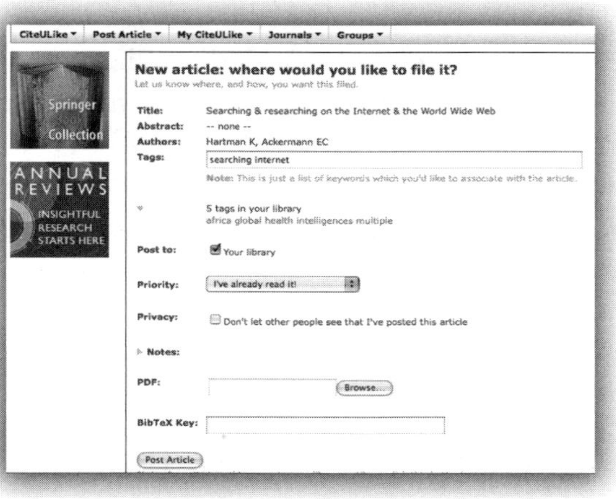

Figure 4.7—Adding an Item to CiteULike

DO IT! Enter the information you want on the form and click **Post Article**.

If we return to CiteULike, and click on **Library** under the **MyCiteULike** tab, we will see the resource added to our list, as shown in Figure 4.8.

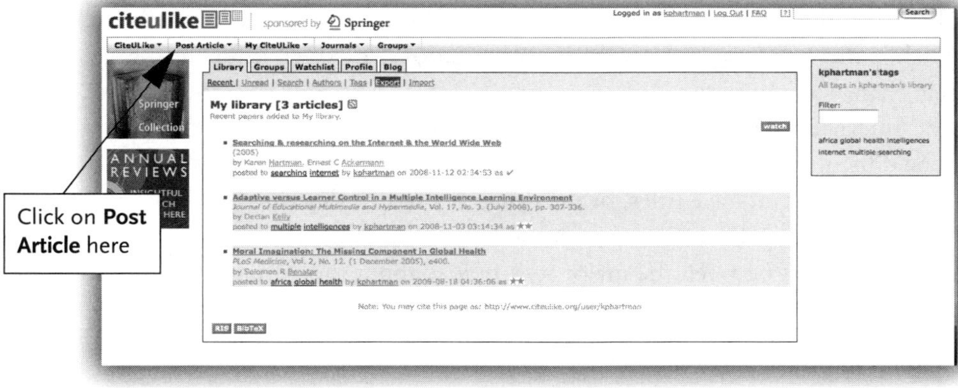

Figure 4.8—My Library in CiteULike

Now that you've learned about a couple of services to help you manage your search results, you can start using these services, or others like them, to organize your own research. There are several other bookmarking services available. We've listed some of those here:

- Connotea: Free online reference management for all researchers, clinicians and scientists, **http://www.connotea.org**
- Digg, **http://digg.com**
- Diigo, **http://www.diigo.com**
- StumbleUpon, **http://www.stumbleupon.com**

Now we'll move on to exploring the nitty-gritty of citing resources properly for scholarly papers and other purposes.

END OF ACTIVITY 4.1

Guidelines for Citing Internet and Web Resources

There are several guidelines and styles for citing works correctly. No single uniform style has been adopted or is appropriate in every case. The styles used for citing electronic works sometimes differ from those for printed works, which have a long tradition of specific formats. Citations for works in print or on the Web have a number of common elements, however. These include the author's name, the work's title, the date on which the cited work was published or revised, and the date you accessed it.

When you're looking for the proper way to cite resources in a report or research paper, you must first see if there is a required or accepted citation style for your situation. If you're preparing a report or paper for a class, then check with your instructor. If you're writing for a journal or some other publication (either in print or electronic form), then see if the editor or publisher has guidelines. Proper format for citations is determined by several organizations. Three commonly used formats are APA (American Psychological Association) style, MLA (Modern Language Association) style, and the Chicago Manual of Style (University of Chicago). In general, researchers in the social sciences use APA format, while humanities scholars use MLA or the Chicago Manual of Style. Each of these organizations publishes a handbook or publication guide, and they also have Web sites that provide guidance on how to cite Internet resources. You will find URLs for these and several other citation style sources later in the chapter in the section entitled "Information on the Web About Citing Electronic Resources."

The following sections will explain some issues and provide tips for solving some of the most common difficulties inherent in citing Web and Internet resources, which are as follows:

♦ URLs, while they are crucial elements of most citations, are often difficult to write or type and may change at any time.
♦ Web and Internet resources may be updated or modified at any time.
♦ It may be difficult or impossible to find a resource's publication or revision date.
♦ Web resources may not have titles, or the titles may not be descriptive.
♦ Web page authors may be difficult to determine.
♦ There are differences between the major style guides about the format of citations for Web resources.

URL Formats

Unlike citations for printed works, a citation for a Web or Internet resource must have information about how to access it. This is often indicated through the work's URL (Uniform Resource Locator). In addition to telling you where to access a work, a URL serves to retrieve the work. Everything on the Web has a URL, indicating where something is located and how to access it. We've seen lots of URLs throughout this text. Here are some examples:

♦ **http://www.loc.gov**, the home page for The Library of Congress
♦ **http://en.wikipedia.org/wiki/Computer_virus**, the entry for the term *computer virus* in Wikipedia
♦ **http://hanlib.sou.edu/searchtools**, a Web site on Internet Searching Tools

You'll find it helpful to think of a URL as having the following form:

how-to-get-there://where-to-go/what-to-get

or, in more technical language:

transfer protocol://domain name/directory/subdirectory/file name.file type

For example, take this URL:

http://www.cs.rice.edu/~druschel/publications/PeerSpective-HotNets.pdf

> **http** is the transfer protocol
> **cs.rice.edu** is the domain name (also called the host computer name)
> **~druschel** is the directory name
> **publications** is the subdirectory name
> **PeerSpective-HotNets** is the file name and **pdf** is its file type

You probably already know some ways in which URLs are used. For example, all hyperlinks on Web pages are represented as URLs. Entries in bookmark and history files are stored as URLs. You type in a URL when you want to direct your browser to go to a specific Web page. When you cite a resource on the World Wide Web, you will usually include its URL. You'll also want to include the URL when you're telling someone else about a resource, such as in an email message. Here's an example:

> If you haven't already seen this fabulous page, you must look at it. It's called "GlobalEDGE" and it's hosted by Michigan State University. The URL is: **http://globaledge.msu.edu**. It's one of the best subject guides I've ever used on international business.

That way, a friend reading the message could use her browser to go directly to the items you mention.

By providing the name of a Web server and the name of a file or directory holding certain information, a URL tells you how to retrieve the information; from the URL alone, you know which Internet protocol to use when retrieving the information and where it's located. If only a server name is present, as in **http://www.loc.gov**, then a file will still be retrieved. Web servers are configured to pass along a certain file (usually named **index.html** or **index.htm**) when the URL contains only the name of the server or only the name of a directory. It's important to be precise when you write URLs because a Web browser uses the URL to access something and bring it to your computer. More specifically, the browser sends a request extracted from the information in the URL to a Web server. Remember, we're talking about having one computer communicate with another; as amazing as some computer systems are, they generally need very precise instructions. Therefore, you have to be careful about spaces (generally there aren't blanks in a URL) and symbols (interchanging a slash and a period won't give appropriate results).

Note that you don't need to type **http://** when accessing a URL, but you should include the **http://** in a proper citation.

The Dates Are Important

You'll see that some citation examples for references to Web or Internet resources contain two dates: the date of publication or revision, and the date of last access. The reason some styles require both dates has to do with the nature of digital media as it's made available or published on the Web. Works in print form are different from digital works; printed documents have a tangible, physical form. We all know we can pick up and feel a magazine or journal in our hands, or we can use a book or periodical as a pillow. It's pretty hard to do that with a Web page! This tangible nature of a printed work also gives an edition or revision a permanent nature. It's usually possible to assign a date of publication to a work, and if there are revisions or different editions of a work, it's possible to date and look at the revisions. If a new edition of a printed work exists, that doesn't mean that older editions or versions were destroyed.

The situation is different for Web documents and other items in digital form on the Internet, for several reasons. They don't have a tangible form. It's relatively easy for an author to publish a work (the work usually only needs to be in a certain directory on a computer that functions as a Web server). It's easy to modify or revise a work. Furthermore, when a work is revised, the previous version is often replaced by or overwritten with the new version. Because of this last point, the most recent version may be the only one that exists. The version you cited might not exist anymore. It is therefore sometimes necessary to include the date you accessed or read a work listed in a citation or reference. This depends on the style you are using. For example, MLA style requires the date you accessed the site, and APA style does not. In any case, you may want to keep a copy of the document in a file (save it while browsing) or print a copy of it to provide as documentation if someone questions your sources.

Ways to Find Out When a Page Was Modified

To find the date a work was last revised, see if the date is mentioned as part of the work. You will often see a line like **Last modified: Tuesday, March 2, 2010** in a Web document, usually at the bottom of the main page. You may also see something like this at the bottom of the Web page:

Copyright ©2008 or **©2007–2010**

If you don't find this information on the Web page or you want to verify the date that is cited, you can try this technique for determining the date of a Web page. When you have a page loaded in your browser, type the following line of JavaScript code directly into the location bar:

javascript:alert(document.lastModified)

This will activate a pop-up box that displays the time stamp. On many automatically generated Web pages, such as the Google home page or the Yahoo! home page, the time stamp will display the current time. If that happens, in your citation the date accessed and the date updated will be the same.

If you are unable to determine the date of the page, you can indicate this in the citation by inserting "n.d." in the appropriate place.

Determining Web Page Titles

The title is what shows up as a hyperlink in the search results if you use a search engine. You may also find the title by selecting **View/Page Info**, or **View/Page Source**. The title is specified in the HTML source for the page and doesn't necessarily show up in the text of the document as you view it with a browser. There are cases when the title is uninformative or not descriptive. In these situations, the first main heading can be used. Some documents have no title. (If a document doesn't have a title, you can construct one by using the major heading or the first line of text. You should enclose this title in square brackets to show that you created it.)

The following is a portion of the HTML code for a Web page mentioned earlier: GlobalEDGE. The exact text of the title of a Web page is surrounded by the tags **<title>** and **</title>** in the HTML source for the page. The source for this page begins with:

```
<!DOCTYPE html PUBLIC "-//W3C//DTD XHTML 1.0 Transitional//EN"
        "http://www.w3.org/TR/xhtml1/DTD/xhtml1-Transitional.dtd">
<html xmlns="http://www.w3.org/1999/xhtml">
<head>
<title>globalEDGE - Your Source for Global Business Knowledge</title>
```

Determining the Author of a Web Page

Look for the author's name at the top or the bottom of a document. If it isn't there, there are a few things you may try.

♦ If a document doesn't contain the name of the author or the institution, and there are no hyperlinks to Web pages that give that information, you can manipulate the URL to try to find it. For example, if you found material at the following URL, **http://scilib.ucsd. edu/howto/guides/patsearch/index.html**, and you wanted to quickly find out the name of the publishing body, you could delete the parts of the URL back to the domain section (everything after **edu/**) and press **Enter**. This would give you **http://scilib.ucsd.edu**, the home page for this institution, which happens to be the University of California, San Diego Science & Engineering Library.

♦ You may find the author's email address in the document. You can use the browser's **Find** function to locate the @ symbol. If an email address is found, you could send a message and ask the person for more information.

♦ Open the Web page's HTML source information by selecting **View/Source or View/Page Source** from your browser's menu. Sometimes the author's name may be viewed there.

Differences Between Styles

While most of the style guides agree as to which elements are essential for citation, they all have different ways of formatting the information. Some formats require the URL in the citation, and others do not. Some advise including the place of publication if the Web resource is a copy of a printed work. Some require the date when the site was last viewed, and others do not. There is, however, considerable agreement on the basic information to be included in a citation of a Web resource.

Citation Examples

In this section, we will provide citation examples using established citation formats. The styles that we will be using are the Modern Language Association (MLA) for the *Works Cited* part of a paper and the American Psychological Association (APA) for the *References* area of a paper. The types of resources that we will cite are Web pages, Web pages that are part of larger works, online journal articles, blog entries, wiki articles, podcasts, and videos. The common elements in citations for different types of resources will be listed, and a citation example for each type of included Internet resource will be given in one of the styles. The information provided is general in nature, and it is not meant to cover every situation. We suggest that if you have a specific citation question that is not covered here, you go to one of the citation guides listed in the section entitled "Information on the Web About Citing Electronic Resources" later in the chapter or visit your library. Because style guidelines change periodically, it's important to check the association's Web sites to make sure you are using the latest information. Librarians are usually willing to assist you in locating and using citation style guides as long as you indicate which style you have been instructed to use.

Web Pages

The major citation styles agree that the following elements should be included in a citation for a Web page:

- Author's name
- Document title
- Title of larger or complete work, if relevant
- Date of publication

Style guides differ on the necessity of including the following elements:

- Date page was accessed
- URL

Citation Examples
MLA Style:

United States. Environmental Protection Agency. Climate Change – U.S. EPA. *Environmental Protection Agency,* 3 November 2008. Web. 15 November 2008.

Note that the URL is not included, the title of the page is italicized, and the word "Web" is inserted between the date of publication and the date the page was viewed. If your instructor requires the URL, then include it at the end of the citation in angle brackets: **<http://www.epa.gov/climatechange/>**

> **TIP!**
> When you have specific questions about citing Internet and Web sources, check some of the Web resources listed later in this chapter and be sure to check with whoever is going to be evaluating or editing your work.

APA Style:

United States. Environmental Protection Agency (2008, November 3). *Climate Change – U.S. EPA.* Retrieved from http://www.epa.gov/climatechange/

Note that APA style requires the URL in the citation. Also note that if the Web site has a date, APA style does not require the date the individual viewed the site.

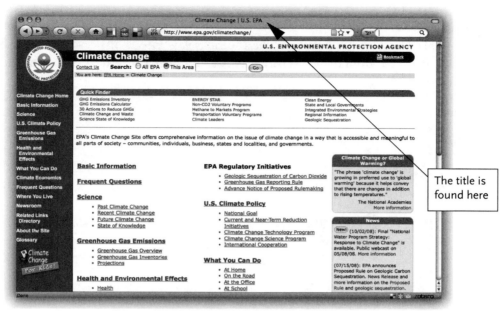

Figure 4.9—Determining the Title of a Web Page

We determined the Web page title by using the title found at the top of the browser window, as shown in Figure 4.9. We found the date the site was updated at the bottom of the page, as shown in Figure 4.10.

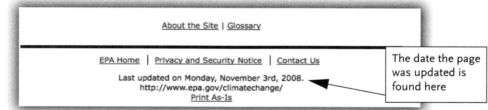

Figure 4.10—The Web Page's Date at the Bottom of the Page

Citing a Web Page That Is Part of a Larger or Complete Work

Many Web pages are parts of larger works or projects. In each of these cases, you need to provide not only the author and title of the individual document, but also the title of the larger work, its editor (especially when using MLA style), and the institution that sponsors the site (if applicable). In many instances, you'll want to include information about the complete work in order to put the document in its proper context and to credit the institution that has helped to make the work available. This additional information may help the reader find the Web page. The following shows how you would cite a page that was part of a larger work.

Citation Examples
MLA Style:
Bales, Jack. "MWP: Willie Morris (1934-1999)." *Mississippi Writers Page.* University of Mississippi. 19 October 2007. Web. 15 November 2008.

Note that the sponsor of the site, the University of Mississippi, is entered after the title of the work.

APA Style:

Bales, J. (2007 October 19). MWP: Willie Morris (1934-1999). In J. Padgett (Ed.), *Mississippi writers page.* Retrieved from the University of Mississippi Web site: http://www.olemiss.edu/mwp/ dir/morris_willie/index.html

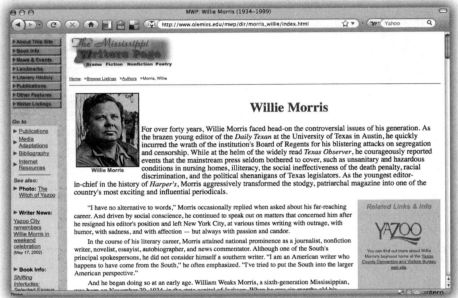

Figure 4.11—A Web Page That Is Part of a Larger Work

In this citation, we determined:

♦ The title of the Web page was found at the top of the browser window. Because MWP is uninformative, we could, if we wished, change the title to simply Willie Morris. If we did so, we would be required to place square brackets around the title, indicating that we had changed it. But in this case, we have decided to leave the Web page title as MWP: Willie Morris (1934-1999). The date range indicates the years Mr. Morris lived.

♦ The writer of this page was found by scrolling down to the end of the article, as shown in Figure 4.12.

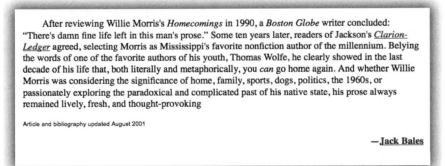

Figure 4.12—Finding the Author of the Willie Morris Page

Determining the date of the last revision proves to be a bit more difficult. Near the author's name there is a statement that the article was updated in August of 2001, but if we scroll down to the end of the page the revision date is listed as October 19, 2007, as shown in Figure 4.13. This is the date we will use.

The editor of the larger work, *Mississippi Writers Page*, is John Padgett. His name is also found at the end of the Web page, as shown in Figure 4.12. Note that MLA requires the editor's name as part of the citation, but APA does not.

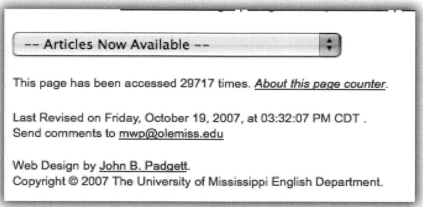

Figure 4.13—Important Information Located at the End of the Web Page

Online Journal Articles

An article in an online journal can be cited very much like any other Web resource. If you were citing an article in a journal, it would be reasonable to include the journal name, volume, issue, and date. If you were citing a resource from a printed journal, you would also include page numbers, but that doesn't usually apply in this case. The URL gives the location of the article. The citation should contain the following elements:

- Author's name
- Title of article
- Title of journal, volume and issue numbers, date of publication
- Date of last revision, if known and different from date of publication

Citation Examples

MLA Style:

Waters, John K. "Unleashing the Power of Web 2.0." *Campus Technology*. 1105Media, June 2008. Web. 16 November 2008.

Note that MLA requires the sponsor of the online journal be included as well, inserted after the title of the journal.

APA Style:

Waters, J.K. (2008, June). Unleashing the Power of Web 2.0. *Campus Technology*. Retrieved from http://campustechnology.com/articles/63551/

Full-text journals that are part of proprietary databases, such as Factiva or Lexis-Nexis, will require more information as part of the citation. When in doubt about how to cite a particular online journal, read the manual of the citation style you are using, or ask a librarian for help.

Blog Entries

Note that the citations for blog entries are very similar to online journal citations.

MLA Style:

Houghton-Jan, Sarah. "Google Blog Search – Viable or Deniable?" *LibrarianInBlack.* 5 Nov. 2008. Web. 16 Nov. 2008.

APA Style:

Houghton-Jan, S. (2008 November 5). Google Blog Search – Viable or Deniable? Message posted to   http://librarianinblack.typepad.com/librarianinblack/2008/11/google-blog-search---viable-or-deniable.html

Wiki Articles

Please note that wikis (like Wikipedia, for example) are collaborative projects. It is therefore difficult to evaluate whether the writing is authoritative or not. You must do a careful evaluation of the wiki entry to make sure that the information is credible.

In the following example, we show an entry in Wikipedia (**http://en.wikipedia.org**) on the topic of fair use. Wikipedia makes it easy for you to cite articles. Please note the link on the bottom left of the screen, **Cite this page**, in Figure 4.14. If you click on this link, Wikipedia will give examples on how to cite this entry in several different bibliographic styles.

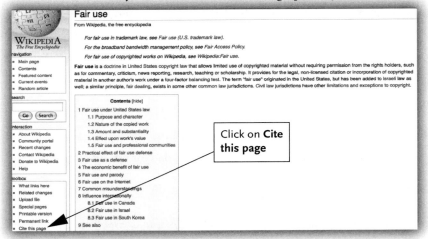

Figure 4.14—Wiki Article in Wikipedia

Figure 4.15 shows the citation examples in MLA and APA for this article.

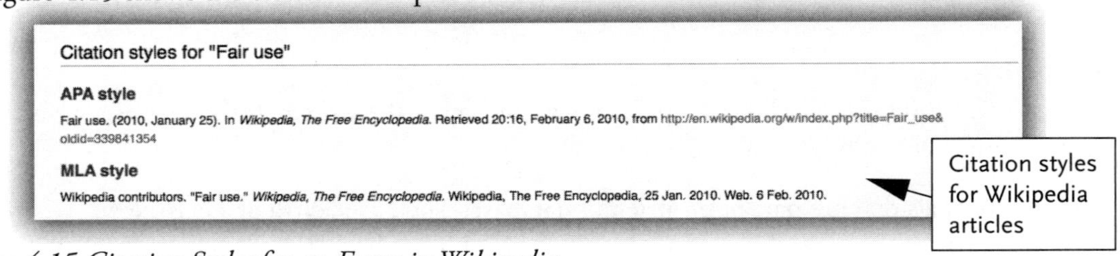

Figure 4.15 Citation Styles for an Entry in Wikipedia

You can use these formats for any wiki article that you choose to cite.

Audio Podcasts

For podcasts, you should provide as much information as possible. Some additional identifiers may include the moderator, producer, or director.

MLA Style:

Phillips, Tony. "Hubble Sees Suspected Asteroid Collision." *Science @ NASA.* NASA. 2 February 2010. MP3 file. 6 February 2010.

APA Style:

Phillips, T. (2010, February 2). Hubble Sees Suspected Asteroid Collision. *Science @ NASA Podcast.* Podcast retrieved from http://science.nasa.gov/podcast.htm

Videos

As with audio podcasts, you should provide as much information as you can. If you know the producer or director you should add this too.

MLA Style:

Russia on Trial: Chechnya and the European Court of Human Rights. Human Rights Watch. Online video. 6 April 2008. Web. 16 November 2008.

APA Style:

Human Rights Watch. (2008, April 6). Russia on Trial: Chechnya and the European Court of Human Rights. Video retrieved from http://www.hrw.org/campaigns/chechnya/focus/

Recording Citation Information

When doing research on the Internet, it's smart to record the document information by either printing the resource or making it a favorite so that you can return to the resource easily, or saving your resources to an online bookmarking service like Delicious. Keeping a record, no matter which service you decide to use, is a good habit to get into. Recording the Web page title and URL accurately is important so you don't have to write it down and risk losing it.

There are some services that assist you in creating citations. One of these is Citation Machine, at **http://citationmachine.net**. You simply select which citation style you are using and add the bibliographic information into the form; a citation will be created in that style.

Wouldn't it be nice if there was a service to help you create bibliographies that are formatted according to the citation system you choose? There are some such commercial services, such as RefWorks, EndNote, and Reference Manager. But recently some new free services have arrived on the scene, and we think it might be useful for you to know about them. One is called Bibme, and you can access it at **http://bibme.org.** Bibme is very easy to use and there is no need to download software on your computer in order to use it. Another is Zotero, and it's also impressive. Zotero was developed by the Center for History and New Media at George Mason University, with funding from the Institute of Museum and Library Services, the Mellon Foundation, and the Alfred P. Sloan Foundation. Zotero is a Firefox extension, and currently can only be used in certain versions of Firefox, Netscape, and Flock. It is not currently available in Internet Explorer. Let's do a brief activity to see how it works.

Zotero (http://www.zotero.org)

Figure 4.16 shows the home page of Zotero. In order to use it, you have to download the software.

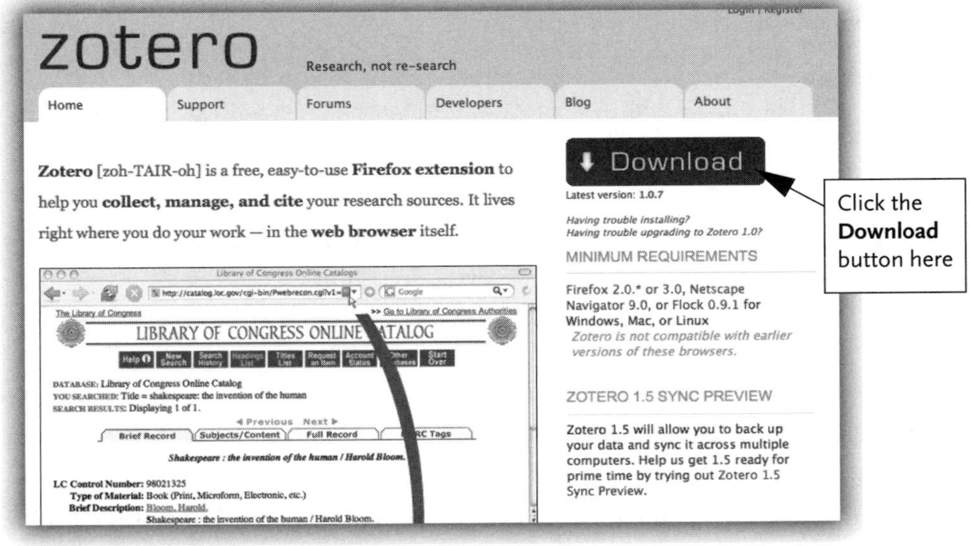

Figure 4.16—Zotero

Once you have Zotero downloaded, you'll notice a Zotero icon located in the bottom right corner of your browser window. When you have found a resource you'd like to add to your collection, you simply click on the Zotero icon and a window pops up. If the resource is a book in a library catalog such as the Library of Congress or WorldCat, Zotero's book icon will show up in Firefox's location bar. Let's say we've found a book in WorldCat that we'd like to add to our collection.

DO IT! Go to WorldCat at **http://www.worldcat.org**. Search for a book entitled "Groundswell: Winning in a World Transformed by Social Technologies," by Charlene Li and Josh Bernoff. Figure 4.17 shows the result.

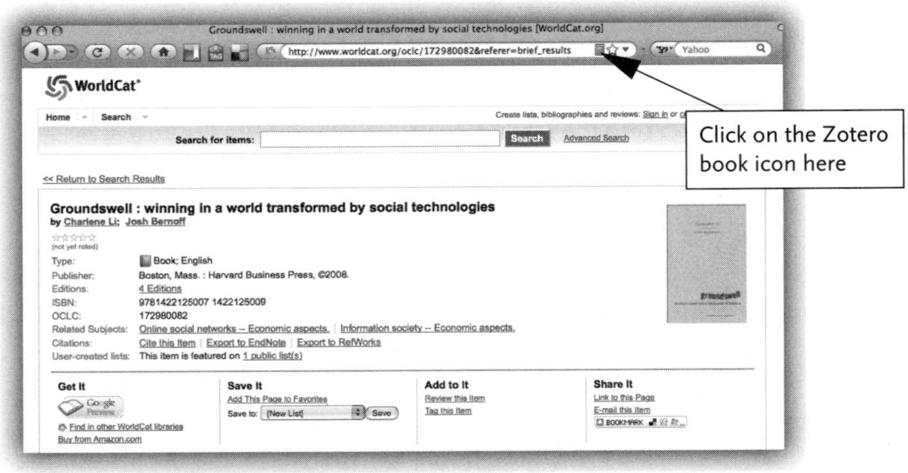

Figure 4.17—Saving a Record from WorldCat to Zotero

Once you click on the Zotero book icon, Zotero will automatically put information about the book into your Zotero collection, including the date your viewed the record. You can add other information, such as the book's call number, notes, tags, or anything else that would help you annotate the resource for your research needs.

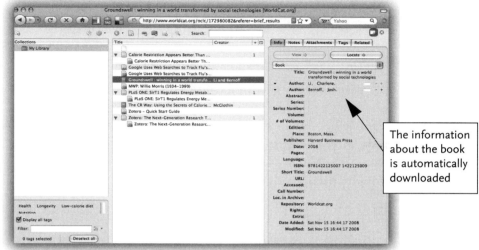

Figure 4.18—Managing Saved Records in Zotero

Zotero is supported by over a hundred online resources and Web sites, and the list is growing daily. It works with dozens of library book catalogs, newspapers, and specialized databases. For a complete list of supported resources, go to **http://www.zotero.org/translators**. For those Web sites that Zotero doesn't support (you can tell when you're in a Web site that Zotero supports, because the Zotero icon will appear in your Firefox location bar, to the right of the URL). You can still use Zotero for recording unsupported Web sites, but you have to add many of the details about the resource yourself.

Zotero Generates Bibliographies

In addition to creating records of your research, Zotero allows you to generate bibliographies in MLA, APA, several Chicago styles, the ASA (American Sociological Association), and several others. You can see which styles the service supports by going here: **http://www.zotero.org/styles**. Zotero also allows you to easily print your resources, post them to the Web, or email them to others. There are a lot of features that Zotero offers that we can't go into here. We suggest you try it and see for yourself. It promises to be a dynamic way for you to keep track of your research.

Information on the Web About Citing Electronic Resources

There are several very good Web pages with information about citing Web and other electronic resources.

The following Web pages have links to several other sources on the subject:

◆ ipl2: Information You Can Trust, Frequently Asked Reference Questions, **http://www.ipl. org/div/farq/netciteFARQ.html**

◆ Karla's Guide to Citation Style Guides by Karla Tonella, **http://bailiwick.lib.uiowa.edu/ journalism/cite.html**

The Web pages in this list contain information about specific styles for citations:

- APA Style Help, **http://www.apastyle.org/apa-style-help.aspx**
- What Is MLA Style? Modern Language Association of America, **http://www.mla.org/style**
- Research and Documentation Online, **http://www.dianahacker.com/resdoc**
- Documenting Electronic Sources: Online Guides to Citing Electronic Sources - The OWL at Purdue, **http://owl.english.purdue.edu/owl/resource/584/03**

These two Web pages contain good, thoughtful discussions about citing work from Web or other electronic sources:

- Citing Electronic Information in History Papers, Maurice Crouse. **http://history. memphis.edu/mcrouse/elcite.html**
- General Guides-The Library- University of California, Berkeley, **http://www.lib.berkeley. edu/Help/guides.html**

Summary

This chapter outlined several ways for you to manage your research using social bookmarking services. These services make it easy for you to organize Web resources for yourself and perhaps share them with others. Citing references or writing a bibliography is usually part of creating a research report. You provide citations so others may check or examine the resources used in the report. There are several style guides provided by organizations for citing both print and electronic resources. This chapter presents guidelines and tips, with examples from some of these style guides, for documenting or citing information obtained from the Web or the Internet.

Citations for documents and other information found on the Web or the Internet usually include the URL (Uniform Resource Locator). A URL includes the names of the Web server and the file or directory holding the information. The URL therefore tells you which Internet protocol to use to retrieve the information and where the information is located. You need to be precise when writing a URL, as a computer will be interpreting it. We listed URL formats for common Web or Internet services. Style guidelines usually suggest that a citation include the author's name, the work's title, the date the information was last revised, the date the information was accessed, and the URL.

The date of access is included because it's relatively easy to modify information on the Web and the information may not always be the same as when it was accessed for research. We discussed methods for determining the date of access and the title of a Web document. The chapter concluded with a list of Web resources that provide more information about citing sources and some suggestions for specific formats.

Selected Terms Used in This Chapter

folksonomy
social bookmarking services
tag cloud

Review Questions

Multiple Choice

1. In citing a Web resource, you may include the following:
   a. The date you accessed the page.
   b. The URL of the page.
   c. The date the page was created or revised.
   d. a and b
   e. all of the above

2. A problem in citing a Web resource is
   a. it may not have a title.
   b. you can't prove that you viewed it.
   c. it may no longer exist.
   d. a and c
   e. all of the above

3. In citing a URL you must include all the following except
   a. the protocol used.
   b. capital letters.
   c. slashes.
   d. All of these are included.

4. URLs are composed in the following fashion:
   a. where to go://what to get/how to get there.
   b. what to get://where to go/how to get there.
   c. how to get there://where to go/what to get.
   d. how to get there://what to get/where to go.

5. Why may it be important to include the date you accessed a Web page when you cite it?
   a. Because Web pages are tangible information.
   b. Because Web pages can be changed easily.
   c. To prove that you saw the page.
   d. a and b

True or False

6. T F A citation for a Web resource must show how to access it.
7. T F All citation styles use the same format when citing a Web resource.
8. T F You must be precise in writing a URL for a source you cite.
9. T F All citation styles require the date the source was accessed.
10. T F Web resources, like books, have a tangible form.
11. T F The only date that is important in a citation is the date a page was last revised.
12. T F The title of a Web page may not appear in the content area of your browser.
13. T F A citation of a newsgroup article includes the name of the newsgroup as the subject of the message.
14. T F You must type **http://** in order to access a Web page.

Completion

15. Tags, or subject headings that are added by individuals to Web sites in a collaborative way, are called _____.

16. The words that appear in the bar at the top of the browser window (and appear within the **<title>** and **</title>** tags in the HTML source) are called the _____.

17. Social science researchers usually use the _____ format when citing their resources.

18. The major difference between Zotero and the other bookmarking sites discussed in the chapter is that Zotero allows you to create _____using several citation styles.

19. Two major types of citation styles are the _____ and the _____.

20. When preparing a report for a class, you should check the citation style with _____.

Exercises and Projects

1. Write a citation to the following document: "Online Social Networks, Virtual Communities, Enterprises, and Information Professionals" using MLA style. *Hint:* This is an online journal article.

2. Go to **http://www.eff.org/deeplinks/2008/11/fcc-unanimously-approves-use-television-white-spac** and write a citation to the document at that address, using APA style. *Hint:* This is a blog posting.

3. Suppose you are doing a research project for a mythology class on the significance of the butterfly in Greek mythology. Go to Google at **http://www.google.com** to find resources on your topic. Do a Web search and look at some of the pages retrieved in your results list. Choose two of the pages in your results list that are relevant to your topic and write citations for them in MLA format.

4. Now return to your results retrieved in question 4 and write citations for those same articles in APA format. (Find a site that gives examples of APA style documentation—you may have luck using "Karla's Guide to Citation Style Guides" at **http://bailiwick. lib.uiowa.edu/journalism/cite.html**)

5. Access the following site and write a citation for the page in APA format and in MLA format: **http://www.cpc.ncep.noaa.gov/products/hurricane/index.shtml**.

6. Now we'll try a citation for an online journal article. Access the article at **http://www. educause.edu/pub/er/erm04/erm0441.asp** and write a citation to the article in APA format.

7. What differences do you see in the requirements for MLA and APA citations of Internet resources? Does one seem more useful than the other? You may want to browse through some other style guides as well. (Go back to Karla's Guide at **http:// bailiwick.lib.uiowa.edu/journalism/cite.html** to find other style manuals.)

CHAPTER
5

A Researcher's Toolkit

In Chapter 2, "Using the Web for Research," we introduced different ways to investigate topics using the World Wide Web. One of those ways is to browse and search directories, which can help you find the best resources on a particular topic. For example, they could help with the questions "What are the best sites on the topic of legal research?" and "What are the most useful American literature resources on the Web?" Some directories collect resources that have been evaluated and judged most useful by information specialists. For example, if you wanted the best Web sites that focus on the Middle East and North Africa, a directory would be a good place to start. In Chapter 2, we covered ipl2: Information You Can Trust. In this chapter, we'll look at another directory and show how to use it. We will introduce the online encyclopedia Wikipedia, and also some Google resources that are very helpful for researchers, such as Google Books and Google Scholar.

As a follow-up to this discussion, we will provide a convenient Researcher's Toolkit, a list of Web sites that will help you find practical information as well as important academic research sites that will get you started on a myriad of scholarly topics.

The sections in this chapter are as follows:

♦ Directories Revisited
♦ Browsing and Searching Directories
♦ Wikipedia
♦ Google Books
♦ Google Scholar
♦ A Researcher's Toolkit

The following are the best directories and guides to evaluated resources on the World Wide Web.

Major Directories on the World Wide Web

♦ Academic Info: Subject Guides,
   http://www.academicinfo.net/subject-guides

♦ Digital Librarian: A Librarian's Choice of the Best of the Web,
   http://www.digital-librarian.com
♦ ipl2: Information You Can Trust,
   http://www.ipl2.org
♦ Infomine: Scholarly Internet Resource Collections,
   http://infomine.ucr.edu
♦ Internet Scout Project,
   http://scout.wisc.edu/Reports/ScoutReport/Current/
♦ Intute,
   http://www.intute.ac.uk
♦ LibrarySpot,
   http://libraryspot.com
♦ Open Directory Project,
   http://dmoz.org
♦ The WWW Virtual Library,
   http://vlib.org
♦ Yahoo! Directory,
   http://dir.yahoo.com

Directories Revisited

Directories are topical lists of Internet resources arranged in a hierarchical way. Although they are organized by subject, directories can also be searched by keyword. They differ from search engines in one major way—the human element involved in collecting and maintaining the information. Directories are created and maintained by people, whereas search engines rely on spiders or robots to crawl the Internet for links. There are a number of differences between directories. One way to determine directories' particular characteristics is to ask the following questions about each of them:

♦ Who selects the included Web resources—directory administrators or people in the Internet community?
♦ Who categorizes the Web pages and sites—the people who submit them or directory administrators?
♦ How are the results displayed—alphabetically, by relevance, or by type of Web page?
♦ Are the resources rated? Are they annotated? Are they reviewed?

Each directory differs from others mainly in the level of quality control involved in its management. For example, some directory managers have very little control over their collections, relying on Web page submitters to provide annotations and decisions about where their resource should be placed in the directory's hierarchy. Other directory managers are much more selective not only about which resources they include, but also about where in the subject hierarchy the pages will be located.

Some directory editors write detailed ***annotations*** of the pages. These annotations can be evaluative, descriptive, or both. Annotations are Web site descriptions that either the Web page submitter or the directory editor attaches to the Web sites. The human element involved in creating and maintaining directories creates both advantages and disadvantages for the user. Some of the inherent strengths of directories can be weaknesses, and vice versa. We'll examine some of these strengths and weaknesses here.

Strengths

The major advantages of using directories are as follows:

- ♦ Directories contain fewer resources than search engine databases.
- ♦ Many directories rate, annotate, or categorize chosen resources.
- ♦ Directories increase the probability of retrieving relevant results.

Because directories rely on people to select, maintain, and update their resource lists, they contain fewer resources than search engine databases. This can be a plus, especially when you are looking for information on a general topic. It's a lot easier and less time-consuming to go through a list of 50 or so Web sites than to sort through the thousands of results that a search engine may present. In addition, many directories rate, annotate, analyze, evaluate, and categorize the resources included, which helps you find resources of the highest quality. With thousands of new resources appearing on the Web each day, it is important that people work to determine which sites and Web pages have the highest quality.

Weaknesses

There are three major disadvantages inherent in World Wide Web directories. They are as follows:

- ♦ Arbitrary hierarchical arrangements
- ♦ Infrequent updates
- ♦ Subjectivity of rating and annotating resources

One of the major disadvantages of using some directories is that the hierarchical arrangements may be arbitrary. For example, let's say we are looking for information on ozone depletion. We want to start by finding a few sites. We decide to use the Yahoo! Directory, **http://dir.yahoo.com**, one of the most established directories on the Web.

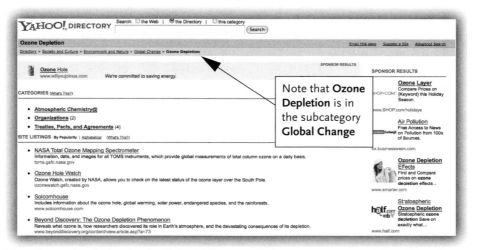

Figure 5.1—Ozone Depletion in the Yahoo! Directory

Note in Figure 5.1 that **Ozone Depletion** is located under the subcategory or subheading **Global Change**, which is located under the category **Environment and Nature**, which is placed under the top-level category **Society and Culture**. The people who organized this directory chose this hierarchy. Another directory might place **Ozone Depletion** under the top-level category **Science**. The ability to search Yahoo! and most other directories by keyword solves this problem of arbitrary hierarchical arrangements.

Another drawback is that selecting and categorizing Web pages takes a lot of time, so directories tend to be less up to date than search engine databases, which are periodically updated by computer programs that automatically gather new Web pages. The third disadvantage inherent in some directories is also an advantage—the resources are chosen by people who subjectively decide which ones are best. What seems to be a good resource to one person may not to the next. This is why it is important for the directory management to have well-stated criteria for selecting resources.

Browsing and Searching Directories

There are two ways to find information in directories. You can browse by subject or search by keyword. These will be discussed in the following section.

Browsing

Browsing a directory is not difficult. You simply click on a subject category that you think will contain the subject you are seeking. This will take you to another level in the hierarchy, where you choose another subject from the list of subjects that appear on your computer screen. You then examine the choices that are returned to you and select the one most closely related to your research topic. You continue this process until your window fills with a list of resources that you can then examine to find the information you need.

Sometimes this process has two levels; other times it has several. It depends on the directory and how detailed the subject is. For example, if we were to browse the Open Directory Project for resources about economics, we would start by clicking on the top-level category **Science**. Next, we would click on **Social Sciences**, and from the resulting list of subcategories, we would choose **Economics**.

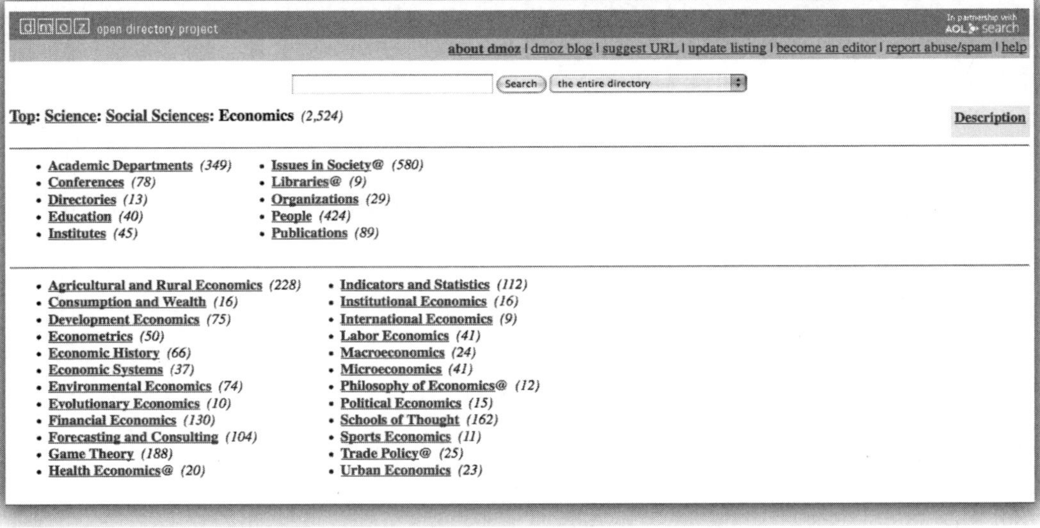

Figure 5.2—Subcategories Under Economics in the Open Directory Project

Now let's try to find economics resources in Yahoo!'s directory. The top-level category we need to click on is **Social Science**. Figure 5.3 shows that **Economics** is a subcategory of **Social Science**. Several subcategories under **Economics** cover specific aspects of the subject.

Figure 5.3—Economics Resources in Yahoo!'s Directory

Searching

By now, you can probably see the advantage of being able to search a directory. It may be difficult to determine where in a directory's hierarchy a particular subject will be found. Searching a directory is not the same as searching the Web using a search engine. The primary difference is that when you search a directory, you have access to only those resources that are included in the directory, not the entire Web. Also, in some directories (such as Yahoo!'s), you do not search the full text of Web pages; you search only the words in the URLs (Uniform Resource Locators), the titles of the Web pages, and annotations (if they exist).

The main difference between directories and search engines is that the resources in directories are selected very carefully. The people who organize directories are usually on the lookout for three major types of information: subject guides, reference works, and specialized databases.

Subject Guides

A *subject guide* is a Web resource devoted to including hyperlinks to most of the important Web pages on a particular subject. For example, a resource devoted to listing Web sites on Middle East & Islamic Studies is a subject guide, as shown in Figure 5.4.

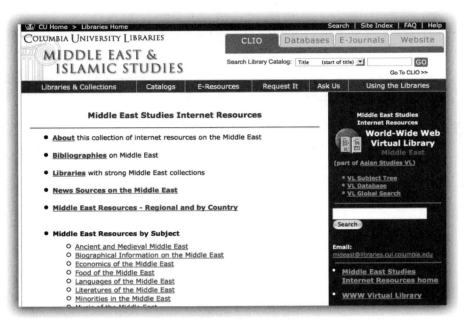

Figure 5.4—Columbia University Libraries' Middle East & Islamic Studies

Reference Works

Another common type of resource collected by directories is a reference work. A ***reference work*** is a full-text document with self-contained information. In other words, it doesn't necessarily contain hyperlinks to other resources. A reference work on the World Wide Web is very similar to its print counterpart. A dictionary on the Web would look very much like a dictionary on a reference shelf. The only difference is that it would allow you to move around the document using hyperlinks instead of turning pages and looking in the index for related topics. There are encyclopedias, handbooks, dictionaries, directories, and many other types of reference works on the World Wide Web. Figure 5.5 pictures a reference work—the U.S. Postal Service's "Zip Code Lookup and Address Information."

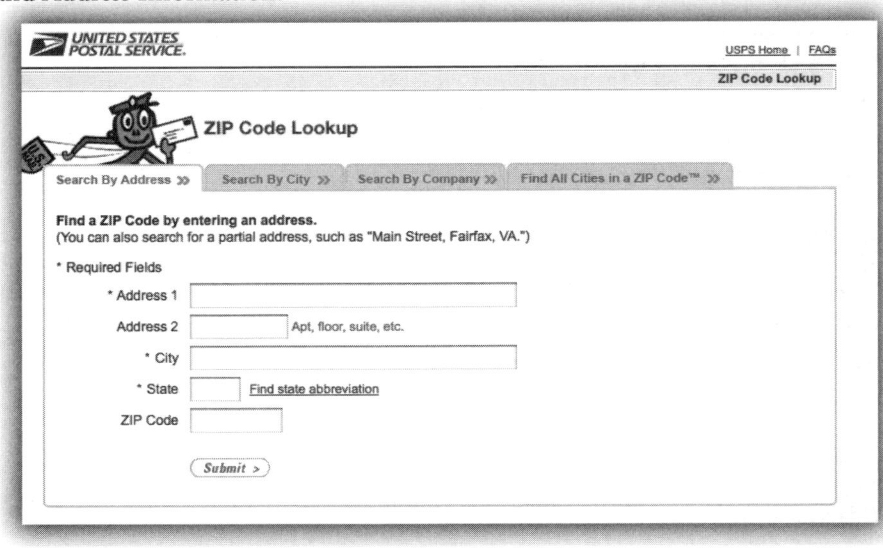

Figure 5.5 —U.S. Postal Service's "Zip Code Lookup and Address Information"

Specialized Databases

Directories can be useful for finding *specialized databases* as well. A specialized database is an index that catalogs certain material, such as patent information, medical journal article citations, company financial data, court decisions, and so forth. Specialized databases can usually be searched by keyword. We'll discuss them in detail in Chapter 7. Figure 5.6 shows a specialized database that covers medical literature—PubMed, a database of Medline citations provided by the National Library of Medicine and the National Institutes of Health.

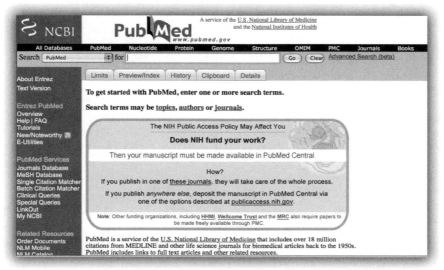

Figure 5.6 —PubMed

Now that you know what types of information are collected in directories, we'll do an activity to illustrate how useful they can be for your research.

ACTIVITY
5.1   FINDING SUBJECT GUIDES FOR INTERNATIONAL BUSINESS RESEARCH

Overview

Let's say you don't know much about doing international business research and you don't know where to start. A subject guide on international business might be exactly what you need. For this activity, we will be using ipl2: Information You Can Trust, a directory run by several universities with graduate programs in library and information science. Every site included in the ipl2 has been chosen and evaluated by a librarian or a graduate student.

We'll follow these steps:
1. Go to ipl2.
2. Browse the categories for a subject guide on international business.
3. Search for international business.

Details

1   Go to ipl2.

DO IT! Type **http://www.ipl2.org** and press **Enter**.

2 Browse the categories for a subject guide on international business.

DO IT! Click on the link for **Resources by Subject**. Your screen should look like the one pictured in Figure 5.7.

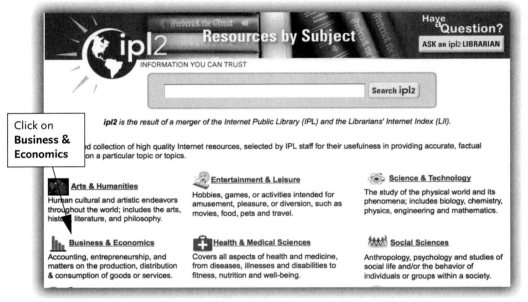

Figure 5.7—Resources by Subject in ipl2

DO IT! Click on the top-level category **Business & Economics**, as shown in Figure 5.7.

Take a look at the subcategories listed under **Business & Economics**. The most promising link is **International Business**. Let's click on that category and see what's available.

DO IT! Click on **International Business** and press **Enter**. Scroll down through the sites listed and read the annotations.

There are several promising sites, but one that looks particularly useful is **International Business Center (CIBER)**, a guide to international business published by Michigan State University. Figure 5.8 shows the annotation for this site.

Figure 5.8—International Business Center (CIBER), an International Business Subject Guide from Michigan State University

Note the magnifying glass icon next to the title of the site. If you click on this icon, you will be able to view the metadata assigned to this record. Let's see what information this provides.

DO IT! Click on the magnifying glass icon, as shown in Figure 5.8.

Figure 5.9 shows the information provided by the metadata.

Figure 5.9—Metadata for the International Business Center (CIBER), Michigan State University

The metadata indicates the subjects assigned to this Web site. It also gives a brief description of the contents of the site, the publisher, language, and the URL. We can access the actual Web site from this window. Let's take a look at it.

DO IT! Click on the URL for the International Business Center (CIBER).

Figure 5.10 shows the front page of this useful Web site.

Figure 5.10—International Business Center (CIBER)

Of particular interest is globalEDGE, a site within CIBER (note the link on the right side of the window), which features country profiles containing business climate, history and politics, and statistics. There are also market indicators and a directory of academic research resources.

3   Search for international business.

That was fairly easy. Now let's try searching ipl2 by keyword.

Returning to the top of ipl2's page, you'll see a search form. Let's search using the phrase **"international business"**. It's important to the put the words in quotation marks because your search results will be much more precise.

DO IT!   Type "international business" in the search form and press **Enter**, as shown in Figure 5.11.

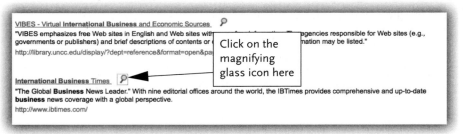

Figure 5.11—Phrase Typed in ipl2's Search Form

Searching the ipl2 for international business results in over thirty more resources that weren't listed in the directory. Let's take a look. One of the resources, as shown in Figure 5.12, **International Business Times**, looks particularly useful. If we click on the magnifying glass icon, we can read the metadata for this site.

DO IT!   Click on the magnifying glass icon, as shown in Figure 5.12

VIBES - Virtual **International Business** and Economic Sources
"VIBES emphasizes free Web sites in English and Web sites with~~~~~~~~~~~~~~~~ agencies responsible for Web sites (e.g., governments or publishers) and brief descriptions of contents or~~~~~~~~~~~~~ nation may be listed."
http://library.uncc.edu/display/?dept=reference&format=open&pa~~

Click on the magnifying glass icon here

International Business Times
"The Global **Business** News Leader." With nine editorial offices around the world, the IBTimes provides comprehensive and up-to-date **business** news coverage with a global perspective.
http://www.ibtimes.com/

Figure 5.12—Partial Results of Keyword Search in ipl2

Figure 5.13 shows the metadata for this site.

International Business Times

Description:
"The Global Business News Leader." With nine editorial offices around the world, the IBTimes provides comprehensive and up-to-date business news coverage with a global perspective.

Publisher:
The International Business Times Inc.

Language:
English

Geographic coverage:
Europe

Source:
http://www.ibtimes.com/

PID= res:ipl-76400

Figure 5.13—Metadata from ipl2 for International Business Times

The metadata can help you decide whether you want to access this site or not. If you want to access it, simply click on the URL that is located under **Source**.

—————————————————————————————————**END OF ACTIVITY 5.2**

This activity showed how useful a directory can be. It's a good idea to browse a directory and search it by keyword in order to retrieve all relevant resources.

Wikipedia

Wikipedia, at **http://en.wikipedia.org**, is a collaborative encyclopedia with millions of entries on a wide variety of topics. The word *Wikipedia* is a combination of the words **wiki** and encyclopedia. It is written by contributions from over 85 thousand people from all over the world, and is available in more than 260 languages. Wikipedia is written with wiki software, where one or more people write and edit documents collaboratively. At the time of this writing, there are more than two million articles in Wikipedia. Wikipedia, with its self-policing nature, strives to be objective. Volunteer fact checkers are constantly editing and removing incorrect content.

Searching Wikipedia

When you do a search in Google or some other search engine, Wikipedia entries on that topic very often appear very high on the results list. You can also search Wikipedia directly. For example, from the Wikipedia home page, **http://en.wikipedia.org/wiki/Main_Page** you can search by keyword or you can try going to a subject portal in the upper right corner, as shown in Figure 5.14.

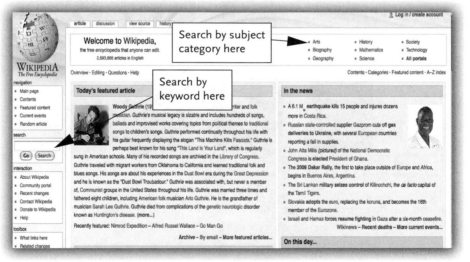

Figure 5.14—Wikipedia

Searching Wikipedia by keyword is straightforward. The following are some examples:
◆ Typing **tribalism Africa** will return all Wikipedia entries where both of these words appear.
◆ Wikipedia also supports fuzzy searching, which is the ability to find all endings or different spellings of words. We'll talk more about this feature in Chapter 6. To do a fuzzy search, simply put the ~ symbol after the word, for example: **labour~ statistic~**
◆ Search for phrases by putting the words in double quotes: **"global warming"**.

For more details on how to search Wikipedia, go to **http://en.wikipedia.org/wiki/ Wikipedia:Searching**.

Google Books

Google Books, at **http://books.google.com**, is an ongoing project between Google, several university libraries, both in the United States and abroad, and book publishers. What Google has done is scan thousands of books and make them searchable by keyword. If the book is not under copyright restriction, then a researcher can read the entire book online. If the book is still under copyright, a person can read parts of the book if the publisher agrees to it. We'll show you some examples of how you can use Google Books for your research.

First, let's explore the Google Books home page.

DO IT! Go to Google Books at **http://books.google.com**.

Figure 5.15 shows the main page of Google Books.

Figure 5.15—Google Book Search Main Page

Note that you can browse the Google Books collection by clicking on any of the links on the left side of the window. You can also click on any of the book covers. The book covers shown change each time you access the database. For this example, we'll choose Up *from Slavery*, by Booker T. Washington. If you are following along with us you may not see this book cover on the main page. If so, click on another book cover of your choice.

Figure 5.16 shows the first page of the book *Up From Slavery*, which has been scanned in its entirely from Stanford University Library. The edition of this book was published in 1919, so it is not under copyright restriction. Therefore, the entire book is available here for us to read.

Figure 5.16—Up From Slavery Scanned in its Entirely in Google Books

There are many things you can do at this point. You can go through the book page by page within this window by clicking the forward arrow as shown in the figure above. You can also download the entire book in PDF format by clicking the **Download** link. You can read book reviews, write a book review, add the book to a library that you have created for yourself within Google Books, or you can order a physical book from a bookstore. You can also find a library near you that has this book so you can check it out. If you click on **Overview** in the upper left corner, you'll find even more information about this book.

DO IT! Click on **Overview**.

This page is filled with very useful information, including links to book reviews, references to scholarly works, links to other editions, and references from Web pages and other books.

Figure 5.17 shows one especially unique feature: a map showing all the places that are discussed in *Up from Slavery*. Your results will be different, based on the book you are viewing.

Figure 5.17—Places Mentioned in Up from Slavery

Let's say you have heard of the book *Team of Rivals: The Political Genius of Abraham Lincoln*, by Doris Kearns Goodwin. You want to know more about the book, perhaps read some reviews, and if possible, read the introduction to the book and possibly the table of contents or index.

DO IT! Simply type in the words **"team of rivals"** in the search form.

Figure 5.18 shows the results of the search.

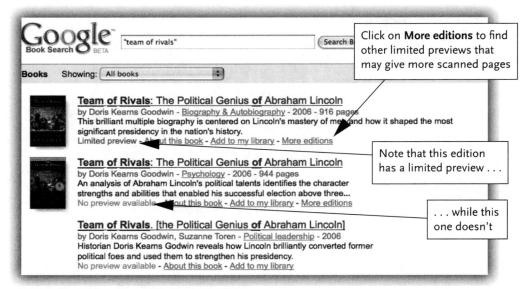

Figure 5.18—Searching Google Books for a Title

Because *Team of Rivals* is a recent book (published in 2006), it is still under copyright restriction. Therefore, we won't be able to read the entire book here. But, depending on the edition and the publisher providing that edition, there may be a limited preview to the book's contents. If you note from Figure 5.18, the first entry listed does have a limited preview. If you clicked on the title you would find much the same value-added information that we found from the first example of *Up from Slavery*. Book reviews, links to libraries and bookstores, scholarly references, and more. You might also be able to read the first chapter or other selected parts of the book that would give you a taste of what the book is about. *Hint:* If the edition you're looking at doesn't have many scanned pages in its preview, click on **More editions**—there may be another edition that has provided more.

Google Scholar

Google Scholar, at **http://scholar.google.com**, is another Google project that is proving to be very useful for the academic researcher. Google Scholar lets you search for scholarly literature in many disciplines and sources. You can use it to locate peer-reviewed papers, theses, books, articles, and abstracts from academic publishers, professional societies, universities, and other organizations. It helps you find the most relevant and important research that has been done on thousands of scholarly topics.

One of the most useful features of Google Scholar is showing the researcher how many other publications have cited a particular article, paper, book, or any other type of resource. For example, if we did a broad search on the topic of global warming, we could find the most important articles written on this topic and also read other articles that have cited a particular article. In Figure 5.19, for example, a search on **"global warming"** found thousands of articles. The first one, a 2003 article published in *Nature* magazine, has been cited over a thousand times.

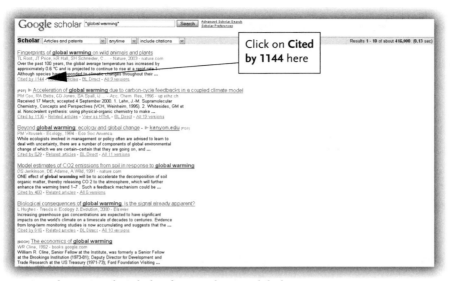

Figure 5.19—Searching Google Scholar for Articles on Global Warming

We could click on the title of the article to find out more about the article and possibly find it in our library, or if it's in the public domain, read the entire article freely on the Web. To find other articles that have cited it, we click on the first link under the annotation—**Cited by 1144**. Figure 5.20 shows a portion of the resulting list. The first article listed is available in its entirety by clicking on the title. If you are following along, your results will vary. An article marked **[PDF]** will be available in its entirety.

Figure 5.20—Articles That Cited the Original Article

Note that you can also click on **Related Articles** to read similar articles on the topic. You can also search Google Scholar by author. Google Scholar has many other features that we won't go into here. We urge you to try it and see for yourself how useful it can be for your research.

A Researcher's Toolkit

The following list of Web sites is organized in two categories. The first part focuses on Web sites that contain practical information you can consult on a daily basis, such as maps, stock information, weather, dictionaries, and so forth. The second section covers some of the best academic research sites that will assist you in preparing for school projects, papers, and presentations. All of the sites listed in this toolkit were found by browsing and searching the directories and virtual libraries discussed in this chapter.

Practical Information Web Sites

Dictionaries, Handbooks, and Almanacs

◆ Bartleby.com, **http://www.bartleby.com**

Bartleby.com is a mega-site consisting of full-text classic fiction and non-fiction, reference works such as *The Columbia Encyclopedia, The American Heritage Dictionary, Roget's Thesaurus, Barlett's Familiar Quotations, Strunk's Elements of Style, Gray's Anatomy,* and more. A one-stop-shop for students and researchers, *Bartleby.com* is a fundamental resource to add to your favorites list.

◆ Infoplease: Encyclopedia, Almanac, Atlas, Biographies, Dictionary, Thesaurus. Free online reference, research & homework help, **http://www.infoplease.com**

Look here for most of the content found in the print *Information Please* almanac: U.S. and international statistics, biographical information, and sports, entertainment, and weather data.

◆ How Many? A Dictionary of Units of Measurement, **http://www.unc.edu/~rowlett/units**

This dictionary describes the relationship between various English and metric units. Look here for measurement information covering almost everything from solar flare intensity to paper sheet sizes to wind-chill charts.

◆ Whatis.com: The IT-Specific Encyclopedia, **http://whatis.techtarget.com**

Whatis.com serves as both a dictionary and an encyclopedia of thousands of computing and information technology terms. This well-designed and useful site is a benefit to users at all levels. It is updated and expanded regularly.

◆ Zip Code Lookup and Address Information, **http://www.usps.com/zip4**

This specialized database will assist you in finding a zip code by address or company name. It will also find all the zip codes of a city or town, and all the cities and towns that use a particular zip code.

Maps

◆ Google Maps, **http://maps.google.com**

Use Google Maps to find locations in the United States and several other countries, including driving directions. You can also find companies or types of companies that are near a particular address. For example, you might search for **"Chinese restaurants" near Ann Arbor, MI**. You can also use Google Maps on your mobile phone. You can also view satellite images of chosen locations.

◆ MapQuest, **http://www.mapquest.com**

MapQuest provides maps and driving directions for individual addresses, airports, and businesses (both by name and by type) in the United States. It also provides similar services for European countries and the United Kingdom.

◆ Perry-Castañeda Library Map Collection, **http://www.lib.utexas.edu/maps**

This collection is a must-see for everyone who is interested in locating a map. The Perry-Castenada Library of the University of Texas has scanned over 4,000 noncopyrighted maps from its own collection, making them available to the public on the Web. While most of the maps in the collection are provided by the U.S. Central Intelligence Agency, there are also maps from obscure agencies and institutions.

Money & Stocks

♦ Oanda, **http://www.oanda.com**

This site contains a currency converter for 164 currencies. Updated daily.

♦ PCQuote, **http://www.pcquote.com**

Look here for securities quotations, stock market information, financial news, and other investment tools.

Telephone Directories

♦ Anywho, **http://www.anywho.com**

This site contains publicly accessible local telephone records for individuals and businesses. It also provides addresses, maps, and driving directions. The user can also find an address by typing in the telephone number if they know it (reverse lookup).

♦ Yellowpages.com, **http://www.yellowpages.com**

Yellowpages.com has most of the same features as Anywho.com. You can find telephone numbers for individuals and businesses, maps, driving directions, and more. You can also find businesses by name or category with the distance calculated from the location you choose.

News

♦ ABYZ News Links, **http://www.abyznewslinks.com**

ABYZ News Links provides access to online news sources from around the world. Newspapers are of primary importance, but the site also includes many broadcast stations, Internet services, magazines, and press agencies. You can browse by region or country. The site is also searchable.

♦ Google News, **http://news.google.com**

Google News covers 4,500 news sources and arranges headlines by relevance, with articles from several newspapers and other sources grouped under each story. The database is updated every 10 to 15 minutes. International in scope, *Google News* uses mathematical algorithms to determine which stories will be listed on its main page.

♦ Kidon Media Link, **http://www.kidon.com/media-link/index.php**

Kidon Media Link provides links to close to 20,000 news sources from around the world. Sources include newspapers, magazines, radio and other broadcast services, and more.

♦ NewsLink, **http://newslink.org**

This site provides links to U.S. and foreign newspapers, college newspapers, radio stations, and magazines. Can also search for radio stations and newspapers by city and state.

Weather

♦ National Weather Service, **http://www.nws.noaa.gov**

This U.S. National Oceanic and Atmospheric Administration site provides up-to-date weather forecasts for all 50 states. You can search the area of interest by zip code or by clicking on a map. Also included are research articles that may be searched by subject.

◆ The Weather Channel, **http://www.weather.com**

This resource provides weather forecasts, traveler's tips, vacation ideas, gardening information, and more.

Academic Research Web Sites

Reference Sites

◆ Biography.com, **http://www.biography.com**

Providing biographical information for over 25,000 people, this A&E network site also includes video clips and educational materials to support classroom discussions.

◆ Guide to Grammar and Writing, **http://grammar.ccc.commnet.edu/grammar**

This site covers virtually everything you'll ever want to know about grammar and writing, including writer's block and how to overcome it, paragraph development, parts of speech, tense consistency, and much, much more.

◆ Research and Documentation Online,
http://www.bedfordstmartins.com/online/citex.html

This site covers details on how to cite electronic sources in the major styles, including APA, Chicago Manual of Style, MLA, and CBE (Council of Biology Editors). Based on a book by Diana Hacker and Barbara Fister.

◆ Online Writing Lab, **http://owl.english.purdue.edu**

This site provides information for students and teachers on writing, including grammar, punctuation, and research skills. English-as-a-second-language resources are included as well.

◆ Plagiarism.org, **http://www.plagiarism.org**

This site provides tips and guidelines for educators and students on the topic of identifying and avoiding plagiarism. It also has information about citing resources properly, with links to Web sites that explain how to use the major citation styles.

◆ Refdesk.com, **http://www.refdesk.com**

You'll find hundreds of links to current news, electronic reference works, statistical information, directories, dictionaries, encyclopedias, and more. The site can also be searched by keyword.

◆ Virtual Reference Shelf, **http://www.loc.gov/rr/askalib/virtualref.html**

Selected Web resources selected by staff members at the U.S. Library of Congress.

◆ Yahoo!'s Babelfish, **http://babelfish.yahoo.com**

Babelfish allows you to translate a section of text or a Web page from English to several languages, and from some other languages to English. The translations aren't always perfect, but the site can be a time saver.

Library Catalogs

◆ Libweb at Berkeley, **http://lists.webjunction.org/libweb**

Use Libweb to find all types of libraries. Be aware that the library catalogs for some of the libraries listed here are unavailable for remote use, especially those of foreign libraries. In some cases, the library's home page is all that is included.

◆ LIBCAT, **http://www.librarysites.info**

   LIBCAT gives lots of information on searching library catalogs. Look here to find a list of special collections and the names of libraries in which they are located.

◆ UNESCO Libraries Portal,
   http://www.unesco-ci.org/cgi-bin/portals/libraries/page.cgi?d=1

   This service lists over 11,000 libraries in the academic, government, national, public, and institutional sectors.

Country Information

◆ CIA World Factbook, **https://www.cia.gov/library/publications/the-world-factbook**

   This is the online version of the CIA's *World Factbook*. Published annually, it contains information on all the countries of the world, including a map of the country, brief historical information, geography overview, population data, description of current government, economic statistics, communications and transportation infrastructure, military conflicts, and more.

◆ United Nations Cyberschoolbus,
   http://www.cyberschoolbus.un.org/infonation/index.asp

   This site, sponsored by the United Nations, allows you to compare statistical data from different countries. Look here to find economic data such as GDP and unemployment rates, infant mortality rates, health statistics, and more.

◆ Nation Master, **http://www.nationmaster.com**

   This site takes information from several public domain data sources, including the CIA *World Factbook* and several United Nations publications. It allows you to compare and contrast statistics between countries. Relevant articles from *Wikipedia* are embedded into the appropriate categories. All entries are cited so that you know from where the data was originally published.

◆ Portal to the World, **http://www.loc.gov/rr/international/portals.html**

   Created by Library of Congress specialists, this site is a collection of links about every country in the world. In addition to geographical information, it also provides links to libraries, regional search engines, science and technology, and more.

Business & Economics

◆ BizLink: Your Online Business Resource, **http://www.plcmc.org/bizlink**

   Developed by Charlotte & Mecklenburg Public Library in North Carolina, this portal is a great place to start researching economic conditions, marketing and demographics, international business, starting a business, and more.

◆ Bureau of Labor Statistics, **http://stats.bls.gov**

   The Bureau of Labor Statistics is a mega-site filled with some of the most useful economic, career, and other workplace-related information available on the Web. For example, you can find the last six months of various U.S. economic data, including the unemployment rate, consumer price index, average hourly earnings, and so forth, with links to historical information on all of these segments. The Employment Projections section develops information about trends in the labor market for ten years into the future. Several publications that are used in career guidance are provided here, including the *Occupational Outlook Handbook* and the *Monthly Labor Review*.

- EDGAR—SEC Filings & Forms, **http://www.sec.gov/edgar.shtml**

    This site provides U.S. Securities and Exchange Commission (SEC) financial statements that are required from all public U.S. companies with less than $10 million in assets and 500 shareholders. Available free from the SEC, EDGAR is a well-designed and reliable resource, with over 1 million documents in its collection.

- GlobalEdge, **http://globaledge.msu.edu**

    This portal, created by Michigan State University, is a useful source for statistical data, economic and political conditions, and historical information for almost 200 countries. It is also a good source for information on industries. GlobalEdge also supports a blog that allows you to discuss topics related to international business and global trade.

- Hoover's Online, **http://www.hoovers.com**

    This is a useful site for the busy student or researcher who needs company information. You can find a brief overview of a company, including street address, telephone and fax numbers, location map, hyperlink to the company's home page, top competitors, company type (whether private or public), key people in the company, links to news, and links to industry information. If the company you have looked up is private, you may get very brief financial information with links to business reports that you will have to pay for prepared by Dun & Bradstreet and other firms.

- Industry Research Desk, **http://www.virtualpet.com/industry**

    This is an excellent starting point for the person researching an industry. The author brings together hyperlinks for industry data, industry home pages, the North American Industry Classification System (NAICS), and office tools such as package costs and tracking devices, and more.

- Market Research Library, **http://www.buyusainfo.net**

    Prepared by the U.S. Commercial Service, this database is for U.S. business people who may want to invest in a country. Also includes links to Country Commercial Guides for each country. Political science and international business students can also benefit from the information found here.

- Resources for Economics on the Internet: RFE, **http://www.rfe.org**

    Sponsored by the American Economic Association, this guide lists more than 2,000 carefully selected resources of interest to academic economics researchers and practicing economists.

- Researching Companies Online, **http://www.learnwebskills.com/company**

    Undoubtedly one of the most-cited business tutorials on the World Wide Web, Debbie Flanagan's *Researching Companies Online* is the best place to start a business-related research project. All of the links provided in the tutorial are free and open to the public without subscription.

Education

- ERIC—The Educational Resources Information Center, **http://eric.ed.gov**

    This is the world's largest source of education information, containing more than one million abstracts of education journal articles, documents, and other resources.

- Lesson Plans Library, **http://school.discovery.com/lessonplans**

    Use this site to find lesson plans written by teachers for teachers. You can browse by subject and grade level.

- MIT Open Courseware, **http://ocw.mit.edu/OcwWeb/web/home/home/index.htm**

  The Massachusetts Institute of Technology (MIT) has posted most of its undergraduate and graduate course content on this site. It is a free service and includes most subjects. Using the materials on this site does not give you an MIT education, nor does it grant degrees or certificates, but for teachers and students, the information can be very useful.

- *New York Times* Learning Network, **http://www.nytimes.com/learning**

  The New York Times Learning Network is a free service for teachers, parents, and students in elementary and secondary schools. Updated each weekday, it contains summaries of news stories from the current day's *New York Times*.

- PBS Teacher Source, **http://www.pbs.org/teachersource**

  One of the best features of the Public Broadcasting System's (PBS) *TeacherSource* is the collection of over 2,500 lesson plans and activities for classroom teachers.

- World Lecture Hall, **http://web.austin.utexas.edu/wlh**

  World Lecture Hall publishes links to pages created by college and university faculty around the world who deliver course materials on the Web in any language. The materials can be used by anyone interested in courseware—faculty, developers, and students.

Humanities

- American Memory from the Library of Congress, **http://memory.loc.gov/ammem/index.html**

  The American Memory Historical Collections consist of digitized documents, photographs, recorded sound, moving pictures, and text from the Library of Congress' Americana collections. Examples of content found here are music from the Civil War, slave narratives, and World War II interviews.

- A Biography of America, **http://www.learner.org/biographyofamerica**

  Created to be a companion Web site to the video series and telecourse of the same name, *A Biography of America* provides a text transcript of each of the 26 videos, maps, timelines, and Webliographies that enhance the content of the series. In-depth articles that complement the series' content are also included.

- EHistory, **http://www.ehistory.com**

  Maintained by Ohio State University's Department of History, eHistory is a portal to history divided by the following broad topics: Ancient, Middle Ages, Civil War, World War II, Vietnam War, Middle East, and World. For each section, there are articles and primary source documents, biographies, maps, timelines, and more.

- Luminarium, **http://www.luminarium.org/lumina.htm**

  This site is devoted to medieval English literature, the Renaissance period, and the early 17th century and is an excellent starting point for students and other interested researchers.

- Stanford Encyclopedia of Philosophy, **http://plato.stanford.edu**

  Each entry in this encyclopedia is written, maintained, and updated by a qualified expert or group of experts in that particular field. Arranged in a simple alphabetical layout, each entry consists of a typical encyclopedic overview of the topic, plus a bibliography of print and Internet resources at the end of the article. The Encyclopedia may also be searched.

- Internet Sacred Text Archive, **http://www.sacred-texts.com/index.htm**

    This site seeks to promote religious tolerance and scholarship by providing electronic texts about religion, mythology, legend, and folklore. Most documents have been translated into English.

Law

- Country Reports on Human Rights Practices, **http://www.state.gov/g/drl/rls/hrrpt**

    These reports review a country's record from the previous year on internationally recognized individual, civil, political, and worker rights, as set forth in the Universal Declaration of Human Rights. Press freedom, religious freedom, democratic trends, treatment of women and children, prison conditions, trafficking in persons, worker's conditions, and arbitrary arrest, detention, or exile, are just some of the subjects covered in these reports.

- Foreign Governments: Constitutions, Laws, and Treaties, **http://www.lib.umich.edu/libhome/Documents.center/forcons.html**

    Part of the incomparable University of Michigan Documents Center at **http://www.lib.umich.edu/libhome/Documents.center**, this directory focuses on the laws, treaties, and constitutions of foreign countries. It's also one of the best places to start if you've got an international law question.

- Copyright Crash Course, **http://www.utsystem.edu/OGC/IntellectualProperty/cprtindx.htm**

    This site focuses on a wide range of copyright issues written in language that the layperson can understand. While the primary audience of the site is college and university faculty, the content may be applied to anyone who is considering reproducing or distributing someone else's work and wants to know the legal limits of doing so.

- FindLaw, **http://www.findlaw.com**

    A major portal to legal resources, *FindLaw* serves several audiences, including legal professionals, students, businesses, and the public. Essentially a directory to a myriad of legal subject areas, its main value lies in its collection of full-text legal opinions.

- LLRX.com, **http://www.llrx.com**

    LLRX.com is a Web journal dedicated to providing professionals with state-of-the-art information on legal research and technology-related issues. It is written by Sabrina Pacifici, and has been in publication since 1996.

Medicine & Health

- AEGIS: AIDS Education Global Information System, **http://www.aegis.com**

    A comprehensive site that covers AIDS treatment, prevention, news services, legal information, and more. It also provides a bulletin board for people to communicate to each other about HIV/AIDS. Founded by the Sisters of St. Elizabeth of Hungary, it is now a non-profit organization in the state of California.

- Drugs.com **http://www.drugs.com**

    This site contains free information on prescription and over-the-counter drugs, provided by independent medical information companies. It is not affiliated with pharmaceutical companies. You can search drugs by name and by medical condition. Also found here are drug interactions.

♦ MedlinePlus, **http://medlineplus.gov**

This site, provided by the National Institutes of Health and the National Library of Medicine, contains carefully selected Web resources on 650 health topics. It also provides a medical dictionary, drug information, interactive health tutorials, and links to preformulated searches of the MEDLINE/Pubmed database.

♦ PLoS: Public Library of Science, **http://www.plos.org**

An open-access collection of peer-reviewed journals in science and medicine.

♦ PubMed, **http://www.ncbi.nlm.nih.gov/PubMed**

This service provides a search interface to the National Library of Medicine's MEDLINE database, which includes over 14 million article citations from more than 4800 biomedical journals, with coverage back to the 1950s.

♦ PubMed Central, **http://www.pubmedcentral.nih.gov**

Also provided by the National Institutes of Health, PubMed Central is a free digital archive of biomedical and life sciences journal literature.

Political Science

♦ Council on Foreign Relations, **http://www.cfr.org**

This site, provided by the publisher of *Foreign Affairs,* contains up-to-date information about U.S. foreign policy.

♦ Foreign Relations of the United States, **http://www.state.gov/r/pa/ho/frus**

This site provides the official documentary historical record of major U.S. foreign policy decisions. Information comes from the Department of State, Presidential libraries, the National Security Council, the Central Intelligence Agency, the U.S. Agency for International Development, and other sources. Coverage on the Web site goes back to the Truman administration.

♦ Political Science Resources on the Web,
http://www.lib.umich.edu/govdocs/poliscinew.html

Provided by the University of Michigan Library, this is a directory to political science resources, arranged by broad subject areas such as reference tools, international relations, think tanks, dissertations, political theory, and more.

Science & Technology

♦ American Chemical Society, **http://portal.acs.org/portal/acs/corg/content**

This portal site from the American Chemical Society contains recent articles, grants information, and career development resources. Educational information is provided for teachers and students from the K–12 level all the way to graduate school.

♦ American Physical Society, **http://www.aps.org**

This is the place to go if you need anything related to physics. It contains homework help, links to journals, Web sites in all areas of physics, exhibitions and special events, and much more.

♦ National Science Digital Library (NSDL), **http://nsdl.org**

The NDSL provides access to high-quality resources that support advances in teaching and learning in science, technology, engineering, and mathematics. It contains science literacy maps, refresher courses for teachers, and includes lists of evaluated science Web sites.

- Programmer's Heaven, **http://www.programmersheaven.com**

    A Programmers Heaven is a portal to tutorials, articles, source code, shareware, news, and other information about a variety of popular programming languages, operating systems, and applications.

Social Sciences

- American Psychological Association, **http://www.apa.org**

    Geared toward psychology students, faculty, and professionals, this site provides information on psychology careers, conferences, ethics, selected articles from APA journals, links to information on AIDS, parenting, depression, aging, and more.

- Social Psychology Network, **http://www.socialpsychology.org**

    Supported in part by the National Science Foundation, Social Psychology Network is one of the largest collections of sites devoted to psychological research and teaching. There are more than 16 thousand selected links here. The site is maintained by Scott Plous of Wesleyan University.

- Social Science Data Archives, **http://www.sociosite.net/databases.php**

    This guide contains links to high-quality resources and texts from all sociological fields relevant to social scientists and students. It is maintained by Dr Albert Benschop of the University of Amsterdam.

- Sociocultural Theory in Anthropology, **http://www.indiana.edu/~wanthro/ sociocultural_theory.htm**

    Maintained by students at Indiana University's Anthropology Department, this site provides resources in sociocultural anthropology. It looks at how the discipline is structured, how it's changed over time, and provides different ways for scholars to think about the discipline.

Statistics

- Statistical Abstract of the United States, **http://www.census.gov/compendia/statab**

    This is the official source of social and economic data for the United States. Some examples of data included are national health expenditures, crime rates, households that have televisions, computers, Internet access, and much more. Statistics dealing with industry and trade, business, natural resources, transportation, agriculture, and some international statistics are also provided.

- Statistical Resources on the Web, **http://www.lib.umich.edu/govdocs/stats.html**

    Perhaps the most useful site for statistics from a wide variety of sources. Resources are arranged in broad categories such as business and industry, foreign governments, housing, labor, politics, and so forth.

Summary

Every good researcher should have a toolkit of resources for their everyday information needs. Directories, topical lists of Internet resources arranged hierarchically to facilitate browsing by subject, can provide many of the most important tools. Most directories have a search capability, which can help you avoid occasionally becoming lost in arbitrary subject categories. Directories depend on the work of individuals who collect, categorize, maintain, and, in many cases, evaluate

Web sites to make it easier for people to find what they are looking for. Directories vary in how they are organized, which sites get to be evaluated, and, if they are, what criteria are used. Because directories rely on people for their selections and maintenance, they are necessarily much smaller than the databases that search-engine spiders or robots create. This difference can be an asset in some cases and a detriment in others. When you are looking for a "few good sites" to start with, a directory can save you time, especially if your subject is broad and you're at the beginning of your research. It is a good idea to know how to use the different directories we covered in this chapter and to explore others. Keep one or two on your favorites list so you can find them quickly.

Wikipedia, the free online encyclopedia, is becoming an important resource tool for scholars. Because it is dependent upon the general public for its content, it is important to critically evaluate the information found there. Also important to researchers are some of the special resources that Google provides, such as Google Books and Google Scholar. This chapter gave a brief overview on how to use these resources, with links to several other useful tools.

Selected Terms Used in This Chapter

annotation
reference work
specialized database
subject guide
wiki

Review Questions

Multiple Choice

1. The following are advantages of using directories *except:*
   a. They may rate and annotate a site.
   b. They contain more resources than search engine databases.
   c. They increase the probability of finding relevant results.
   d. They rely on people to select their resources.
2. Wikipedia
   a. is an online encyclopedia that is seldom updated.
   b. relies on volunteers who constantly edit and revise the information.
   c. is a directory.
   d. should never be used for serious research.
3. If you wanted to use Boolean searching to search in a directory for scholarships available in the field of physics, you could phrase your search
   a. physics or scholarships
   b. scholarships for physics
   c. physics and scholarships
   d. A directory cannot be searched.

4. To browse a directory for the topic of electronic books, you would start with the category
   a. computers.
   b. literature.
   c. technology.
   d. any of the above

5. If you were looking for a specialized database on a subject, you could start your search with a
   a. reference work.
   b. directory.
   c. hyperlink.
   d. subdirectory.

6. A disadvantage of using a directory is
   a. resources are selected by a spider or robot.
   b. the ratings of sites are subjective.
   c. they decrease the probability of finding relevant results.
   d. they include more sites than a search engine.

7. A searchable index that catalogs a specific type of material (such as medical articles or court decisions) is known as a
   a. subject guide.
   b. specialized database.
   c. reference source.
   d. multi-search tool.

True or False

8. T   F   One weakness of using directories to look for information is they are updated infrequently.

9. T   F   A directory would be a good first choice to find information about a broad subject.

10. T   F   When you perform a keyword search in ipl2: Information You Can Trust, you are searching the entire Web.

11. T   F   One strength of directories is that they all use the same subject headings.

12. T   F   Descriptions of Web sites in a directory are always written by the editors of the directory.

13. T   F   Directories list the most popular Web pages first since they are the best on a subject.

Completion

14. A _____ is a topical list of Internet resources arranged hierarchically.

15. Wikipedia is a _____ encyclopedia with millions of entries.

16. A Web page description that evaluates, rates, or otherwise describes a Web site is called a(n) _____.

17. In Yahoo! a(n) _____ is a category or heading with the search phrase in the category heading.

18. Google Books is a project between Google, _____, and _____.

19. Google Scholar indexes scholarly literature. The most useful feature is finding which publications have _____ a particular article, paper, book, or any other resource.

20. The three major types of information included in directories are _____, _____, and _____.

21. A Web resource that includes hyperlinks to sites on that particular topic is called a(n) _____.

Exercises and Projects

1. It's helpful to learn more about a directory before deciding whether it fits your needs. A good way to start is to look at that small print at the site's home page. See if you can find selection criteria for sites to be included at the following directories and describe how the criteria differ.
   a. Yahoo!, **http://dir.yahoo.com**.
   b. Intute, **http://www.intute.ac.uk/**
   c. Open Directory Project, **http://dmoz.org**
   d. ipl2: Information You Can Trust, **http://www.ipl2.org**

2. Let's compare two resources for the same topic:
   a. Using the Open Directory Project at **http://dmoz.org**, browse through the categories to find information on the subject of immigration. In what category did you find it? Now search the directory for the topic. How many results did you find?
      How do they compare to your results from browsing? Which method worked better for the topic?
   b. Now go to ipl2 at **http://www.ipl2.org**.
      Browse this directory for the topic of immigration. How many sites are included here? Can you find a subject guide?
   c. For this topic, did you find the Open Directory Project or the ipl2 more helpful? Why?

3. See if you can find Moroccan recipes by browsing the Open Directory Project at **http://dmoz.org**. Write down the categories and subcategories you chose as you browsed. Print a recipe for couscous.

4. One of the remarkable aspects of Google Books is the ability to obtain full texts of literary works. Find the full text of Shakespeare's *Romeo and Juliet* by using Google Books at **http://books.google.com**. When you find the play, click on **About This Book**. Find the most popular passages in the play and write one of them down.

5. Now find a work that's not in English. Go to the Open Directory at **http://dmoz.com**. Find the full text of St. Augustine's *Confessions* in Latin by performing a keyword search at the directory. Describe how the search results are presented. Give the URL of a site where the Latin text of the *Confessions* is located.

6. Go to ipl2 at **http://www.ipl2.org**. See if you can find information about Internet filtering in public libraries. How did you find it? How many Web sites did you find? Go to one of them and describe what Internet filtering is. Give the URL of the site you used. Now use Wikipedia, **http://en.wikipedia.org/wiki/Main_Page**, and look for the same topic. Did you find information on Internet filtering in public libraries?

What was the title of the most relevant entry that you found?

7. Aromatherapy is a fast-growing aspect of alternative medicine.

   a. Does Intute, **http://www.intute.ac.uk**, list any resources about the topic?

   b. Go to the Yahoo! directory at **http://dir.yahoo.com** and look for aromatherapy. How many resources did you find at this directory? What categories did you browse to find them? Go to one of the sites listed, find out what aromatherapy is, and give a definition and the URL of the page you visited.

8. Go to Google Scholar at **http://scholar.google.com** at and search to see what you can find about Johannes Gutenberg and the invention of the printing press.

   How did you find the information? Click on some resources that cite the first resource on your list. Write down one article or book that cites the publication you found.

CHAPTER 6

Search Strategies for Search Engines

In Chapter 2, "Using the World Wide Web for Research," we introduced basic keyword searching in search engine databases. In this chapter we will explore searching these databases in greater detail. We will focus our discussion on global search engines such as Google and Yahoo!, but the guidelines and search strategies will also work in smaller search engines. For example, specialized databases such as PubMed, Factiva, and Lexis-Nexis have search engines that support searching by keyword, and many other search features. The strategies in this chapter will help you search any database effectively. The chapter features a detailed discussion on different search and output features of typical search engines, and also provides a 10-step search strategy that will help guide you through research questions in any database. Also provided will be activities in three global search engines, each showcasing different approaches and strategies.

This chapter will include the following sections:
♦ Search Engine Similarities and Differences
♦ How Search Engines Work
♦ Search Features Common to Most Search Engines
♦ Output Features Common to Most Search Engines
♦ A Basic Search Strategy: The 10 Steps

Search Engine Similarities and Differences

All of the major search engines are similar in that you enter keywords in a ***search form***. After clicking on **Search**, **Submit**, **Find**, or some other similar command button, the database returns a collection of hyperlinks, usually listed according to their ***relevance*** to the keyword(s) you typed in, from most relevant to least relevant. Even though most of the major search engine databases attempt to index as much of the Web as possible, each one has a different way of determining which pages will be listed first. Some databases list results by term relevancy, employing algorithms that measure how closely a Web document matches the search expression used. Others list them by using link analysis, which takes into account the context of the Web pages in relation to the search expression, how many quality Web pages link to the pages, or how "popular" they are.

The major search engines differ in several ways:

◆ Size of index
◆ Search features supported (many search engines support the same features but require different syntax to initiate them)
◆ How frequently the database is updated
◆ Ranking algorithms
◆ How deeply each Web site is indexed

It is important to know these differences because to do an exhaustive search of the World Wide Web, you must be familiar with a few different search tools. No single search engine can be relied upon to satisfy every query.

How Search Engines Work

In search engines, a computer program called a *spider* or *robot* gathers new documents from the World Wide Web. The program retrieves hyperlinks that are attached to these documents, loads them into a database, and indexes them using a formula that differs from database to database. Then, when you consult the search engine, it searches the database looking for documents that contain the *keywords* you used in the *search expression*. No search engine actually indexes the entire Web. There is information that is inaccessible to search engines, commonly referred to as the *invisible Web* or the *hidden Internet*. Much of this content can be located in special databases, which we will discuss in Chapter 7. Although robots have many different ways of collecting information from Web pages, the major search engines all claim to index most of the text of each Web document in their databases. This is called *full-text indexing*. In some search engines, the robot skips over words that appear often, such as prepositions and articles. These common words are called *stop words*.

How a Spider Works—Searching the Internet for New Documents

Spiders automatically do this gathering of documents at intervals that differ from service to service. You need to keep in mind that it may be that some portions of a search engine's database may not have been updated in a few weeks. People can also submit their Web pages to be included in the database. This often results in a robot visiting the page and collecting information for the search engine's database. Some robot programs are intuitive; they know which words are important to the meaning of the entire Web page, and some of them can find synonyms to the words and add them to the index. Some full-text databases use robots that enable them to search on concepts as well as on the search query words. Some Web page authors include *meta-tags* as part of the HTML code in their pages. Meta-tags may contain keywords that describe the content and purpose of a Web page, but may not appear on the page. They appear only in the HTML source file. You can view the HTML source code by looking at the page source. Click on **View,** and then select **Source.** Meta-tags allow Web pages that don't contain a lot of text to come up in a keyword search. The two most important meta-tags are the *description* and *keywords* tags. Some search engines will use the description section as the short summary that appears next to the URL in the results list.

Becoming proficient in search techniques is crucial in a full-text environment. The chance of retrieving irrelevant material is high when you can type in a word and conceivably retrieve thousands of Web pages that have that word in it. The following two sections define search features and can be referred to when formulating search expressions.

Search Features Common to Most Search Engines

It's important to understand the different search features before you begin using a search engine for research. The reason for this is that each search engine has its own way of interpreting and manipulating search expressions. In addition, many search engines have *default settings* that you may need to override if you want to obtain the most precise results. Because a search can bring up so many Web pages, it is very easy to have a lot of hits with few that are relevant to your query. This is called *low precision/ high recall*. You may be satisfied with having very precise search results with a small set returned. This is defined as *high precision/ low recall*. Ideally, using the search expression you enter, the search engine would retrieve all of the relevant documents you need. This would be described as *high precision/high recall*.

> **A Note About Google**
>
> Google is currently the most popular global search engine. It has one of the largest databases, and has many services that are useful for searchers, including Google News, Google Books, Google Scholar, Google Blogsearch, and Google Image Search. Google's successful ranking algorithm using link analysis gives most searchers a satisfying search experience, returning highly relevant Web sites near the top of search results lists. We recommend that searchers not depend solely on Google, however. It is important to know how to use a couple of other global search tools because not all search engines index the same documents, and if they do, they don't index them in the same way. For example, research has shown that Google doesn't index documents as deeply as Yahoo! In addition, each search engine calculates relevancy in different ways. Therefore, it's a good idea to search more than Google when trying to do comprehensive research.

Search engines support many search features, though not all engines support each one. If they do support certain features, they may use different *syntax* in expressing the feature. Before you use any of these search features, you need to check the search engines' help pages to see how the feature is expressed or if it is supported at all. We will now list the most common search features and explain how each feature is used.

Boolean Operators

We discussed Boolean operators briefly in Chapter 2. Knowing how to apply Boolean operators in search expressions is extremely important. The diagrams show the different operators and how they are used.

hiking AND camping

Use an AND between search terms when you need to narrow your search. The AND indicates that only those Web pages having both words in them will be retrieved. Some search engines automatically assume an AND relationship between two words if you don't type AND between them. This would be a default setting of the search engine.

hiking OR camping

An OR between search terms will make your resulting set larger. When you use OR, Web pages that have either term will be retrieved. Some databases automatically place an OR between two words if there is nothing typed between them. This would be a default setting of the search tool.

hiking NOT camping

The NOT operator is used when a term needs to be excluded. In this example, Web pages with *hiking* would be retrieved but not those with the word *camping*. Some search engines require an AND in front of the NOT. In that case, the expression would be *hiking AND NOT camping*.

hiking AND (camping OR swimming)

This example shows ***nested Boolean logic***. Use this technique when you need to include ANDs and ORs in one search statement. For example,

> **Note About Boolean Logic**
>
> Even if you have never typed in AND, OR, or NOT in a search expression, you have used Boolean logic. The reason for this is that most search engines incorporate Boolean logic automatically. For example, whenever you type two words in a search form without quotation marks around them, the search engine is searching for the two words with an AND between them. It's easier to see Boolean logic at work when you use the advanced search option in most search engines. In forms and pull-down menus asking you to find "any of the words" or "should have" you are essentially OR'ing words together. In a form asking for "all of the words" or "must have" you are AND'ing words together. And in those forms that ask you to "exclude words" or "must not have" you are essentially using the NOT operator.

say that there is a term that must appear in your results. You want to search for this term along with a concept that you can describe with synonyms. To do this, you will need to tell the search engine to find records with two or more synonyms and then to combine this result with the first term. In the example above, the parentheses indicate that *camping OR swimming* will be processed first, and that this result will be combined with *hiking*. If the parentheses were not there, the search engine would perform the search from left to right. All pages with both the words *hiking* and *camping* would be found first, and then all pages with the word *swimming* would be included. This would give you an unacceptable result, so you must be careful when using ANDs and ORs together in a search expression.

Implied Boolean Operators

Implied Boolean operators, or pseudo-Boolean operators, are shortcuts to typing AND and NOT. In the search engines that support this feature, you type + (plus sign) before a word or phrase that must appear in the document and − (minus sign) before a word or phrase that must not appear in the document.

Phrase Searching

A *phrase* is a string of words that must appear next to each other. *Global warming* is a phrase, as is *chronic fatigue syndrome*. Use phrase-searching capability when the words you are searching for must appear next to each other and must appear in the order in which you type them. Most search engines require double quotation marks to differentiate a phrase from words searched by themselves. The two phrases mentioned above would be expressed like this: **"global warming"** and **"chronic fatigue syndrome"**. In some search tools, a phrase is assumed when more than one word is typed together without a connector between them. You should read the help pages of the database you are using to find out how ***phrase searching*** is performed.

Proximity Searching

Proximity operators are words such as *near* or *within*. For example, you are trying to find information on the effects of chlorofluorocarbons on global warming. You might want to retrieve results that have the word *chlorofluorocarbons* very close to the phrase *global warming*. By placing the word NEAR or WITHIN between the two segments of the search expression, you would achieve more relevant results than if the words appeared in the same document but were perhaps pages apart. (Some search tools that use this operator allow a **W/# of words** between the two segments to indicate how close the two words need to be, so a search phrase such as *Hillary W/2 Clinton* would look for the two words to occur not more than two words apart, allowing, for example, for both "Hillary Clinton" and "Hillary Rodham Clinton" to be returned in the search.) This is called *proximity searching*.

Truncation

Truncation looks for multiple forms of a word. Some search engines refer to truncation as *stemming*. For example, to research postmodern art, you might want to retrieve all the records that had the root word *postmodern*, such as *postmodernist* and *postmodernism*. Most search engines support truncation by allowing you to place an asterisk (*) at the end of the root word. You will need to see the help pages in the search engine you are using to find out which symbol is used. For example, in this case, we would type **postmodern***. Some search engines automatically truncate words. In those databases, you can type **postmodern** and to be sure to retrieve all the endings. In these cases, truncation is a default setting of the search engines. If you don't want your search expression to be truncated, you need to override the default feature. You can find out how to do this by reading the search engine's help pages.

Wildcards

Using *wildcards* allows you to search for words that have most of the letters in common. For example, to search for both *woman* and *women,* instead of typing **woman OR women**, we place a wildcard character (most often an asterisk) to replace the fourth letter, like this: **wom*n**. In addition to searching for both the American and British spellings of certain words, wildcards are also useful when searching for those words that are commonly misspelled. For example, take the word *genealogy*. By placing the wildcard character where the commonly mistaken letters are placed, like this: **gen*logy**, you can be sure to get documents with the word spelled correctly. Of course, you'll also get pages where the word is misspelled!

Field Searching

Web pages can be broken down into many parts. These parts, or *fields,* include titles, URLs, text, summaries or annotations (if present), and so forth. (See Figure 6.1.) *Field searching* is the ability to limit your search to certain fields. This ability to search by field can increase the relevance of the retrieved records. In Google, for example, you can search for Web pages that contain certain words in the title of the page by typing **allintitle:obama afghanistan taliban**. You can also limit your search to a specific domain, such as educational institutions (**.edu**), commercial sites (**.com**), and so forth. In addition, a search can be limited to a particular host, such as a company or institution Web site.

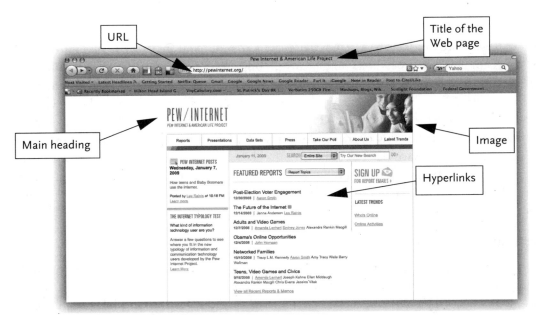

Figure 6.1—The Parts of a Web Page

Language Searching

The ability to limit results to a specific language can be useful. Several search engines support this feature, including Yahoo! and Google. Some search engines also provide a translation service.

Searching by File Format Type

The ability to search for files of a particular file type can also be a useful feature. For example, let's say you need to create a presentation on a particular topic, such as the environment, and you want some ideas of how others have presented similar information. In Google, you would enter **environment filetype:ppt** and retrieve links to PowerPoint presentations on the topic of the environment. In Yahoo, the search would look like this: **environment originurlextension:ppt**.

Link Searching

This feature allows you to search for sites that link to a particular URL. In Google and Yahoo! you type link: before the URL that you are searching for. For example, if you want to see all the Web sites that link to Wikipedia's main page, you would enter **link:en.wikipedia.org**.

Limiting by Date

Some search engines allow you to search the Web for pages that were added or modified between certain dates. In *limiting by date*, you can narrow your search to only the pages that were entered in the past month, the past year, or a particular year.

Output Features Common to Most Search Engines

The way a search engine displays results can help you decide which search engine to use. The following features are common to many engines, but as we saw earlier with the search features, the engines all have different ways of determining and showing these features.

Results Ranking

Many search engines measure each Web page's relevance to your search query and arrange the search results from the most relevant to the least relevant. This is called *relevancy ranking*. Each search engine has its own algorithm for determining relevance, but it usually involves counting how many times the words in your query appear in the Web

To read more about search features in several search engines, the Web site Search Engine Showdown at **http://www.searchengineshowdown.com** is an excellent resource.

pages. In some search engines, a document is considered more relevant if the words appear in certain fields, such as the title or summary field. In other search engines, relevance is determined by the number of times the keyword appears in a Web page divided by the total number of words in the page. This gives a percentage, and the page with the largest percentage appears first on the list. Most search engines determine relevancy by how many Web pages link to it or how many people have accessed particular pages in response to similar questions in the past.

Annotations or Summaries

Some search engines include short descriptive paragraphs of each Web page they return to you. These annotations, or summaries, can help you decide whether you should open a Web page, especially if there is no title for the Web page or if the title doesn't describe the page in detail.

Results Per Page

In some search engines, the *results per page* option allows you to choose how many results you want listed per page. This can be a time saver because it sometimes takes a while to go from page to page as you look through results.

Meta-tag Support

Some search engines acknowledge keywords that a Web page author has placed in the field in the HTML source document. This means that a document may be retrieved by a keyword search, even though the search expression may not appear in the document.

A Basic Search Strategy: The 10 Steps

The following list provides a guideline for you to follow in formulating search requests, viewing search results, and modifying search results. These procedures can be followed for virtually any search request, from the simplest to the most complicated. For some search requests, you may not want or need to go through a formal search strategy. If you want to save time in the long run, however, it's a good idea to follow a strategy, especially when you're new to a particular search engine. A basic search strategy can help you get used to each search engine's features and how they are expressed in the search query. Following the 10 steps will also ensure good results if your search is multifaceted and you want to get the most relevant results.

The 10 steps are as follows:

1. Identify the important concepts of your search.
2. Choose the keywords that describe these concepts.
3. Determine whether there are synonyms, related terms, or other variations of the keywords that should be included.
4. Determine which search features may apply, including truncation, proximity operators, Boolean operators, and so forth.
5. Choose a search engine.
6. Read the search instructions on the search engine's home page. Look for sections entitled Help, Advanced Search, Frequently Asked Questions, and so forth.
7. Create a search expression using syntax that is appropriate for the search engine.
8. Evaluate the results. Were the results relevant to your query?
9. Modify your search if needed. Go back to Steps 2 through 4 and revise your query accordingly.
10. Try the same search in a different search engine, following Steps 5 through 9 above.

Search Tips

If you feel that your search has yielded too few Web pages (low recall), there are several things to consider:

- Perhaps the search expression was too specific; go back and remove some terms that are connected by ANDs.
- Perhaps there are more terms to use. Think of more synonyms to OR together. Try truncating more words if possible.
- Check spelling and syntax
- Read the instructions on the help pages again.

If your search has given you too many results and many are unrelated to your topic (high recall/low precision), consider the following:

- Narrow your search to specific fields, if possible.
- Use more specific terms; for example, instead of *cancer,* use the specific type of cancer in which you're interested.
- Add additional terms with AND or NOT.
- Remove some synonyms if possible.

In order to explain these concepts in the most practical way, we'll do short activities in three different search engines.

ACTIVITY
6.1   SEARCH STRATEGIES IN GOOGLE

Overview

In this activity, we are going to search for resources on a multifaceted topic. We want to find information on U.S. policy in Afghanistan during former President Bill Clinton's administration.

Following most of the steps of the basic search strategy, we need to examine the facets of our search, choose the appropriate keywords, and determine which search features apply. Then, we'll go to Google and read the search instructions. Let's see how this search engine handles this multifaceted topic.

We'll follow these steps:

1. Identify the important concepts of your search.
2. Choose the keywords that describe these concepts.
3. Determine whether there are synonyms, related terms, or other variations of the keywords that should be included.
4. Determine which search features may apply, including truncation, proximity operators, Boolean operators, and so forth.
5. Choose a search engine.
6. Read the search instructions on the search engine's home page. Look for sections entitled Help, Advanced Search, Frequently Asked Questions, and so forth.
7. Create a search expression using syntax that is appropriate for the search engine.
8. Evaluate the results. Were the results relevant to your query?
9. Modify your search if needed. Go back and revise your query accordingly.
10. Try the same search in a different search engine, following Steps 5 through 9 above.

> **TIP!**
> Remember that the Web is always changing and that your results may differ from those shown here. Don't let this confuse you. The activities demonstrate fundamental skills. These skills don't change, even though the number of results obtained or the actual screens may look very different.

Details

1 Identify the important concepts of your search.

The most important concepts of this search are Bill Clinton, foreign policy, and Afghanistan.

2 Choose the keywords that describe these concepts.

The main terms or keywords include the following: *Bill Clinton*, *foreign policy*, and *Afghanistan.*

3 Determine whether there are synonyms, related terms, or other variations of the keywords that should be included.

> For Bill Clinton: none
> For foreign policy: none
> For Afghanistan: Taliban

4 Determine which search features may apply, including truncation, proximity operators, Boolean operators, and so forth.

When developing a search expression, keep in mind that you place OR between synonyms and AND between the different concepts, or facets, of the search topic. If you write down all the synonyms you choose, it may help with the construction of the final search phraseology.

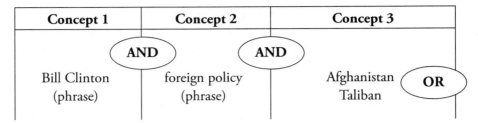

Table 6.1—Formulation of the Search Strategy

Table 6.1 shows the three major concepts, or facets, of the search topic with their synonyms connected with the appropriate Boolean operators. Keep in mind there can be different ways to express the same idea. Before you get online, take a few minutes to determine whether you've included the major keywords and the appropriate search features. It can save you a lot of time in the long run.

5   Choose a search engine.

Because this chapter focuses on search engines, we will do this search in Google, Yahoo!, and Exalead. Exalead is not a major search engine but it has search features that we'd like to introduce you to. If you had access to a commercial database such as Factiva or Lexis-Nexis, you might get even better results there. But for the purposes of explanation, we will use Google first. Google supports Boolean searching and phrase searching, and it is the largest search engine database on the Web, so it makes sense to start there.

DO IT!   Click on the location bar, type **http://www.google.com**, and press **Enter**.

6   Read the search instructions on the search engine's home page. Look for sections entitled Help, Advanced Search, Frequently Asked Questions, and so forth.

DO IT!   From Google's home page, click on **About Google**.

DO IT!   On the next page, click on **Help**. On the next page, click on **Web Search Help**.

Your screen should look similar the one shown in Figure 6.2.

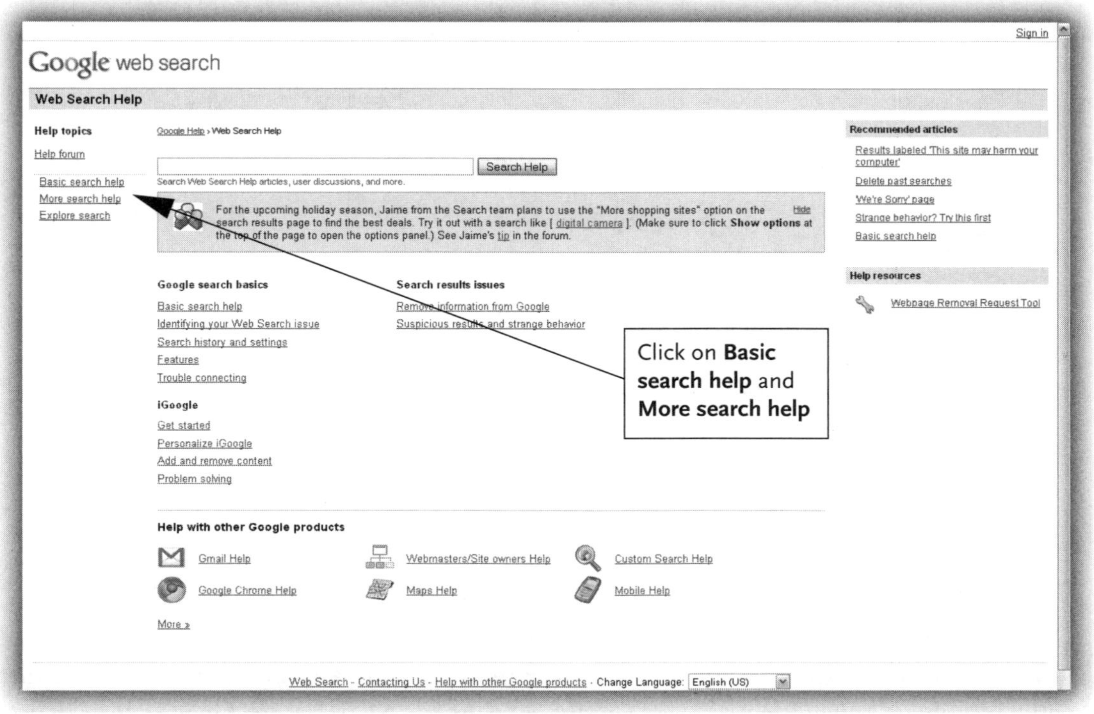

Figure 6.2—Google Help

DO IT! Click on **Basic search help** and **More search help**, as shown in Figure 6.2 above.

The information provided in the search help section tells us that it is necessary to use quotation marks around phrases. Because we want to search for synonyms, it will be necessary to use the OR connector. Google's help section tells us that it is possible to do this, but **OR** must be capitalized.

7   Create a search expression using syntax that is appropriate for the search engine. Now that you've read the search help, it's time to formulate the search expression. It will help to write it out before you type it in the search form. Here is a possible way to express this search:

> **"Bill Clinton" "foreign policy" Afghanistan OR Taliban**

There is no need to capitalize the proper nouns in the search expression, but we have shown them capitalized here for grammatical accuracy.

Keep in mind that you can always modify your search later. Let's try entering it in Google's search form.

DO IT! Type the following search expression in the search form provided:

> **"Bill Clinton" "foreign policy" Afghanistan OR Taliban**

DO IT! Click on **Google Search**.

8   Evaluate the results. Are the results relevant to your query?

Look at the results of the search query, as shown in Figure 6.3. Your results may differ.

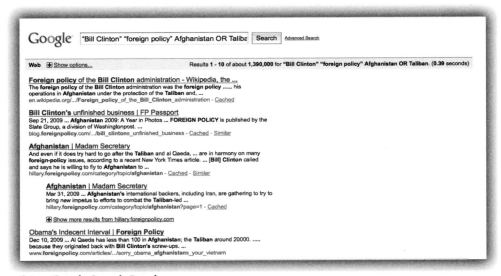

Figure 6.3—Google Search Results

9 Modify your search if needed. Go back and revise your query accordingly.

The results seem fairly relevant to our topic. After opening a few Web sites, however, we find that many of the documents discuss Iraq. We are curious to see if we can find some resources that are primarily about Afghanistan. This is a good time to use the NOT feature. Google's help section told us that NOT can be expressed by typing a – just before the term(s) that you don't want to appear in the results. We will go back and modify our search by adding the term Iraq with a – in front of the word.

DO IT! In the search form that appears at the top of the page, add **–iraq** to the end of the search expression. Make sure that there is no space between the hyphen and the word.

The search results appear in Figure 6.4. Note that by deleting the word **Iraq**, we've cut our search results dramatically!

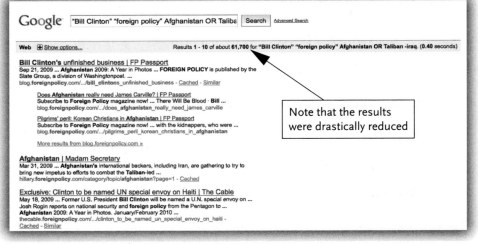

Figure 6.4—Results of Modifying Google Search

You could now go back and revise your search again. For example, if you wanted to limit your results to U.S. government resources, you could limit the search to only those documents ending in a **.gov** domain, by adding **inurl:.gov** to the end of your search expression.

10   Try the same search in a different search engine, following Steps 5 through 9 above.

See Activity 6.2 for this step.

————————————————————————————————————END OF ACTIVITY 6.1

As we saw in this activity, Google handled this search query quite well. There are pros and cons to using any of the search engines. Sometimes it comes down to which service you are more comfortable with using. In the next activity, we'll search for the same topic in Yahoo!. We will again follow the steps laid out in the basic search strategy.

ACTIVITY 6.2   SEARCH STRATEGIES IN YAHOO!'S ADVANCED SEARCH MODE

Overview

We'll be searching for the same information that we did in Activity 6.1—U.S. foreign policy in Afghanistan during President Bill Clinton's administration. Because we have already done Steps 1 through 4 of the basic search strategy in Activity 6.1, we can move on to the following steps, which correspond to Steps 5 through 10 of the strategy:

1. Choose a search engine.
2. Read the search instructions on the search engine's home page. Look for sections entitled Help, Advanced Search, Frequently Asked Questions, and so forth.
3. Create a search expression using syntax that is appropriate for the search engine.
4. Evaluate the results. Were the results relevant to your query?
5. Modify your search if needed. Go back and revise your query accordingly.
6. Try the same search in a different search engine.

Details

1   Choose a search engine.

We'll be searching Yahoo!, another popular search engine. We'll try Yahoo!'s advanced search mode so that you can see how useful it is. Let's go to Yahoo! and see how it handles our topic.

DO IT!   Click on the location bar, enter **http://www.yahoo.com**, and press **Enter**.

You should now be at Yahoo!'s home page.

2   Read the search instructions on the search engine's home page. Look for sections entitled Help, Advanced Search, Frequently Asked Questions, and so forth.

DO IT!   Click on **Help** at the bottom of Yahoo!'s home page or enter **help.yahoo.com** in the location bar.

Your screen should look like the one in Figure 6.5.

Figure 6.5— Yahoo!'s Help Page

DO IT! Click on **Search**, as shown in Figure 6.5.

You can read through Yahoo!'s search instructions here. After reading through these searching help tips, we determine:

♦ Yahoo! supports phrase searching by requiring quotes to be placed around words that must be together.

♦ Yahoo! supports the OR Boolean operator in order to search for synonyms or related terms

♦ The AND operator is implied between terms (no need to type AND).

After reading through the information provided, we decide to use Yahoo!'s Advanced Search form to search for resources on this topic.

DO IT! Click on **Go Back to Yahoo! Search**, as shown in Figure 6.6.

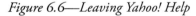

Figure 6.6—Leaving Yahoo! Help

You should now be at a screen that looks like the one pictured in Figure 6.7.

DO IT! Click on **more** and select **Advanced Search**.

Figure 6.7—Choosing Yahoo!'s Advanced Search Mode

3   Create a search expression using syntax that is appropriate for the search engine.

DO IT!   Type **Clinton** in the search form next to **all of these words**. This will guarantee that every Web page that has this word will be included in the text. Note that we are not including **Bill** with this term because there doesn't seem to be a way to search for two phrases in the Advanced Search mode. We want to search **foreign policy** as a phrase, so we should insert those two words in the **the exact phrase** box. Note that it is not necessary to place quotation marks around the phrase when using this field-based search form. Then type **Afghanistan Taliban** in the search form next to any of these words. Typing words into this field is essential telling the search engine to place an OR between each term. Finally, type **Iraq** in the form next to none of these words. For safe measure, let's add the word Hillary as another term that we don't want in the results, to make sure that we limit our results to those that concern former President Bill Clinton. Your window should look like the one pictured in Figure 6.8.

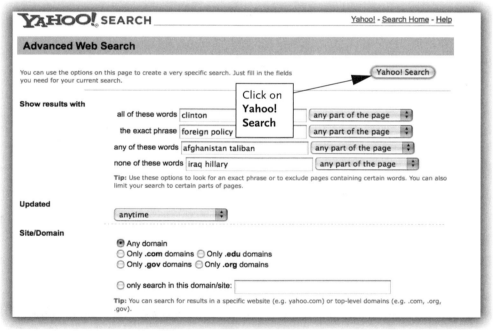

Figure 6.8—Searching in Yahoo!'s Advanced Search Mode

DO IT!   Click on **Yahoo! Search** to begin.

4   Evaluate the results. Were the results relevant to your query?

This search retrieved over 500,000 documents. From scanning the titles, the first 10 to 20 appear to be relevant. Because we left out one important aspect of the search, the date range, we have obtained many thousands more results than the Google search. Yahoo! doesn't support the feature of searching for number ranges as Google does. Another possible reason why there are so many more results is that Yahoo! indexes the first 500KB of the content of Web pages, whereas Google indexes only the first 100KB.

5   Modify your search if needed. Go back and revise your query accordingly.

Figure 6.9 shows how we could limit the search to U.S. government resources. We simply clicked on the radio button next to **Only .gov domains** in the **Site/Domain** section of the Advanced Search page.

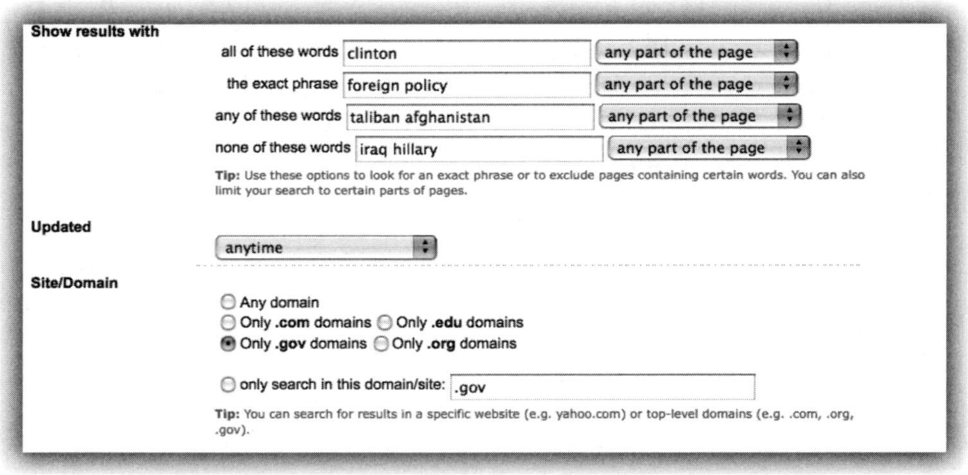

Figure 6.9—Limiting the Results to the .gov Sites

6   Try the same search in a different search engine.

Next we'll try the same search in Exalead in Activity 6.3.

END OF ACTIVITY 6.2

ACTIVITY 6.3   SEARCH STRATEGIES IN EXALEAD

Overview

In this activity, we'll look for information on the same topic in Exalead. Exalead is a relatively new search engine, appearing on the scene in late 2004. It is much smaller than Google and Yahoo!, and may not be updated as frequently, but it has some very nice features that neither Google nor Yahoo! provide. It supports truncation, proximity searching, and provides unique options for narrowing search results. Let's see how Exalead handles our search query. We will be following Steps 5 through 10 of the basic search strategy, as we did in Activity 6.2.

1. Choose a search engine.
2. Read the search instructions on the search engine's home page. Look for sections entitled Help, Advanced Search, Frequently Asked Questions, and so forth.
3. Create a search expression using syntax that is appropriate for the search engine.
4. Evaluate the results. Were the results relevant to your query?
5. Modify your search if needed. Go back and revise your query accordingly.

Details

1   Choose a search engine.

Let's go to Exalead.

DO IT! Click on the location bar, type in the URL for Exalead, **http://www.exalead.com/ search**, and press **Enter**.

Your screen should look like the one shown in Figure 6.10.

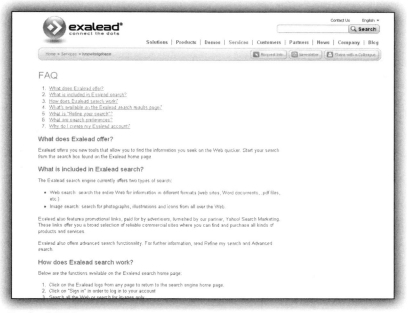

Figure 6.10—Exalead's Home Page

2 Read the search instructions on the search engine's home page. Look for sections entitled Help, Advanced Search, Frequently Asked Questions, and so forth.

In order to find out how to use Exalead, read its documentation.

DO IT! Click on the link **FAQ** located at the bottom of the screen.

Figure 6.11—Exalead FAQ

After reading the FAQ, we determine that Exalead

- offers a personalized version of its search interface. In order to customize Exalead, you need to sign up for a free account.
- supports phrase searching by putting quotation marks around the phrase, supports the OR operator, and uses a – for the NOT operator
- has an advanced search option that allows you to truncate words, do proximity searches, and more.
- indexes several different file types, including images, pdfs, and more.
- also offers a helpful "refine your search" option on the results page.

3   Create a search expression using syntax that is appropriate for the search engine.

DO IT!   Return to the Exalead home page by clicking on the Exalead icon in the upper left corner.

DO IT!   Type **"bill clinton" "foreign policy" afghanistan OR taliban –hillary** in the search form.

DO IT!   Click on **Search**.

Figure 6.12 shows the results of the search. Note that there are several related terms listed and site types (blogs, forums, etc.) that you can click on to narrow your results.

Figure 6.12—Searching Exalead

Now we will try the Advanced Search mode. Click on the Exalead icon in the upper left corner to return to the home page.

DO IT!   Click on **Advanced Search**.

Your window should look like the one in Figure 6.13.

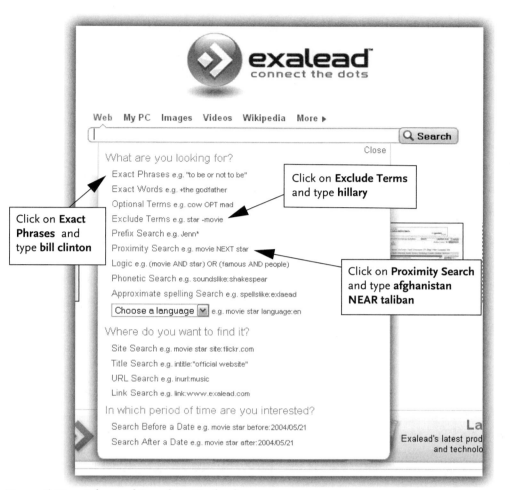

Figure 6.13—Advanced Search in Exalead

DO IT! Click on **Exact Phrases** and type **bill clinton**.

DO IT! Click on **Exact Phrases** again and **type foreign policy**.

DO IT! Type **afghanistan**, then click on **Proximity Search** and type **taliban**.

DO IT! Change the word **NEXT** to **NEAR**.

DO IT! Click on **Exclude Terms** and type **hillary**.

Your screen should look like the one pictured in Figure 6.14.

Figure 6.14—Advanced Search in Exalead

DO IT! Now click on **Search**.

Figure 6.15 shows the first page of results.

Figure 6.15—Results of the Advanced Search in Exalead

4 Evaluate the results. Were the results relevant to your query?

Note that the number of results have been greatly reduced from over three million to just over a thousand. One reason for this is that we searched for Afghanistan NEAR Taliban and not

Afghanistan OR Taliban. When you use OR, the search terms may be separated by several pages of information, whereas when you use the NEAR option, the words are near each other. Also note that the Web sites seem to be quite relevant to the topic.

5 Modify your search if needed. Go back and revise your query accordingly.

This search seemed to provide many relevant hits, but let's say you want to narrow your results a bit more. You could choose one of the related terms that are located on the right side of the window, as shown in Figure 6.15, or you could click on one of the "related terms" located just below the search form. For example, if we clicked on **National Security**, Exalead would narrow the existing results by focusing on that term.

DO IT! Click on **National Security**, as shown in Figure 6.15. After this modification, we note that even more choices appear in the **Related terms** section. Let's try clicking on **Clinton Administration**, as shown in Figure 6.16.

Figure 6.16—Focusing Results in Exalead by Selecting Related Terms

Figure 6.17 shows the result of focusing in on the topic of the Clinton Administration. Note that we have narrowed our results to around 300 and they look to be quite relevant and useful.

Figure 6.17—Results of Searching Exalead

6 Try the same search in a different search engine.

If you like, you could try the same search in a different search engine on your own.

END OF ACTIVITY 6.3

In Activities 6.1, 6.2, and 6.3 we searched for information on the same topic in three different search engines. Each one had its own particular syntax and individual search and output features. We saw the importance of reading each search engine's documentation before initializing the search. All of the search engines gave relevant results, but none of them gave the same results.

Summary

Search engines are information-retrieval systems that allow us to search the vast collection of resources on the Internet and the World Wide Web. A search engine consists of three components: a computer program called a spider or robot that retrieves hyperlinks attached to documents, a database that indexes these documents, and software that allows users to enter keywords in search forms to obtain ranked results.

Each search engine database is unique and accesses its database differently. Even though many search engine databases claim to cover as much of the Web as possible, the same search performed in more than one database never returns the exact same results. If you want to do a thorough search, you should become familiar with a few of the different search engines. To this end, it is important to understand the major search features, such as Boolean logic, phrase searching, truncation, and others before you get online. It is also necessary to read each search engine's documentation before you enter the search request in the search form. You may want to check the documentation often, since search engines are constantly changing their search and output features.

In this chapter, we introduced the basic search strategy, a 10-step procedure that can help you formulate search requests, submit them to search engines, and modify the results retrieved. We have focused on the major search engines on the World Wide Web, but there are several hundred smaller search engines on the Web that search smaller databases. We'll discuss these in some detail in Chapter 7, "Specialized Databases." Our intent in this chapter was to give you a foundation in searching any database, no matter whether it is large or small, fee-based or not. All of the steps in the basic search strategy apply to any searchable database.

Selected Terms Used in This Chapter

default setting	limiting by date	robot
field	low precision/high recall	search expression
field searching	meta-tag	search form
full-text indexing	nested Boolean logic	spider
hidden Internet	phrase searching	stemming
high precision/high recall	proximity searching	stop word
high precision/low recall	relevance	syntax
implied Boolean operator	relevancy ranking	truncation
invisible Web	results per page	wildcard
keyword		

Review Questions

Multiple Choice

1. A results list, or hit list, that has many results with few that are relevant to your query would be described as
   a. high precision/low recall.
   b. high precision/high recall.
   c. low precision/low recall.
   d. low precision/high recall.

2. The configuration a search engine automatically uses for a search unless you override it is called the
   a. syntax.
   b. nested Boolean logic.
   c. default setting.
   d. field searching.

3. A search engine that indexes all or most of the words of each Web document in its database is doing
   a. abstracting.
   b. full-text indexing.
   c. citation indexing.
   d. subject indexing.

4. The following is an example of truncation:
   a. psyche near soul.
   b. +internet.
   c. -unix.
   d. colleg*.

5. The expression **mining and (coal or iron)** shows the concept of
   a. phrase searching.
   b. implied Boolean operators.
   c. nested Boolean logic.
   d. proximity searching.

6. If a search returns too many results and they are not relevant to your topic, you could
   a. narrow your search by using more specific terms.
   b. add additional terms to your search with **OR**.
   c. a and b
   d. none of the above

True or False

7. T F Typing a **+** or **–** before a word in a search is making use of implied Boolean operators.

8. T F Truncation is also known as stemming.

9. T F Every search engine determines relevancy in the same way.

10. T F Some search engines allow you to limit a search to a part of the page, such as the title.

11. T   F   The first step in planning a search is to choose a search engine.
12. T   F   All search engines allow you to limit your results by date.
13. T   F   The related terms option in Exalead can help you narrow your results.
14. T   F   Each global search engine indexes every single word in all the Web pages indexed.

Completion

15. Common words that a search engine skips over, such as *of* or *the*, are known as _____.

16. In a search expression, the words *near* or *within* are known as _____.

17. Typing a search expression with one character that stands in for a group of characters, such as m*n, is making use of a(n) _____.

18. The _____ is that part of the Internet that is in special databases and isn't easily searchable with search engines.

19. A keyword that does not appear on a Web page but is included in the source code of the page and may be indexed by a search engine is called a(n) _____.

20. A part of a Web page, such as a title or URL or annotation, is known as a(n) _____.

Exercises and Projects

1. Using the Advanced Search mode in Google, **http://www.google.com**, and in Yahoo!, **http://www.yahoo.com**, look for relevant resources on the following topics:
    a. The life expectancy of a Sun Conure.
    b. Mary Kingsley's travels in Africa.
    c. Maria Mitchell's contributions to astronomy

    Write down the titles of the first three Web pages retrieved by each search engine. Were any of these the same in the two search engines? Write down the search expression you used in each database.

2. Sometimes it is helpful to look for specific types of Web sites about a topic. Go to Google at **http://www.google.com** and look for Web pages about the inventor Nikola Tesla. Can you tell how many results are found? Now go to Google's Advanced Search page and do the same search, limiting your results to domains that end with **.edu**. How many results do you find now? Change your search to look for results with the **.gov** domain which were updated in the last year. How many results do you find?

3. Find the most recent annual report and a mission statement for Pfizer. What would be the best strategy to use to find this information?
    a. Go to Exalead at **http://www.exalead.com**. What search expression(s) did you use to find the annual report and mission statement? Give the URLs of the page(s) where they are found.
    b. Try the same search in Google at **http://www.google.com**. Which search engine gave you more relevant results?

4. Look for information on how genetically altered corn is affecting Monarch butterflies.
   a. First, write down your search strategy. What keywords will you use? What other words might be used instead of "genetically altered?" What search expression will you start with?
   b. Try your search at Ask, at **http://www.ask.com**. How many results did you find? Go to the first three sites listed. How relevant are they to your search? Give the URLs of the sites you visited. Do you need to modify your search expression?

5. Virtual Humans have become a topic of interest. Besides being the stuff of speculative fiction, they are becoming the stuff of reality!
   a. Go to Google at **http://www.google.com** and search for virtual humans. How many results do you find? Look at some of the first ten sites in your results list. What is a virtual human? Give the URL of the site where you found your answer.
   b. Now search for pages that show Peter Plantec's contribution to the field of virtual humans. What was your search expression? How many results did you find? Who is Peter Plantec? Give the URL of the page where you found the answer.

6. Using the advanced search mode in Yahoo!, **http://search.yahoo.com/web/advanced**, look for information on how mad cow disease (also known as Bovine Spongiform Encephalopathy) causes Creutzfeldt-Jakob disease in humans.
   a. Write down your search expression and the total number of results. Do you need to modify your search expression?
   b. Were your results relevant to your request? Write down three of the most relevant titles and their URLs.

7. Go to Yahoo! at **http://www.yahoo.com**, to find comparison studies of the drugs venlafaxine XR and fluoxetine. What search expression did you use? Go to the first three Web sites listed. What are the brand names of these drugs? Give the titles and URLs of the three sites you visited. Which was most relevant?

8. Just as the Web constantly changes, search engines do as well. Go to Google at **http://www.google.com** and do a search for comparisons and reviews of search engines. Scan through the search results and go to the most promising sites. Give the titles and URLs of the sites you visited. Which was the best? Why? You may want to put one of these sites in your list of favorites or bookmarks. (A good site for keeping up with the rapid pace of change in search engines is Internet Tutorials at **http://www.internettutorials. net/engines.asp**.

9. From cuneiform writing to the printing press, written communication kept changing and becoming more pervasive. By the 19th Century, a new invention made a big difference. Try a search for the history of the ball point pen.
   a. Who invented it? When did the invention take place?
   b. Tell what search engine you used, what search expression you used, and give the URL of the site where you found your answer.

CHAPTER
7

Specialized Databases

Much of what is available on the World Wide Web that is not accessible from the major search engines is to be found in specialized databases. Some folks describe this group of resources as the *invisible Web* or the *hidden Internet.* Databases containing public information or material not proprietary in nature commonly appear on the Web. These databases, many of which are maintained by government agencies and nonprofit organizations, can quickly provide you with a wealth of information that formerly was difficult or time-consuming to obtain. *Specialized databases* are indexes that can be searched, much like the search engines explored in Chapter 6. The main difference is that specialized databases are collections on particular subjects or types of documents, such as books, journal article abstracts and citations, company financial data, court decisions, phone numbers, email addresses, maps, census data, patents, and so forth. Specialized databases can also be limited to specific collections, such as a library catalog. You can find information in specialized databases that you often would not locate by using a global search engine. For example, if you want to know if a library has a particular book, you would search an online library catalog, which is a type of specialized database and not a global search engine such as Google.

If you know there is a specialized database on the subject you are researching, using that database can save you time and give you reliable, up-to-date information. We covered subject guides in Chapter 5. The difference between a subject guide and a specialized database is that subject guides are collections of URLs in a particular area, whereas a specialized database contains the actual data or information you are seeking.

This chapter will include the following sections:
- Overview of Specialized Databases
- Information in Specialized Databases Is Often Not Accessible Via Search Engines
- How to Find Specialized Databases
- Using Specialized Databases

Overview of Specialized Databases

There are several different types of specialized databases. A ***bibliographic database*** includes citations that describe and identify titles, dates, authors, and other parts of written works. It doesn't usually contain the full text of the works themselves, although if an article is available for free, a link will be provided to it. Examples of bibliographic databases are PubMed, which we'll cover in Activity 7.1, and WorldCat, a ***library catalog*** that we'll cover in Activity 7.3. A ***full-text database***, on the other hand, includes the entire text of the indexed works. A full-text database can contain books, articles, poetry, and more, and is searchable by keyword. The major difference between a bibliographic and a full-text database is that a bibliographic database describes an entity, whether it be an article, a book, a work of art, or any other product, whereas a full-text database includes a description *and* the work itself. An example of a full-text database is Bartleby.com, which we'll also cover in this chapter. Another type of specialized database is a ***numeric database***, which contains statistical data, usually in chart or spreadsheet formats. An example of a numeric database is the Statistical Abstract of the United States, which we will briefly cover here. Another type of database is a ***directory database***. Directory databases usually provide brief information about people, businesses, or places. We'll include a brief discussion about using these databases as well. There are also databases that provide a mix of directory information with numeric information. Hoovers.com is one of these databases. We will show how to search Hoovers for company information. There are also ***multimedia databases***, which index images, videos, podcasts, and more. These databases will be covered in Chapter 9, "Searching for Multimedia."

Proprietary Databases

There are hundreds of ***proprietary*** or ***commercial databases*** on the World Wide Web, but these are available only if you or your organization has purchased access to them. For example, Factiva, **http://www.factiva.com**; DIALOG, **http://www.dialog.com**; STN, **http://stnweb.cas.org**; and Lexis-Nexis, **http://www.lexisnexis.com**, all provide proprietary databases.

Proprietary databases have certain value-added features that databases in the public domain do not have. Here are some examples of that enhanced content:

- ◆ Proprietary, or commercial databases often contain information that is under copyright restriction. You will be prompted to pay or enter a password to see full text. Your library may have the right to access the database, so it's important that you check with a librarian before you pay for an article that you need.

- ◆ Proprietary databases allow you to download information easily. For instance, some of these databases include financial information that is commonly free to the public, but they charge for the use of their databases because they have made it much easier for the user to download the information to a spreadsheet program.

- ◆ Proprietary databases often index material that others do not. The information is distinguished by its uniqueness, its historical value, or its competitive value (for example, private company financial information).

- ◆ Proprietary database systems are more responsive to their users. Because they charge fees to use, they are more apt to provide training and other user support, such as the distribution of newsletters that update their services. There are also databases on the Web that are free to the public but charge for the full text of the articles, for example, High Beam Research,

http://www.highbeam.com/library/index.asp. Many newspaper archives work the same way. You can search the archive, but if you want a copy of the newspaper article, there is a fee involved.

Accessing Fee-based Databases

Ask a reference librarian at your local library about accessing proprietary databases. The library may have purchased access to databases via the Internet. If it is an academic library, use from your home computer may require you to be a current student at the institution, but most college libraries will allow visitors to search the databases from the library. Many public libraries provide access to databases from home for members with a library card. The specialized databases covered in this chapter are all free and open to anyone.

Information in Specialized Databases Is Often Not Accessible Via Search Engines

The major search engines discussed in earlier chapters build their databases by collecting URLs that exist on the World Wide Web. The Web pages that are attached to the URLs are then indexed. When you type a word or words in a search engine's search form, you retrieve a list of URLs that already exist in the search engine's database. To put it simply, a search engine typically cannot search a specialized database because of the following reasons:

◆ A database usually cannot search another database without some very special programming. The search engine you are using may come across a specialized database but then may be stopped from going any further because the special database has a search form that requests information from the user. For example, you wouldn't look in Google, **http://www.google.com**, to see what books are in your library; you'd look at your library's Web-based catalog.

◆ Many specialized databases contain information that is retrieved dynamically every time a request is made, and the URLs that are generated are different each time. A search engine usually cannot build its database with URLs that may work today and not tomorrow. (Although we have seen that a search engine occasionally picks up information from a dynamic Web site and indexes the unstable URL. If you retrieved that page from your results list, your keywords would not appear.)

◆ While search engines such as Google, **http://www.google.com**, have made great progress with their attempts to reach the invisible Web, by indexing PDF files and including some dynamically generated Web pages in its search results, there are still some types, such as audio and video files, that aren't always accessible in a basic search.

How to Find Specialized Databases

There are thousands of specialized databases on the World Wide Web. How do you find them? Sometimes you'll stumble across specialized databases while doing a keyword search in a search engine. Occasionally, a Web page will have a hyperlink to a database, or a friend or colleague will tell you about a particular site. There are more precise ways to find them, but even these are not always foolproof.

♦ You can go to a search engine and type in the kind of database you're searching for along with the word **database**. For example, each of these search expressions typed in Google's search form provides excellent databases in the areas requested:

> **medical database**
> **flags database**
> **"zip codes" database**

♦ Directories are often the best sources to use when looking for specialized databases. Following is a list of some of the most popular ones.

Tool, URL	Description
Beaucoup **http://www.beaucoup.com**	Beaucoup lists more than 2,500 specialized databases and directories and also serves as a meta-search tool.
The Digital Librarian **http://www.digital-librarian.com**	The Digital Librarian is maintained by Cortland, NY, librarian Margaret Vail Anderson.
ipl2: Information You Can Trust **http://www.ipl2.org**	The ipl2 is a virtual library that provides a good starting point for finding reference works, subject guides, and specialized databases.
Intute **http://www.intute.ac.uk**	Intute provides access to the very carefully selected Web resources for education and research. All sites are evaluated and selected by a network of subject specialists.
LibrarySpot **http://libraryspot.com**	LibrarySpot collects links to quality reference resources and provides links to more than 2,500 libraries around the world.
Open Directory Project and Yahoo! Directory **http://dmoz.org** and **http://dir.yahoo.com**	Two of the most comprehensive directories on the Web; these are also good places to find subject guides and specialized databases.
The Scout Report **http://scout.cs.wisc.edu**	The Scout Report is a good way to keep up with new search tools, especially specialized databases. You can view its weekly report and its archive of previous Scout Reports on the Web.

Table 7.1—Some Tools That List Specialized Databases

Using Specialized Databases

Just like search engines, specialized databases support different search features. Most of these databases support many of the same search features covered in Chapter 6, such as Boolean searching and phrase searching. Many databases have search instruction pages, just as the major search engines do.

In this chapter, we'll be doing a few activities that will familiarize you with some of the most useful types of databases on the World Wide Web. We've chosen databases that cover medical research, statistical information, books and other materials, people, and businesses. We selected these areas because the Web is an excellent medium for research in these fields. Much of the useful information needed for research in these areas is in the public domain. We'll search first for medical information. While you move through the activities, you may want to review the search features and the basic search strategies introduced in Chapter 6.

In the first activity, we'll look for a specialized database to help us find scholarly journal articles on a medical topic. In the example, we'll use the ipl2 to help us find a database devoted to medical journal literature.

Remember that the Web is always changing and that your results may differ from those shown here. Don't let this confuse you. The activities demonstrate fundamental skills. These skills don't change, even though the number of results obtained or the actual screens may look very different.

ACTIVITY 7.1   SEARCHING PUBMED

Overview

We are doing research on the nutritional aspects of vegetarian diets. We need to find recent articles from medical journals that would update our general knowledge of this topic. We know that the National Library of Medicine publishes a database of research journal articles and we've heard that it may be available on the Web for free. How can we find it? Let's try ipl2. After we find it, we'll search it and view the results. We will take the following steps:

1. Go to the home page for ipl2: Information You Can Trust (ipl2).
2. Starting with the list of health and medicine resources, locate and select PubMed.
3. Look at basic search help.
4. Type in search terms and retrieve results.
5. Choose a citation from the list of results.
6. Display the full record of the selected citation.

> **F Y I**
> **Searching for Medical Information**
>
> The World Wide Web can be a useful source for health and medical information. Medical centers and physicians create home pages that discuss specific aspects of health care, and you can find these pages by doing searches in the major search engines. Medical reference books are also appearing on the Web. For example, the entire Merck Manual Medical Library, **http://www.merck.com/mmpe/index.html**, a well-known medical diagnostic handbook, is online.

Details

1   Go to the home page for ipl2: Information You Can Trust (ipl2).

DO IT!   Click on the location bar, type **http://www.ipl.org**, and then press **Enter**.

DO IT!   Click on **Health & Medical Supplies** from the ipl2 home page, as shown in Figure 7.1.

2   Starting with the list of health and medicine resources, locate and select PubMed. You will see a listing of several health and medical resource from which to choose, as shown in Figure 7.1.

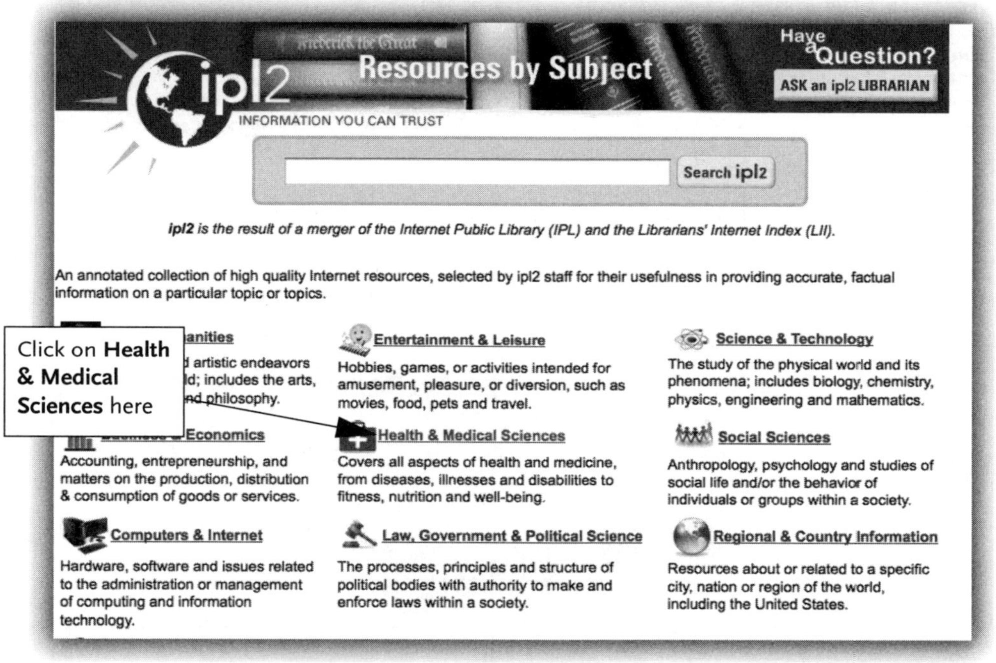

Figure 7.1—Health and Medicine Resources in the ipl2

Scroll down this page until you find some general health resources listed. From this list, there are several resources that might provide the information you need, but we are looking specifically for articles from the database that the National Library of Medicine provides. It looks like PubMed is what we want. The annotation tells us the following:

> PubMed provides access to bibliographic information which includes MEDLINE as well as additional life science journals. MEDLINE is the National Library of Medicine's (NLM) premier bibliographic database covering the fields of medicine, nursing, dentistry, veterinary medicine, the health care system, and the preclinical sciences.

DO IT!   Click on the hyperlink titled **PubMed**, as shown in Figure 7.2.

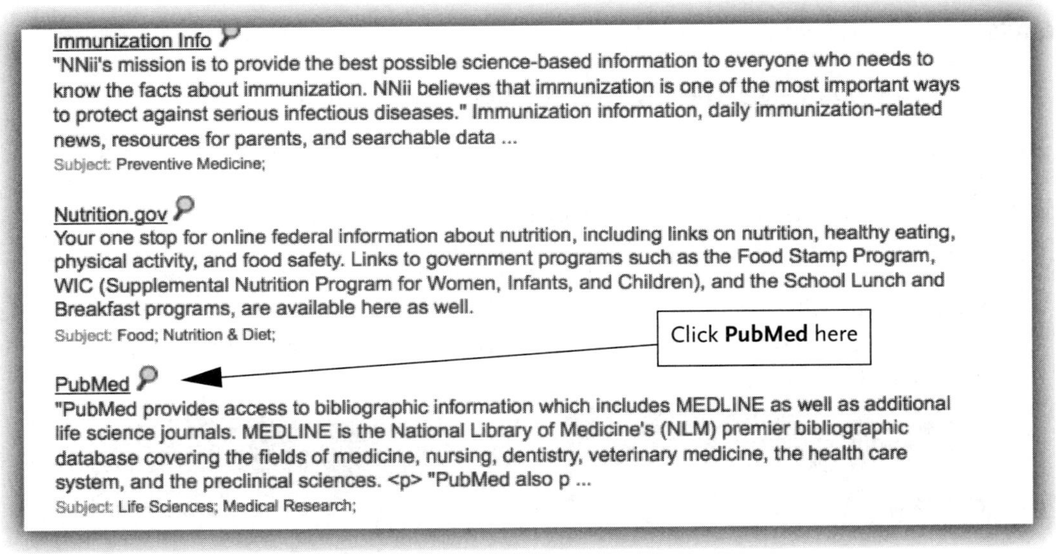

Figure 7.2—PubMed Listing in the ipl2

3   Look at basic search help.

The home page tells us that PubMed "comprises more than 19 million citations for biomedical articles from MEDLINE and life science journals. Citations may include links to full-text articles from PubMed Central or publisher web sites."

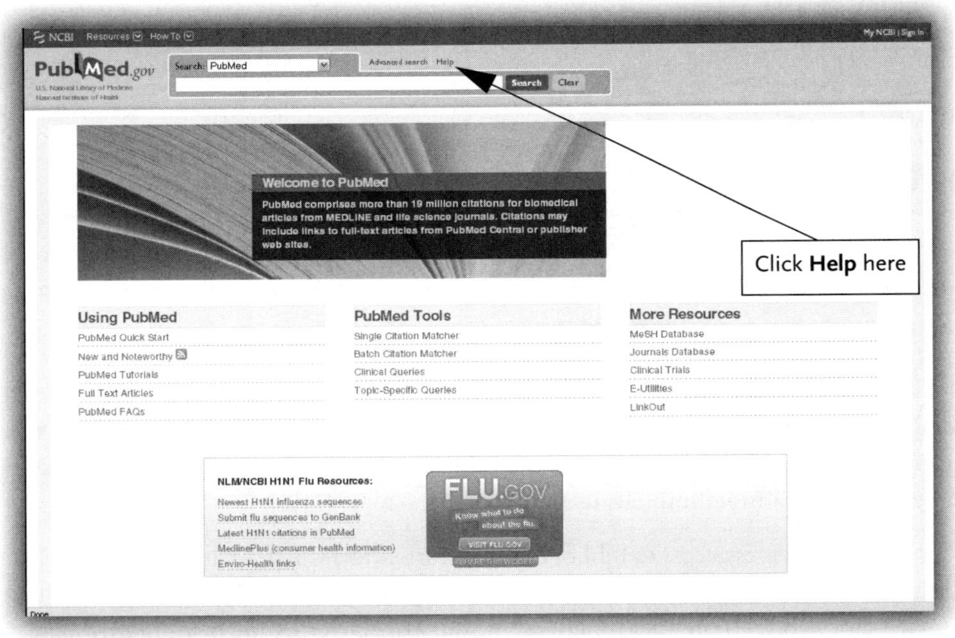

Figure 7.3—PubMed Home Page

Now that we know a bit more about what PubMed consists of, let's find out how to search it effectively by reading the help section. Help is located above the Search box on PubMed's main page.

DO IT   Click on **Help**.

Reading the **Searching PubMed** section of the Help page, we discover the following:

♦ Searching using Boolean operators is supported in the Advanced Search mode only.

♦ AND is assumed between words in the main search mode.

♦ Phrase searching is supported by placing quotation marks around the phrase. Searching by phrase turns off the automatic term mapping feature, so it should be used with care.

♦ PubMed allows you to easily limit your search to particular fields, such as individual journal titles, article types (for example, review articles and clinical trials), certain years, languages, links to free full-text articles, and many other specifications.

PubMed is an extremely well-indexed database. Even though it supports many advanced search features, when you're doing a broad subject search, it is wise to keep it simple. The reason for this is that the terms you enter are mapped to other terms such as the subject headings that PubMed uses—called MeSH terms. If you use too many search features, such as phrase searching, you might not retrieve as many useful citations, because the automatic term mapping will be turned off. Let's do a search to show you how it works.

4   Type in search terms and retrieve results.

DO IT!   From the Help window, click the **PubMed** icon at the top of the page.

Our search has two facets, nutrition and vegetarian diet. We also want to limit our search to those articles that are in the English language, and we would like to retrieve citations to articles that are available for free. We learned from the Help section that to limit results to those in certain fields, it's best to use the **Limit** section, found on the Advanced Search page.

DO IT!   Click **Advanced search** at the top of the PubMed home page.

DO IT!   Type **nutrition vegetarian diet** in the search form, as shown in Figure 7.4.

To narrow the search to those articles that are written in English, scroll down in the **Limit by Topics, Languages, and Journal Groups** section to find the **Languages** heading.

DO IT!   Click on the boxes next to **Links to free full text** and **English** under the **Languages** section, as shown in Figure 7.4.

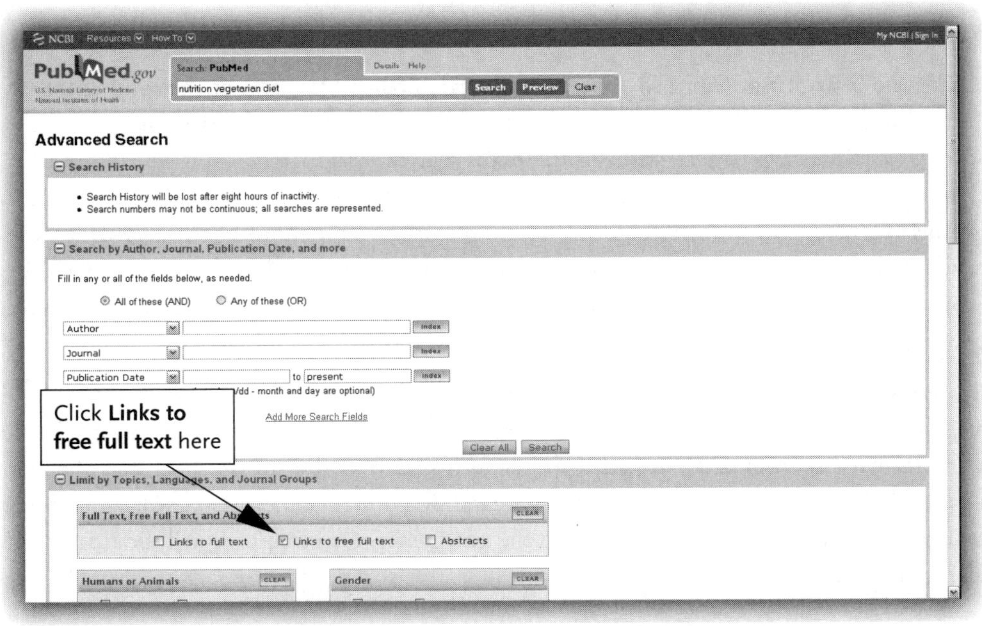

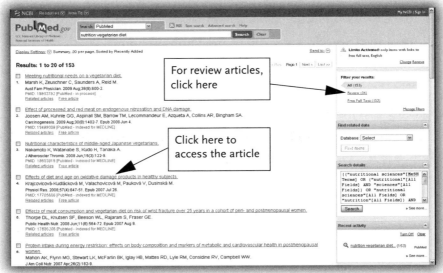

Figure 7.4— Setting Limits in PubMed

DO IT! Click **Search** at the top of the page.

Figure 7.5 shows the results of the search. Note that PubMed gives a history of your searches on the right hand side of the window, under **Recent Activity**.

Figure 7.5—Results of the Search in PubMed

One helpful tip when searching PubMed is to access review articles. Review articles provide an overview of a topic and usually have extensive bibliographies that give you other articles to read on that topic.

DO IT! To see the list of review articles, click on the **Review** tab, as shown in Figure 7.5.

Figure 7.6—Review Articles on the Nutritional Aspects of Vegetarian Diets in PubMed

5   Choose a citation from the list of results.

Figure 7.6 shows the list of review articles on our topic. Article number 4 looks like something that would be useful. Let's access this article.

6   Display the full record of the selected citation.

DO IT!   Click on **Free article** under the article titled **Nutrition ecology: the contribution of vegetarian diets**.

Figure 7.7 shows us more information about this article. You can read an abstract of the article, and you can also link to related articles on the topic. To read the full text, you'll need to access the article at the site that provides it.

DO IT!   Click on **Full Text**, as shown in Figure 7.7.

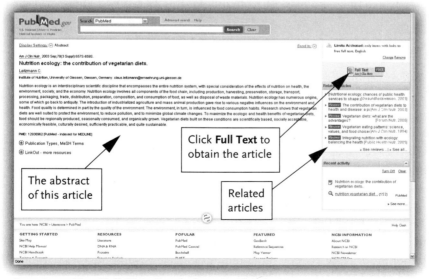

Figure 7.7—Accessing a Free Full-Text Article from PubMed

Figure 7.8 shows the beginning of the article.

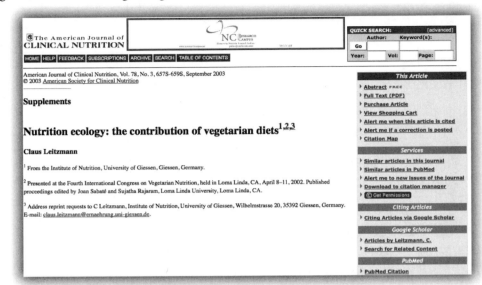

Figure 7.8—An Article From The American Journal of Clinical Nutrition

When we performed this search, we limited the results to free full-text articles that are on the Internet. If we hadn't limited our search to these types of articles, we would have found thousands more. If you wanted to access some of these articles that are not freely accessible, you could find out if your local library has the journal, either in paper or in a commercial database that the library subscribes to.

                                                                    — **END OF ACTIVITY 7.1**

PubMed can provide you with the most up-to-date medical research information available anywhere. This example barely scratches the surface of the searching possibilities in this database. Whether you're researching an illness or gathering information for a biology paper, PubMed is an invaluable resource.

Searching for Company and Industry Information

The World Wide Web has become a useful place to conduct business research. Most companies use their Web sites as marketing or communications tools. These home pages may include annual reports, press releases, and biographies of the people in top-level management. Company Web sites may also include information about the companies' products and services, including catalogs. If you want to do industry research, you can use business-related subject guides. These contain hyperlinks to businesses within the particular industry that interests you. You can easily find subject guides in the directories listed at the beginning of this chapter.

Keep in mind that companies that provide the most financial information on the Web are usually publicly traded. Public companies are required to provide very detailed information about themselves to the U.S. government, whereas privately held companies are not. If a private company is listed in a nonproprietary (open-to-the-public) database, some financial information will be available, but not nearly as much as if it were a public company.

ACTIVITY 7.2   FINDING COMPANY INFORMATION

Overview

In this activity, we'll find information about a specific company. The company we'll be searching for is The Gap. Suppose you need to find a Web site, physical address, annual financial information, and recent news about this company. There are several company directories on the Web that would provide a starting place for this type of research. Virtual libraries and meta-search tools list databases by subject. In this activity, we'll use LibrarySpot, **http://libraryspot.com**, which is a directory. After we find a company database that gives general information, we'll search it. We'll locate general information about the company and financial information that can be accessed from the page. Let's get started!

We'll follow these steps:

1. Go to LibrarySpot and find a company directory database.
2. Search Hoovers to find the company's address, home page, and other basic information.
3. Find financial information and news about the company.

Details

1 Go to LibrarySpot and find a company directory database.

DO IT! Click on the location bar, type **http://libraryspot.com**, and press ⌐Enter⌐.

Along the left side of the LibrarySpot's home page is a list of subject categories.

DO IT! Click on **Business**, located under **REFERENCE DESK**, as shown in Figure 7.9.

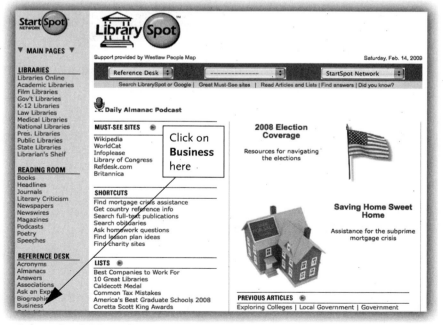

Figure 7.9—LibrarySpot's Home Page

Figure 7.10 shows a partial view of the current page. Let's access Hoover's Online.

DO IT! Click on **Hoovers Online**, as shown in Figure 7.10.

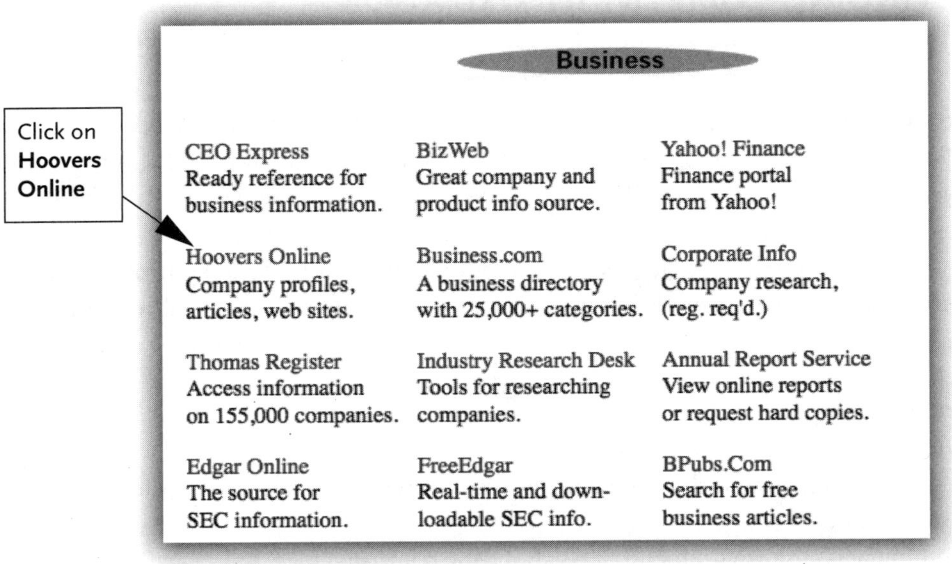

Figure 7.10—Business Resources in LibrarySpot

2   Search Hoover's to find the company's address, home page, and other basic information.

Figure 7.11 shows Hoover's home page.

DO IT! Type **gap** in the search form.

DO IT! Click on the search icon as shown in Figure 7.11.

Figure 7.11—Hoover's Home Page with Company Name Entered

Your screen will fill with companies that have the word *gap* in them, as shown in Figure 7.12. The hyperlink we need is **The Gap Inc**.

DO IT! Click on **The Gap Inc.**, as shown in Figure 7.12.

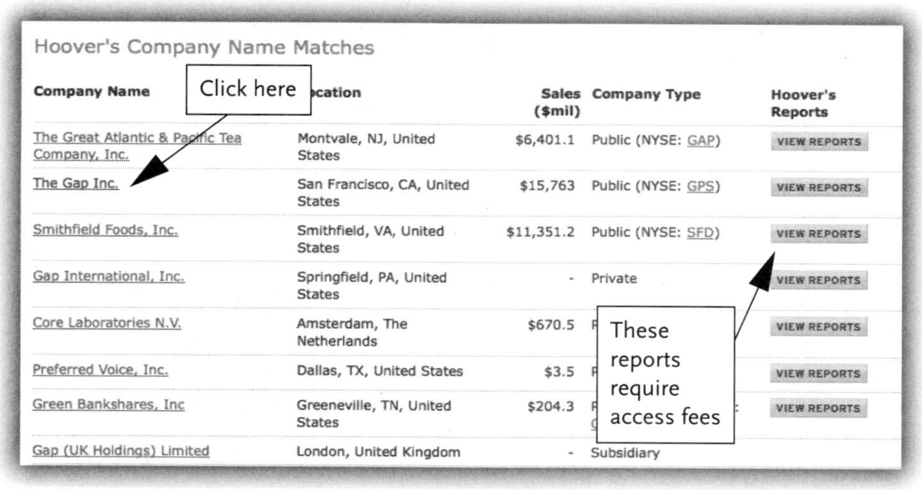

Figure 7.12—Results of Searching for The Gap in Hoover's

Figure 7.13 shows the entry for The Gap Inc. Note the information provided by Hoover's. It provides The Gap's corporate address, a map, phone and fax numbers, and a link to The Gap's Web site. There are also links to financial information, people, and industry data. While much of the information provided requires a subscription fee, there is still a lot of data provided for free.

Figure 7.13—Basic Information About The Gap in Hoover's Online

3   Find financial information and news about the company.

DO IT!   Click on **More The Gap Financials**, as shown in Figure 7.13.

Figure 7.14 shows several financial statements for The Gap. There are income statements for recent years, stock quotes, financial ratios, and competitive intelligence information. There are also links to the annual report and investor relations information.

Figure 7.14—Financial Information About The Gap in Hoovers.com

The purpose of this activity was to provide an overview of what's involved with researching a company. Using special databases for information like this can be more effective than searching with global search engines, since you can more precisely pinpoint the information you need.

Searching Library Catalogs

Numerous types of libraries exist in the world, and every one has a catalog of its holdings. In addition to large national libraries (such as the Library of Congress), academic libraries (such as the Harvard University Library), and public libraries (such as the New York Public Library), there are thousands of special libraries that are part of larger organizations, corporations, and government agencies. Most of the libraries in all of these categories, in the United States and in foreign countries, are rapidly making their catalogs accessible to the public through the Internet. Libraries all over the world upload their catalog records to the Online Computer Library Center, or OCLC, which is a nonprofit research organization that provides cooperative services for libraries. OCLC and more than 69,000 libraries worldwide produce and maintain WorldCat, which is OCLC's online catalog.

ACTIVITY 7.3   SEARCHING LIBRARY CATALOGS USING WORLDCAT

Overview

WorldCat is an international bibliographic database that holds millions of library records. The great thing about WorldCat is that you can search for books, journals, multimedia, and other information and find out whether a library near you owns the material you need. In this activity, we will show you how to find materials on the topic of homebased business, and see if there is a library in your area that has the material you want.

In this activity, we'll show how to:

1. Go to the home page for WorldCat.
2. Search for information on your topic.
3. Find the material in a library near you.

Details

1   Go to the home page for WorldCat.

DO IT!   Click on the location bar, type **http://www.worldcat.org**, and press **Enter**.

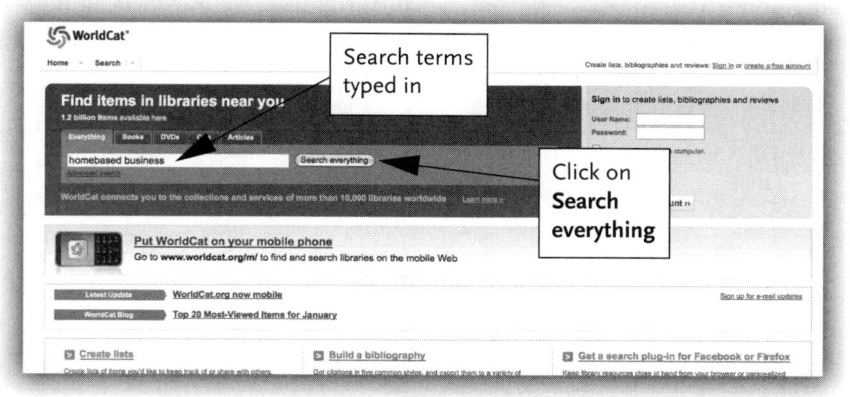

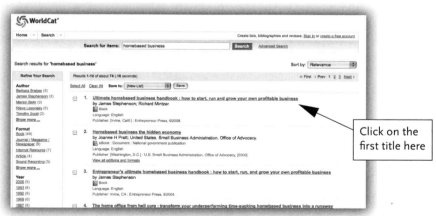

Figure 7.15—WorldCat Home Page With Search Terms Inserted

2   Search for information on your topic.

We are looking for material on the topic of homebased business. Let's go ahead and insert those keywords.

DO IT!   Type **homebased business** in the search form and click on the button **Search everything**. Note that we are searching the entire catalog, including articles and multimedia such as DVDs and CDs. If we wanted to limit our search to books only, we would click on the **Books** tab.

Figure 7.16—Results of Searching for Homebased Business in WorldCat

The search results are shown in Figure 16. The first title listed is a book, and it looks like it could be useful. It is a recent book, published in 2008. Let's click on the title and see if we can find more information about this title.

DO IT! Click on the first title, **Ultimate homebased business handbook: how to start, run and grow your own profitable business**.

Figure 7.17 shows the record for this book. If you want more information about the book, you scroll down to the **Details** section. If you'd like to read reviews of the book, you can scroll down to the **Reviews** section.

3   Find the material in a library near you.

After reading about the book, we decide to see if it is held by our local library. In order for WorldCat to know where we are, we need to insert your zip code in the space provided. We have inserted a zip code in order to show you how this works.

DO IT! Insert your zip code in the space provided and click on **Find libraries**, as shown in Figure 7.17.

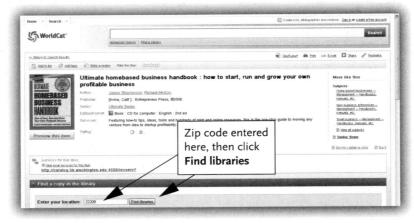

Figure 7.17—Bibliographic Record in WorldCat

Scroll down the page a little to view the results, as shown in Figure 7.18. Note that WorldCat also provides links to online bookstores where you can purchase the book.

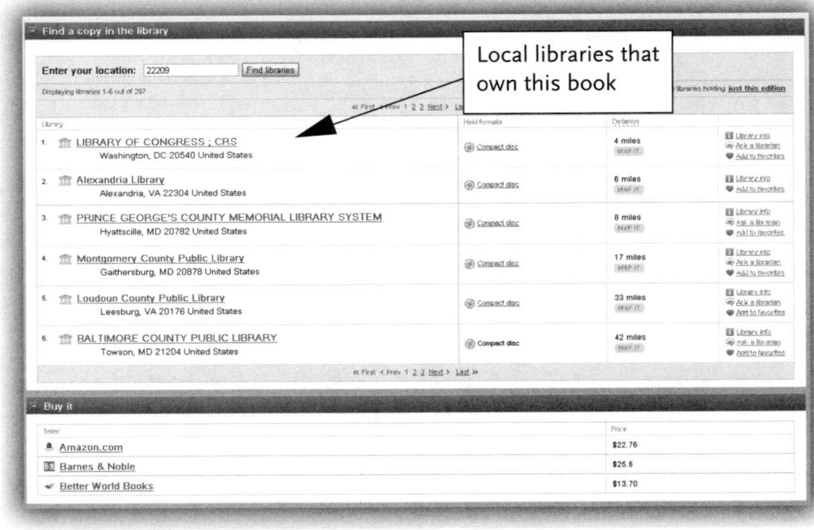

Figure 7.18—Location Information in WorldCat

WorldCat is a great resource to use if you want to find materials in libraries. You can also search your local library's catalog directly. For a list of library catalogs in your location, check out these Web sites:

♦ Lib-web-cats, **http://www.librarytechnology.org/libwebcats**
♦ Libdex, **http://www.libdex.com**

———**END OF ACTIVITY 7.3**

The following two brief activities will show you the basics of searching Bartleby.com for full-text materials and finding statistics in the U.S. Statistical Abstract.

Full-text Database Example: Bartleby.com

Bartleby.com is a Web site that contains a database of hundreds of resources, including books, dictionaries, encyclopedias, and more. We'll do a brief activity to show you how to use it.

Go to Bartleby.com at **http://www.bartleby.com**.

Let's say you want to find the book *Origin of Species*, by Charles Darwin. The easiest way to do this is first select **Non-fiction** from the pull-down menu, as shown in Figure 7.19. Then type **Charles Darwin** in the search form. Click on **Go**.

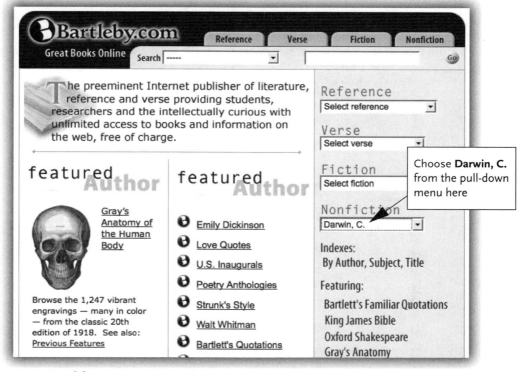

Figure 7.19—Bartleby.com

Figure 7.20 shows the list of resources found. The first is a link to *The Origin of Species*, the book we want. To obtain the entire book, simply click on this link.

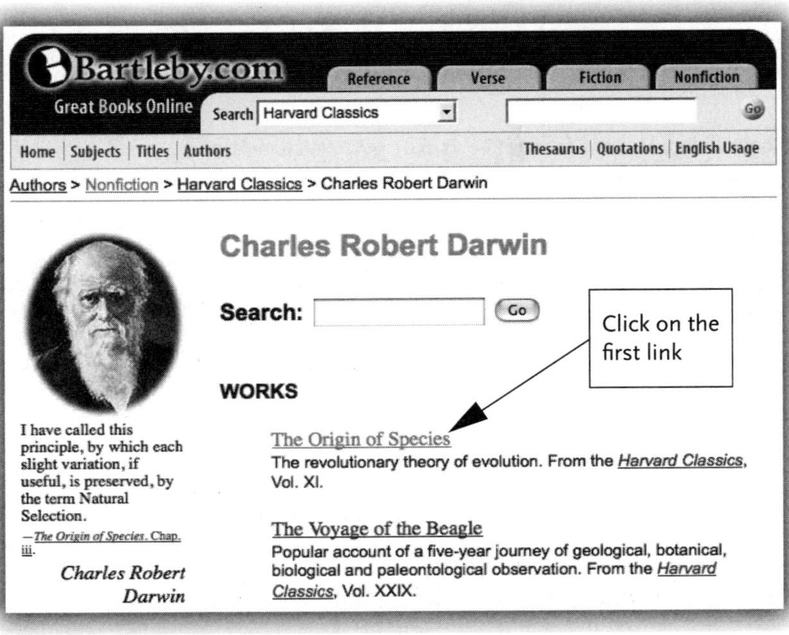

Figure 7.20—Results of Searching for Works by Charles Darwin

Figure 7.21 shows the beginning of the work *The Origin of Species*. Note that because Bartleby.com is a full-text database, you can search the entire work by the words or phrases that you are interested in.

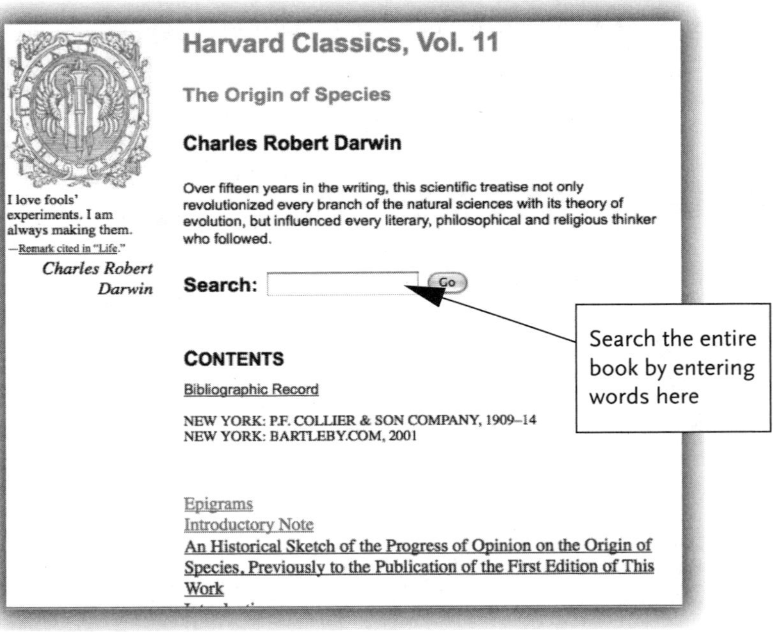

Figure 7.21—The Origin of Species in Bartleby.com

Numeric Database Example: U.S. Statistical Abstract

The Statistical Abstract of the United States is an annual publication that consists of statistics gathered from hundreds of U.S government agencies and private organizations. It has appeared in print since 1878. It is a very useful tool for finding information on several topics, including labor, education, health issues, population, and more. We will do a brief example to show you how it works.

First of all, go to the Abstract at this URL:

http://www.census.gov/compendia/statab

We are looking for statistics about child poverty. You can find this information in two ways: by searching the site by keyword, or by accessing a table from the categories on the left side of the window. We'll show how to find a table that covers child poverty. Figure 7.22 shows the home page of the 2009 Statistical Abstract. Note the sections on the left side of the window. Scroll down until you see the section entitled **Income, Expenditures, Poverty & Wealth**. Click on the arrow and a sub-menu will appear. Click on the **Poverty** link.

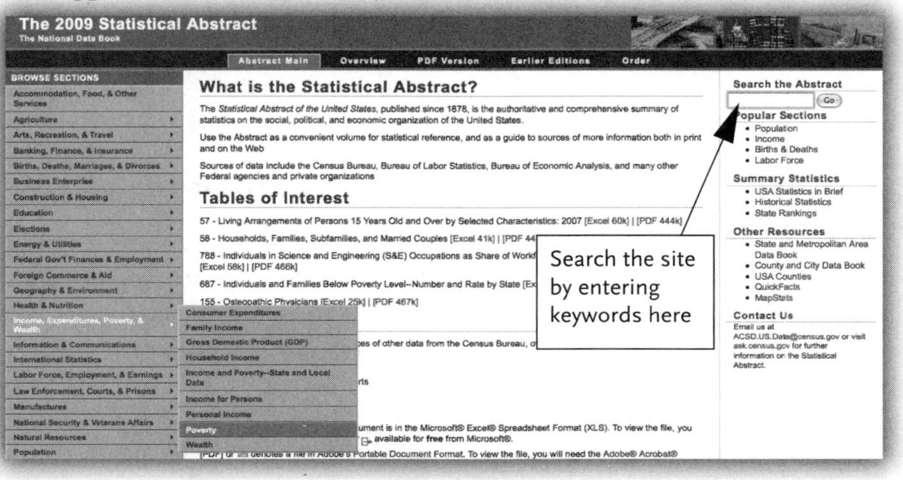

Figure 7.22—The Statistical Abstract of the United States: http://www.census.gov/compendia/statab

Figure 7.22 shows several different tables on the subject of poverty. One of them, table 690, is entitled **Children Below Poverty Level by Race and Hispanic Origin**. Note that you can view this table as an MS Excel spreadsheet as well as a PDF file.

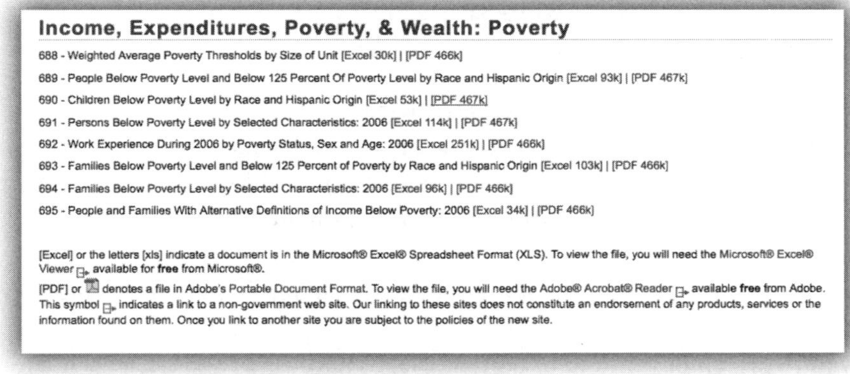

Figure 7.23—Poverty Tables in the Statistical Abstract

Access the Excel spreadsheet by clicking on the link. Figure 7.24 shows the part of the file. This table shows the number of U.S. children below the poverty level for each year since 1959. In order to understand the table, it's important to click on the **See notes** link in the upper left corner. The notes will give you definitions of the data, which will make it more meaningful to you and your research.

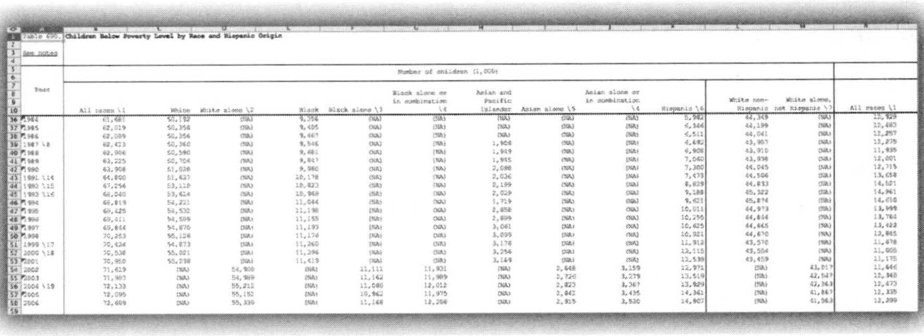

Table 696. Children Below Poverty Level by Race and Hispanic Origin

See notes

Year	Number of children (1,000)												
	All races \1	White	White alone \2	Black	Black alone \3	Black alone or in combination \4	Asian and Pacific Islander	Asian alone \5	Asian alone or in combination \4	Hispanic \6	White non-Hispanic	White alone, not Hispanic \7	All races \1
1984	61,681	50,192	(NA)	9,356	(NA)	(NA)	(NA)	(NA)	(NA)	5,982	44,349	(NA)	12,929
1985	62,019	50,358	(NA)	9,405	(NA)	(NA)	(NA)	(NA)	(NA)	6,346	44,199	(NA)	12,483
1986	62,009	50,356	(NA)	9,467	(NA)	(NA)	(NA)	(NA)	(NA)	6,511	44,041	(NA)	12,257
1987 \8	62,423	50,360	(NA)	9,546	(NA)	(NA)	1,908	(NA)	(NA)	6,692	43,907	(NA)	12,275
1988	62,906	50,590	(NA)	9,681	(NA)	(NA)	1,949	(NA)	(NA)	6,908	43,910	(NA)	11,935
1989	63,225	50,704	(NA)	9,847	(NA)	(NA)	1,945	(NA)	(NA)	7,040	43,938	(NA)	12,001
1990	63,908	51,028	(NA)	9,980	(NA)	(NA)	2,098	(NA)	(NA)	7,300	44,045	(NA)	12,715
1991 \14	64,800	51,627	(NA)	10,178	(NA)	(NA)	2,036	(NA)	(NA)	7,473	44,506	(NA)	13,658
1992 \15	67,256	53,110	(NA)	10,823	(NA)	(NA)	2,199	(NA)	(NA)	8,829	44,833	(NA)	14,521
1993 \16	68,040	53,614	(NA)	10,969	(NA)	(NA)	2,029	(NA)	(NA)	9,188	45,322	(NA)	14,961
1994	68,819	54,221	(NA)	11,044	(NA)	(NA)	1,719	(NA)	(NA)	9,621	45,874	(NA)	14,610
1995	69,425	54,532	(NA)	11,198	(NA)	(NA)	2,858	(NA)	(NA)	10,011	44,973	(NA)	13,999
1996	69,411	54,599	(NA)	11,155	(NA)	(NA)	2,899	(NA)	(NA)	10,256	44,844	(NA)	13,764
1997	69,844	54,870	(NA)	11,193	(NA)	(NA)	3,061	(NA)	(NA)	10,625	44,665	(NA)	13,422
1998	70,253	55,126	(NA)	11,176	(NA)	(NA)	3,099	(NA)	(NA)	10,921	44,670	(NA)	12,845
1999 \17	70,424	54,873	(NA)	11,260	(NA)	(NA)	3,178	(NA)	(NA)	11,912	43,570	(NA)	11,678
2000 \18	70,538	55,021	(NA)	11,296	(NA)	(NA)	3,256	(NA)	(NA)	12,115	43,584	(NA)	11,005
2001	70,950	55,238	(NA)	11,419	(NA)	(NA)	3,169	(NA)	(NA)	12,539	43,459	(NA)	11,175
2002	71,619	(NA)	54,900	(NA)	11,111	11,931	(NA)	2,648	3,159	12,971	(NA)	43,017	11,646
2003	71,907	(NA)	54,989	(NA)	11,162	11,989	(NA)	2,726	3,279	13,519	(NA)	42,547	12,340
2004 \19	72,133	(NA)	55,212	(NA)	11,080	12,012	(NA)	2,823	3,367	13,929	(NA)	42,363	12,473
2005	72,095	(NA)	55,152	(NA)	10,962	11,975	(NA)	2,842	3,436	14,361	(NA)	41,867	12,335
2006	72,609	(NA)	55,330	(NA)	11,168	12,288	(NA)	2,915	3,530	14,907	(NA)	41,563	12,299

Figure 7.24—Children Below Poverty Level by Race and Hispanic Origin from the Statistical Abstract

If you wanted to search the site instead of browsing the tables, you could enter keywords such as **children poverty** in the search form on the main page.

Searching for Telephone Numbers, Email Addresses, and Maps for Individuals and Businesses

There are several directory databases for finding information about people or businesses, and their Web sites are relatively easy to locate. Because these services are used to look up addresses and phone numbers, they're often called ***white page services*** for individual information and ***yellow page services*** for business listings. You can find them listed in directories such as The Open Directory Project, **http://dmoz.org**, and the ipl2, **http://ipl2.org**. You can also find them by doing a search in a global search engine such as Google, using the keywords **people finders** or **white pages** or **yellow pages**.

The following are some of the most popular services to use to find people and businesses:

- Anywho.com, **http://www.anywho.com/wp.html**
- Pipl – People Search, **http://www.pipl.com**
- Switchboard.com, **http://www.switchboard.com**
- WhitePages.com, **http://www.whitepages.com**
- Yahoo!'s People Search, **http://people.yahoo.com**

Advantages and Disadvantages of Using These Services

White and yellow page services give you fast access to very large databases of phone numbers, street addresses, and other information. Some services also provide maps, driving directions, email addresses (very rarely for free), and information about businesses in a specific area. Here are several good reasons to use these services:

- You met people at a conference, business meeting, or another situation, and you want to get in touch with them again.
- You wonder which of your old or current friends have email and what their addresses might be.
- You're applying for a job or interviewing at a company, so you want the company address, a map of the surrounding area, information about the community in which it's located, and directions by car.

The main disadvantage is that many times you can't find the information you'd like for an individual. The overwhelming majority of entries in these databases are related to businesses. Listings for individuals usually appear only when people register in these directories. Individual listings also come from addresses people use when they post an article in a discussion forum. It is impossible to find a directory of everyone with access to the Internet—there's no central control of registry service for Internet users, and no single agency could keep pace with the increasing numbers of people using the Internet and World Wide Web. There are many companies that charge money for this information, but even then you can't be sure of its accuracy. The surest way, if you can do it, is to ask people directly for their email addresses! If this is impossible, you could try posting a message to the Google Group soc.net-people at **http://groups.google.com/group/soc.net-people**.

Privacy and Ethics Issues

Services such as these make it possible to search a centralized collection of millions of records in seconds. This capability raises a number of questions related to privacy and the ethical use of the information in such records. An example of such a question is this: Where does the information in these databases originate? Most of the services obtain their information from public sources, such as published phone books and registration lists for online services. All services encourage individuals to register with them. If you register, you must provide information about yourself. In return, you gain access to some features not available to the general public. What control does an individual have over the information in these databases? As much of it comes from public sources, accuracy, and issues of whether a listing appears at all sometimes need to be addressed at the source of the information. You can request that you not be listed in such services. Most of the online white page services make it relatively easy for you to do that.

The problem is that you have to send an email request or fill out a form for *each* service. There's no way to ask that information about you be hidden or removed from every service.

Can users perform so-called reverse searches? For example, can they type in a phone number and find the name and address of the person with that number? This feature is available in several services. Using this capability would help someone identify a person based on the phone number.

Questions related to ethical use of the information almost all deal with using the information for online junk mail—mass mailings related to commercial activity. Such unsolicited email (usually advertising something or soliciting money) is called **spam**. Phone listings in online databases could also be used to generate lists for commercial calls for telemarketing. Most of the services on the Web include a policy statement saying that the information they provide isn't to be used for commercial purposes, but the services don't police the people searching their databases. In their statements, they only promise to respond to complaints from others. It's really up to individuals to protect their privacy and to demand ethical behavior on the Web and the Internet.

Before registering for any Internet service, you need to read policies about how your personal information will be used. You can usually find such policies by clicking on hyperlinks labeled **Help**, **Privacy Policy**, **Acceptable Use Policy**, or **FAQ** from the service's Web page. The questions raised by the use of this technology are typical of what we need to be aware of and concerned about as more information becomes readily available electronically. There are many advantages to using these tools, but we need to think about, and act on, the ramifications of making this type of information so easily accessible.

Summary

Specialized databases are searchable collections on particular subjects or formats. The difference between a specialized database and a subject guide is that a subject guide is a collection of URLs in a particular subject area, whereas a database contains the actual data or information you are seeking. Many databases provide hyperlinks that take you from one related field to another. The major types of databases are bibliographic, full-text, numeric, and directory databases. You can easily find them by accessing directories such as ipl2: Information You Can Trust. Specialized databases are also found in subject guides. These databases are like search engines in that they all support different search features. Most databases have search instruction pages that you should read before you start searching. This chapter covered the bibliographic database, PubMed, an excellent resource for finding journal articles in the medical field. Also covered was a directory-type database, Hoover's, which focuses on company information. We explored searching a library catalog by using the bibliographic database WorldCat, and showed briefly how to use a numeric database, the U.S. Statistical Abstract. Full-text searching in Bartleby.com was also given as an example. We listed several services that let you search for phone numbers, mailing addresses, and other information about individuals and businesses available on the World Wide Web. These provide electronic access to the white and yellow pages of a phone book. Instead of searching an individual phone book, you can search a very large collection of phone books. Having rapid access to this type of information raises questions about privacy and the ethical use of this information. Most services have a hyperlink from their home page that provides policy statements regarding these issues. You need to be aware of your rights and responsibilities when you register with or use these services. Also, be sure not to give these services information that wouldn't be safe to share with a complete stranger. Putting information on these services is like tacking it up on thousands of bulletin boards throughout the world.

Selected Terms Used in This Chapter

bibliographic database

commercial database

directory database

full-text database

hidden Internet

invisible Web

library catalog

multimedia database

numeric database

proprietary database

spam

specialized database

white page services

yellow page services

Review Questions

Multiple Choice

1. The best place to start a search for a specialized database on your subject is often
   a. a general search engine.
   b. a directory, such as ipl2: Information You Can Trust.
   c. a news archive.
   d. a commercial database.

2. Which statement is true of specialized databases?
    a. They all use the same search syntax.
    b. They are available on the Web for free.
    c. They are also called subject guides.
    d. They include information you often wouldn't find on a search engine.
    e. a and b

3. The following are characteristics of commercial databases except
    a. they may be searched by a general Web search engine.
    b. they may include extra information unavailable elsewhere.
    c. they make it easy to download information.
    d. they may provide training to users.

4. A bibliographic database includes
    a. the full text of the works it indexes.
    b. directories.
    c. citations that identify the works it indexes.
    d. a and c

5. One problem with white pages services is
    a. they may infringe on people's privacy.
    b. they sometimes have inaccurate information.
    c. there is centralized control of all email addresses.
    d. a and b
    e. all of the above

6. The following is true of white pages services:
    a. You cannot have your name removed from a listing.
    b. They prohibit users from obtaining addresses for spam.
    c. They have privacy policies that you should read before using them.
    d. all of the above

True or False

7. T   F   The information in a specialized database can be easily found using a Web search engine.

8. T   F   A bibliographic database includes the full text of the works it indexes.

9. T   F   There is one central registry that holds all email addresses on the Internet.

10. T   F   PubMed allows you to limit your search to find articles available only in English.

11. T   F   It is more difficult to find information online about publicly traded companies than those that are privately held.

12. T   F   By searching WorldCat, you can find books and other information that is in a library near you.

Completion

13. Many specialized databases are maintained by _____ and _____.

14. A _____ includes the full text of the indexed works.

15. A database that includes citations that describe titles, dates, and authors, but does not include the works themselves is called a(n) _____.

16. A database that is available only if you or your organization has purchased access is known as a(n) _____.

17. Typing in a phone number to find the person's name and address is called a(n) _____.

18. _____ is the database published by the National Library of Medicine.

19. _____ is a specialized database that gives access to the world's library materials.

Exercises and Projects

1. Do the following:
    a. Go to PubMed at **http://www.ncbi.nlm.nih.gov/PubMed** and do a search for *fibromyalgia*. How many results do you find?
    b. Following the instructions given at the site (on the Advanced search page described in this chapter), limit the search to articles in English published during the last two years. How many articles are listed now?

2. Here is a specialized database on a completely different topic than those we studied in the chapter: the Internet Broadway Database at **http://www.ibdb.com/default.asp**. Let's look for some information about the production of *The Lion King*. Type the title into the search box, choose the proper category, and click **Submit**.
    a. What date did the production open? What is the name of the theater?
    b. Who wrote the music for the show? Who choreographed all those dances in the production? Did he win any awards for it?
    c. Now look up the production of *Ragtime*. When did it open? When did it close? Who sang the role of Sarah on opening night?

3. Suppose you want to invest in the stock market and need information about a company or two you are considering in the food industry. Let's try a search for information about Mars, who you know makes wonderful candy bars. You know you can search for the company at Hoover's Online, as we did in the chapter. Access their site at **http://hoovers.com** and look for Mars.
    a. What is the URL that is given for Mars? Is this a publicly traded company or a private one? What is the corporate address?
    b. Now try looking for Hershey Foods. What is the URL for the company?
    c. Is Hershey a publicly traded company? Go to their Web site. (*Hint:* Click on **Map** to get to their URL) Where do you find their latest annual report?
    d. Does Hershey have a direct purchase plan for buying its stock? Where did you find this information?

4. You are doing some research on food and nutrition and want to find some statistical and other data. Go to Intute at **http://www.intute.ac.uk** and try to find some databases that cover this topic. How many did you find? How did you find them?

5. Go to WorldCat, **http://www.worldcat.org**, and do an author search on the name **Charles Baxter**. See if you can find the title *A Feast of Love*. Type in your zip code and see if any local libraries own that particular book.

6. Go to the ipl2 at **http://www.ipl2.org** and find the Internet Movie Database. How did you find it?

   a. Access the site, and search for the actress Adrian Booth. What was her real name? What other name did she use? In what films did she appear with John Wayne?

   b. Now look for The Lord of the Rings movies. If you just type **Lord of the Rings** into the search box, how many results do you see? Click on the 2003 film, **Lord of the Rings: The Return of the King**. On the left side of the page, click on **Awards and Nominations**. How many Academy Awards did it receive?

   c. Now click on **Trivia**. Give a fun fact about the film.

7. Another excellent government-produced database is Thomas, at **http://thomas.loc.gov**. Thomas is the U.S. Congress Web site.

   a. Access the site and search for bills currently in Congress about hate crimes legislation. How many results do you find?

   b. Is the Congressional Record searchable as well? What about bills that are still in committee?

8. Go to FindLaw at **http://www.findlaw.com**. Click on **Learn About the Law**. See if you can find the rules for common law marriage in Pennsylvania.

9. Go to Yahoo!'s People Search at **http://people.yahoo.com** and to WhitePages.com at **http://www.whitepages.com**. Look for their privacy policies and compare them. Is it easy to find their policies? Is one more strongly protective of privacy than another? Can you remove your name from either listing?

10. Go to Switchboard at **http://switchboard.com**.

    a. Find the address and phone number of the Ordway Center in St. Paul Minnesota.

    b. Print a map that shows the location of the theater, and print driving directions from your location to the theater.

    c. Find the same information (address, phone number, map, driving directions) for the MacArthur Park restaurant in New York City.

Searching for News and Keeping Up to Date Using RSS

The nature of the Web makes it a perfect medium for news. With the ability to update content throughout the day, to include color images, video, and audio clips; and for readers to easily write comments in reaction to stories, news on the Web is engaging, lively, and interactive. In the not-so-distant past, daily newspapers came only in paper form once or twice a day. Now most newspapers have online versions that are updated around the clock. This is also true about magazines. *Time* and *Newsweek* may be available weekly on the newsstand, but the content changes daily on their Web sites. There are also e-zines, Web-based magazines that do not have print counterparts. Some news services include text transcripts of television and radio shows, as well as video and audio transcripts. In addition to major news organizations, thousands of individuals and institutions publish Web logs, or ***blogs***, that may be updated several times a day. Many news services, magazines, professional reporters, and citizen reporters also update the news throughout the day and night using micro-blogs, such as Twitter. This chapter will help you systematically search for news by using the hundreds of news search tools that are available. How do you avoid being overwhelmed trying to keep up with news coverage?

Staying current with news stories that interest you has been made easier by technology that provides tracking of news stories or news alerts. ***RSS***, or Really Simple Syndication, makes it possible to have headlines from sources that you subscribe to brought to your own personal news aggregator.

This chapter includes the following sections:
- ♦ Searching for News
- ♦ Blogs, Microblogs. and E-zines
- ♦ News Tracking and Alerts
- ♦ RSS and News Aggregation

Searching for News

Before you start searching for news on a particular topic, it helps to think about what the nature of that news is. Is it an international story that is being covered on major news television channels and will be covered on the front page of major newspapers? Or is it a local story that will likely be of limited interest: for example, to a small community, city, state, or region? Another very important issue is the period of time in which the story took place. If it is a current major story from today to 30 days ago, you will most likely find what you need by using one of the major search engines' news services. If it took place before that, you'll need to search individual online newspapers' archives.

Search Engine News Sites

General search engines' home pages aren't the best place to start when searching for news, especially recent news, because their databases get updated too infrequently. Most of the major search engines have developed their own separate news search tools. These are primarily used for big news and fast-breaking stories that have national and international interest. The better-known ones are listed below.

◆ Google News, **http://news.google.com**

   Google News covers 25,000 news sources and arranges headlines by relevance, with articles from several newspapers and other sources grouped under each story. The database is updated every 10 to 15 minutes. International in scope, Google News uses computer algorithms to determine which stories will be listed on its main page. By using its advanced news search mode, you can limit your search to a specific source title, to a particular country or state, and by date. The news coverage goes back 30 days. Google News also has an alert feature, which we will explore later in the chapter.

◆ Yahoo! News, **http://news.yahoo.com**

   Yahoo! News covers over 7,000 sources in 35 languages. It relies extensively on wire services such as Reuters and Associated Press. Archives are kept from seven days to one month, depending on the source. Advanced searching allows searching for stories written in foreign languages and limiting results to a specific source or location (country or state). Yahoo! News also has a news alert service.

Newspaper Directories

If you are looking for information of a local nature—for example, stories from a small town newspaper—you can go to directories that list newspapers all across the United States and around the world. The following directories have links to thousands of newspapers.

◆ Kidon Media-Link, **http://www.kidon.com/media-link/index.php**
◆ NewsLink, **http://newslink.org**
◆ NewsVoyager, **http://www.newspaperlinks.com/voyager.cfm**
◆ Onlinenewspapers.com, **http://www.onlinenewspapers.com**

News Archives

Several newspapers provide archives of their stories on their Web sites, but they often require a fee to obtain the articles. For example, *The New York Times* allows free access to articles back to 1987 but if you want to search its archives back to 1922, you will have to pay for access. Before 1922 articles are free because they are in the public domain. Here is a list of some news archives:

- Documents in the News—Current Events Research,
  http://www.lib.umich.edu/govdocs/docnews.html
- Google News Archives, **http://news.google.com/archivesearch**
- New York Times Article Archive,
  http://www.nytimes.com/ref/membercenter/nytarchive.html
- NewsLibrary (fee-based), **http://www.newslibrary.com/nlsite/**
- U.S. News Archives on the Web, **http://www.ibiblio.org/slanews/internet/archives.html**

Television and Radio News

The following are some mainstream television and radio news Web sites:

- ABC, **http://abcnews.go.com**
- BBC, **http://www.bbc.co.uk**
- CBS News, **http://www.cbsnews.com**
- CNN.com, **http://www.cnn.com**
- MSNBC, **http://www.msnbc.msn.com/**
- NPR, **http://news.npr.org**

Commercial News Databases

Your school, college, or public library may have access to commercial databases such as Lexis-Nexis or Factiva. These databases index thousands of newspapers and magazines and provide the full text of the articles. Most of the titles are archived here as well. It is important to know that these services usually index the paper versions of the publications, so the content may be different from the online versions. Both Lexis-Nexis and Factiva provide text transcripts of radio and television programs.

Blogs, Microblogs, and E-zines

A blog is a frequently updated Web page that contains links to resources, personal commentaries, and opinions. In the mid-1990s, when blogs first made their appearance on the Web, there were maybe a few dozen in existence. According to Technorati's State of the Blogosphere 2008, **http://www.technorati.com/blogging/state-of-the-blogosphere** there are over 133 million blogs. In 2004, the number was around 4.3 million. One of the reasons why blogs have become so popular is the simplicity of publishing them. There is no need for the author to know HTML, and there are free blog automated publishing tools, such as Blogger, **http://www.blogger.com**, that make it easy for anyone to create a blog. Blogs are often defined as personal online journals, operated by individuals who compile lists of links and comment on these links to provide information that interests them, with new links on the top of the page, and older ones at the bottom. Recently, however, blogging culture has grown to include political campaigns, institutions such as libraries and museums, and virtually any entity that wants to create a community of interest around particular topics. Blogs are also a good way to uncover news that the regular media cannot or will not cover. It is important to keep in mind that because virtually anyone can publish a blog, you must evaluate the information the blogger has provided. Make sure you can verify the author's credentials before relying on the information that he or she has published.

What Makes a Blog Unique from a Web Site?

- Blogs tend to be more dynamic than Web sites—it is expected that a blog will be updated each day and perhaps several times a day.
- Blog entries may be added from any browser that's connected to the Internet.
- Each entry is time- and date-stamped automatically by the blogging software.
- Blog entries are automatically archived.
- Readers may comment on individual blog entries.

How to Find Topical Blogs

To find blogs on a particular topic, there are a few good directories to try. We have listed some of them here:

- Best of the Web: Blogs,
  http://blogs.botw.org
- Blog Catalog,
  http://www.blogcatalog.com/directory
- FindBlogs.com,
  http://findblogs.com
- Technorati's Blog Directory,
  http://technorati.com/blogs/directory

In addition, general directories, such as Yahoo!'s Directory or the Open Directory Project, are good places to search for blogs on particular topics. You can also search a social bookmarking site such as Delicious for blogs on a particular topic. Simply explore Delicious tags for the term *blog* with your topic of interest. For example, Figure 8.1 shows how to search Delicious tags for blogs on the topic of Pakistan. You'll want to click on **Tags**, as shown, and choose **Explore**.

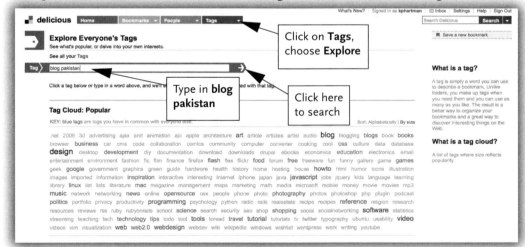

Figure 8.1—Searching Delicious for Pakistani Blogs

When we did this search in Delicious, we found 627 blog articles that were tagged with both *blog* and *Pakistan* by folks.

Searching the Content of Blogs

Search engines, including Google and Yahoo!, integrate blog content in their search results. Ways to limit results to only blogs in both Google and Yahoo! are shown here:

Google: Enter search terms followed by **~blog inurl:archives**.
For example, **"global warming" ~blog inurl:archives**

Yahoo!: Add **blog inurl:archives** to your search keywords.
For example, **"global warming" blog inurl:archives**

There are specialized blog search engines that allow you to search the content of blogs:

- Google Blog Search, **http://blogsearch.google.com**
- Technorati, **http://www.technorati.com**
- Bloglines, **http://www.bloglines.com**

Microblogs

A *microblog* is a site that creates a network of users who write short updates on just about anything they want to write about. These updates are limited in size, usually around 140 characters. The most popular microblogging service is Twitter, **http://www.twitter.com**. When you sign up for a Twitter account, you are not only able to contribute your own content to the service, but you are able to "follow" others that you want to keep in touch with. People in a few countries, including the United States, can set Twitter up so that they are able to receive and send updates, or "tweets" via their cell phones. This capability means Twitter can be an amazingly powerful news source, especially for news that is fresh and not reported in traditional news sources yet. If a person has a Web-enabled phone, he or she can post tweets about a news event immediately, and possibly take a picture of what's happening with their cell phone camera. The person on the street, or "citizen journalist" can be a powerful source of information. In addition to individuals, many news services and other organizations have Twitter feeds that you can follow. In Chapter 10, we will show you how to contribute your own content to Twitter. Even if you have no desire to sign up for Twitter, you can use Twitter as a source of news by searching its content. Searching Twitter feeds is straightforward. Simply go to **http://search.twitter.com** and search for the news you are interested in. The following example shows how this works.

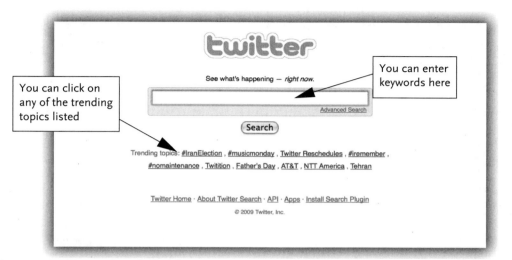

Figure 8.2—Twitter Search Window

You can type keywords in to the search form as shown in Figure 8.2, or you can click on an existing "Trending topic." Figure 8.3 shows the results of clicking on the topic **#IranElection**.

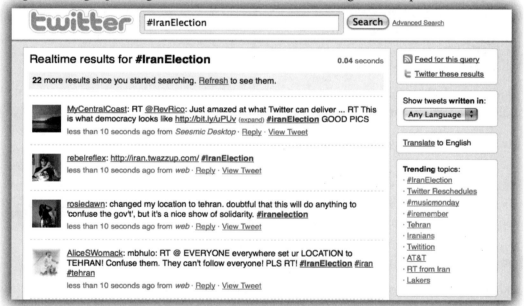

Figure 8.3—Results of Searching Twitter for #IranElection

As more people post "tweets" on this topic, you can see them added in real time by clicking on the **Refresh** link.

Of course, if you have a Twitter account you can follow news sources and journalists directly without having to do searches in **search.twitter.com**. Figure 8.4 shows NBC's Ann Curry's Twitter site.

Figure 8.4—Ann Curry, of NBC News, has a Twitter Site

Twitter is not the only microblogging service, although it is currently the most popular. Other microblogging sites include:

♦ Identi.ca, **http://identi.ca**
♦ Jaiku, **http://www.jaiku.com**
♦ Plurk, **http://www.plurk.com**
♦ Tumblr, **http://www.tumblr.com**

Another microblogging site, Yammer, **http://www.yammer.com**, is used on companies' or institutions' intranets. Yammer is a useful way for co-workers to share information.

E-zines or Online Magazines

These publications are periodicals that are published solely online. They cover most topics and can provide extremely useful information that will not be found in the more mainstream publications. These two resources will help you find them: Ezine Directory, **http://www.ezinedir.com**, and John Labovitz's E-Zine-List, **http://www.e-zine-list.com**.

News Tracking and Alerts

Tracking news stories can be done by continually searching in a news database for information on a particular story you're following. This can be time-consuming, and you can never be sure if you're finding everything that is available. News alerts are requests made to the database using keywords that describe the subject. When a new story is published on the issue, the search tool will email you the link to the article(s) immediately. Google has a very effective alert program, available for the entire Web, or just for blogs, news, video, or groups. Let's say that you want to track news developments on a topic such as the development of a vaccine for the H1N1 virus, or "swine flu."

1. Go to Google Alerts at **http://www.google.com/alerts?hl=en**.
2. Click on the **Type:** drop-down box, select **News**.
3. In the box next to **Search terms:**, type keywords that describe a topic you want to track, such as **"H1N1 vaccine"**.
4. In the box next to **How often:**, choose **as-it-happens**.

5. In the **Email length:** box, select **up to 10 results**. This will prevent an overwhelming number of alerts coming in all at once.

6. Verify your email address in the box titled **Deliver to:**. If you are not registered and signed in with Google, this box will be labeled Your Email:, and you will enter your email address here.

Your alert setup should look much like the one in Figure 8.5 (your own email address will be inserted in the **Deliver to:** box).

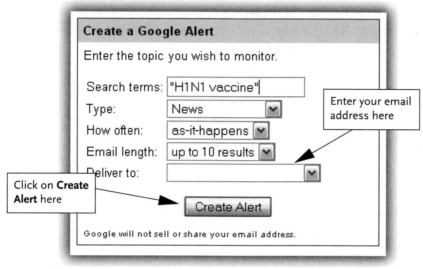

Figure 8.5—Google News Alert

7. Click on **Create Alert**, as shown in Figure 8.5.

The news alert will be initiated after you click on the link that is sent to you in a verification email message. The news alert will remain in effect until you cancel it.

News alerts can help you because you can avoid wasting time searching for and keeping up with news on a topic—the search tool does it for you. The following section covers news aggregators and RSS technology, which is another way to keep up with the news.

RSS and News Aggregation

You can set up news alerts, arrange for email updates from online newsletters and e-zines, or save frequently used blogs and news Web sites to your favorites list; but if you want to monitor several sites on a regular basis, it makes sense to use news readers or aggregators. These use RSS technology. RSS stands for Really Simple Syndication, or RDF Site Summary or Rich Site Summary. Really Simple Syndication seems to be the term most people use to describe it. RSS is an *XML (Extensible Markup Language)*-based format for distributing and aggregating Web content. *Syndication* in this media can be described very much like syndication in the newspaper or radio business. A columnist may be syndicated, which means that his or her material is distributed to newspapers all over the world: for example, Garrison Keillor's articles, or opinion pieces by Thomas Friedman. RSS allows someone to distribute content on a large scale. A small newspaper or newsletter, with sought-after content, can compete with bigger news sources.

RSS Readers/Aggregators

RSS readers, or aggregators, are software packages that allow you to receive, within one page, news sources that you choose, including blogs and newspapers such as *The New York Times*, broadcast news, and so forth. Headlines are updated regularly throughout the day, and if you want to read the entire article, you can easily click on the headline to go to it. It is important to note that not all news sources are RSS-enabled. If the source is available via a newsreader, the source will usually clearly indicate this by using an icon on its main page labeled **XML** or **RSS**. RSS readers or ***news aggregators*** may be Web-based services that are free and accessible from any computer that is connected to the Internet. If you choose a Web-based service, you may set up an account for free and be assigned a user name and password to protect your privacy. There are also aggregators that require software that you may download to your computer—some of these packages are free and others are fee-based.

Finding News Readers

The following resources provide links to several news readers that are either Web-based or available for downloading to your computer. These services list dozens of RSS readers, both free and fee-based, Web-based and downloadable.

- RSS Specifications, **http://www.rss-specifications.com/rss-readers.htm**
- News on Feeds: Web-based Aggregators, **http://www.newsonfeeds.com/faq/aggregators**

Popular free Web-based RSS readers are:
- Bloglines, **http://www.bloglines.com**
- Google Reader, **http://www.google.com/reader**
- MyYahoo!, **http://my.yahoo.com/s/about/rss/index.html**

Finding RSS Feeds

These databases collect RSS-enabled news sources. Search these to find resources to add to your reader. You can also search for feeds in the RSS reader you are using.

- Bloglines, **http://www.bloglines.com**
- NewsIsFree, **http://www.newsisfree.com**

In addition to providing a free Web-based newsreader, NewsIsFree updates its more than 32,000 new sources every 15 minutes. It lists RSS feeds, or channels, by topic and by headline.

ACTIVITY 8.1   SETTING UP A PERSONAL RSS READER

Overview

In this activity, you'll learn how to find and establish your own personal Web-based news reader or feed aggregator, and how to search for resources that are RSS-enabled that you can add to it. Although there are RSS readers that you pay for, and there are those that you must download to your computer, the reader we will show is free and Web-based, so you won't need to download any software. Some feed aggregators that are downloaded have more features than the Web-based versions, and of course the ones you pay for would also have more features than the free tools.

In this activity, we will create a personal news reader and add a couple of news-related resources to it. We will use the Google Reader for this activity.

We will follow these steps:

1. Create an account in Google Reader.
2. Select a resource from Google Reader and add it to your reader.
3. Subscribe to an RSS feed directly from a Web site.

Details

1   Create an account in Google Reader.

DO IT!   Type **http://www.google.com/reader** in the location bar.

Your window will look much like the one pictured in Figure 8.6.

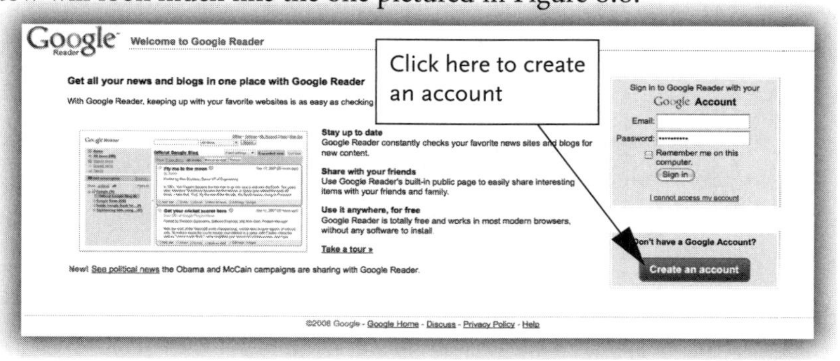

Figure 8.6—Google Reader

In order to use Google Reader, you'll need to create an account. After creating an account, you will need to enter a user name and password whenever you use the service. Because Google Reader is Web-based, you can access it from any computer that is connected to the Internet. If you have already created an account with another Google service, for example, Gmail, you won't need to create a new account to use the Reader.

DO IT!   Click on the **Create an Account** button, as shown in Figure 8.6.

You will now be instructed to fill in a registration form. You'll need to insert your name and your email address, and accept the Google Terms of Service. Your email address will serve as your user name, and this is where your activation key will be sent. You can create your own password. After submitting the form, Google will send you an email message with a link that you must click on to activate your account.

DO IT!   Access your email account, find the message from Google, and click on the activation hyperlink.

2   Select a resource from Google Reader and add it to your reader.

Now we will add some news feeds to the reader. There are several ways to do this. Google Reader, like most aggregators, has hundreds of RSS feeds indexed at its site. Let's say you like National Public Radio's news program *All Things Considered* and would like to subscribe to its feed. Let's see if Google Reader indexes it.

DO IT!   From the Google Reader page, click on **Add a subscription**, as shown in Figure 8.7.

Figure 8.7—How to Add an RSS Feed in Google Reader

DO IT! In the form that appears, type **NPR All Things Considered**, then click **Add**, as shown in Figure 8.8.

Figure 8.8—Searching for an RSS Feed in Google Reader

After clicking on the **Add** button, Google Reader will list the feeds that include the search term you searched for. Figure 8.9 shows the feeds available. Let's say you that you want to get the feed from the NPR Program *All Things Considered*.

DO IT! Simply click on the **Subscribe** button below the annotation describing *All Things Considered*, as shown in Figure 8.9.

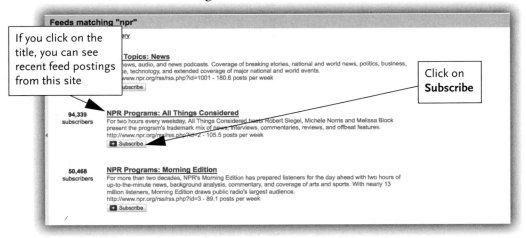

Figure 8.9—Subscribing to NPR's All Things Considered RSS Feed

After clicking on **Subscribe**, you will have the option to put the feed in an existing folder that you have created, or to create a new folder to put it into.

DO IT! To create a folder entitled **News**, click on **Add to a folder**, as shown in Figure 8.10.

DO IT! Select **New folder**, as shown.

You will be then prompted to give the folder a name.

DO IT! In the form provided, type **News**, then click **OK**.

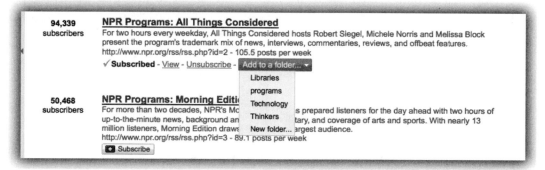

Figure 8.10—Creating a Folder for an RSS Feed in Google Reader

Now, if you take a look at the left side of your window, you'll see the NPR feed listed under the **News** folder.

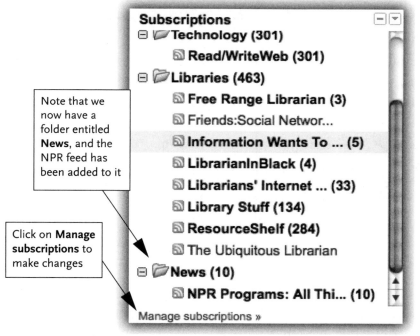

*Figure 8.11—Feeds Under the **News** Folder*

To manage your feed subscriptions, such as deleting them or adding to them to a different folder, you need to access the Manage Subscriptions section.

DO IT! Click on **Manage Subscriptions**, as shown in Figure 8.11.

Figure 8.12 shows what the subscription management section looks like. You can delete feeds, add them to different folders, and more. Remember to click on the subscription feed first.

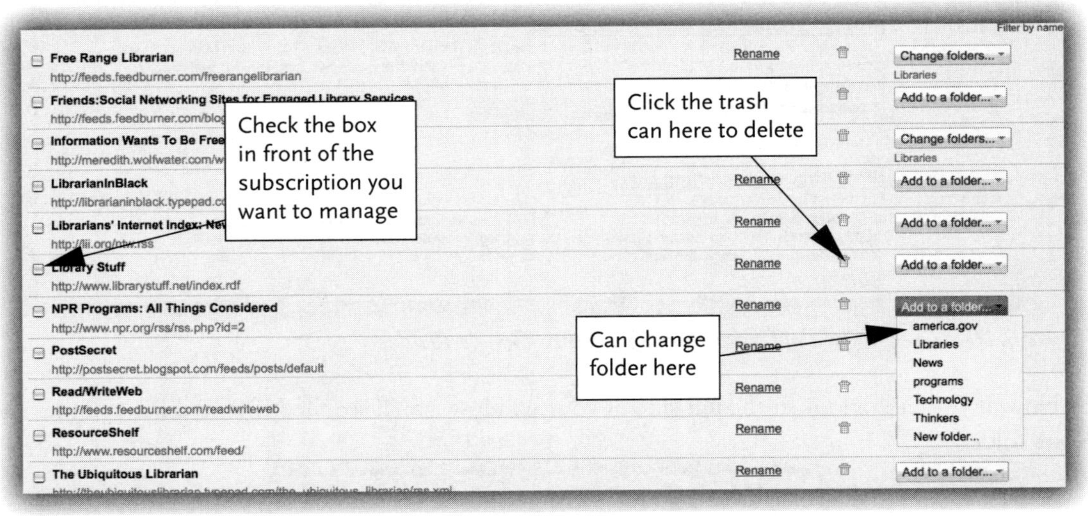

Figure 8.12—Subscription Management in Google Reader

3   Subscribe to an RSS feed directly from a Web site.

Now we will show you how to add a feed directly from a Web site. Let's say you want to receive automatic news feeds from *The New York Times*. You are primarily interested in news related to Africa.

DO IT! Go to *The New York Times* at **http://www.nytimes.com**.

From the *New York Times* home page, scroll down to the bottom of the page and click on RSS.

Figure 8.13 Accessing RSS Feeds on The New York Times Web site

Figure 8.14 shows some of the RSS feeds available. Because we are interested in African news, we will start by selecting **World** from this primary listing.

DO IT! Click on **World**, as shown in Figure 8.14.

Figure 8.14—The New York Times RSS Feeds

DO IT! In the next window, click on **Africa**, as shown in Figure 8.15.

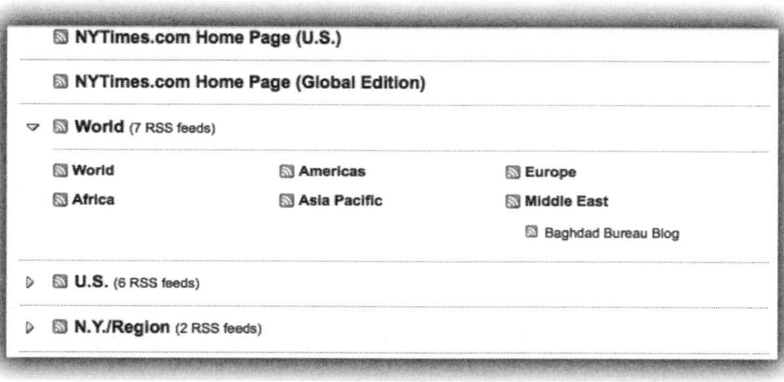

Figure 8.15—Choosing Africa From the New York Times' World RSS Feeds

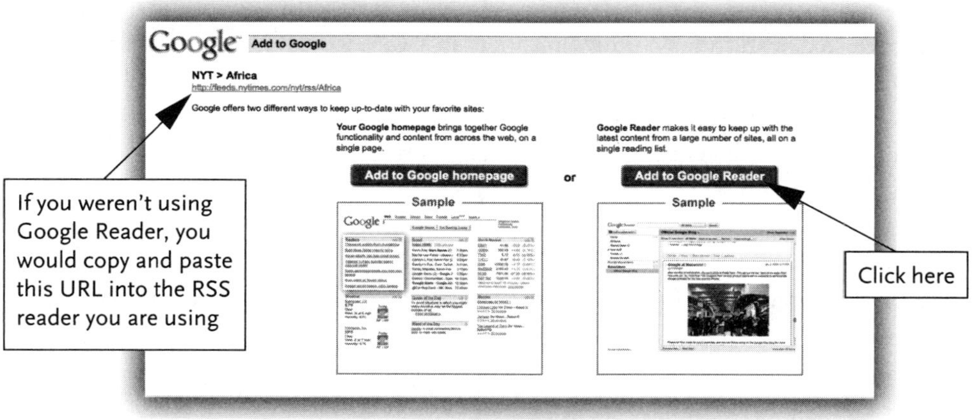

Figure 8.16—Adding the New York Times' Africa Feed to Google Reader

DO IT! Click on the **Add to Google Reader** link, as shown in Figure 8.16.

After clicking on **Add to Google Reader**, you will be taken immediately to your reader (if you are logged in). Recent postings from this site will be shown immediately. To add this feed to the News folder we created, simply click on **Feed settings** and select **News**.

Figure 8.17—Adding the Africa RSS Feed to the News Folder

END OF ACTIVITY 8.1

This activity showed how simple it is to set up your own personal RSS reader and find resources to add to it. Now you can go to the Web-based aggregator by typing in the URL (in this case, **http://www.google.com/reader**), log in with your user name and password, scan headlines from the many resources that you have chosen, and go to the actual articles themselves without having to keep the items in your favorites list or receiving email alerts. You can check these items from wherever you happen to be—at a conference, on vacation, or wherever there is an Internet connection. It's an excellent way to keep up to date with news on just about any topic you choose.

ACTIVITY 8.2   SEARCHING FOR BLOGS ON A PARTICULAR TOPIC AND ADDING THEM TO GOOGLE READER

Overview

Let's say you're interested in starting your own business and want to read blogs on entrepreneurship. The business you're starting is a coffee shop, so you'd like to find some blogs related to the coffee industry as well. You've heard that following blogs is a good way to do track business developments and perform competitive intelligence; in other words, know what your competitors are up to. In this activity we'll show you how to find blogs on these topics, using a few different blog search services. We'll then add the blogs' feeds to the RSS reader that we set up in Activity 8.1.

This activity will follow these steps.

1. Use Blogcatalog.com to find a blog that focuses on entrepreneurship and add it to your RSS reader.
2. Use FindBlogs.com to find a blog that focuses on the coffee business and add it to your RSS reader.
3. Subscribe to an RSS feed from several blogs on a particular topic.

Details

1   Use Blogcatalog.com to find a blog that focuses on entrepreneurship and add it to your RSS reader.

DO IT! Type **http://www.blogcatalog.com/directory** in the location bar and press **Enter**.

DO IT! From the Blog Directory home page, click on the **Business** category, as shown in Figure 8.18.

Figure 8.18—Accessing Blogcatalog.com's Directory

From the list of subcategories that appear, click on **Entrepreneurship**, as shown in Figure 8.19.

Figure 8.19—Blogs Focusing on Entrepreneurship in Blogcatalog.com's Directory

Blogcatalog.com lists over 2,000 blogs that focus on entrepreneurship. Let's select one and add it to our RSS reader. We went through the first several blogs listed and decided upon one that interests us. You could pick a different one. The blog we selected is the The Green Market. The examples below will use this resource.

DO IT! Click on **The Green Market**.

Blogcatalog.com provides a useful feature. When you select a blog, it provides details of the blog's content, including the country that the author is from, language, ratings, tags associated with it and more, as shown in Figure 8.20

Figure 8.20—Blog Detail for The Green Market

To access the blog you'll need to click on the URL located beneath the blog's title.

DO IT! Click on the URL for The Green Market, as shown in Figure 8.20.

Figure 8.21 shows the home page of the blog, The Green Market. Note that the blog is embedded in a Blogcatalog.com window.

To subscribe to the blog's RSS feeds, you'll need to click on the RSS icon. This is usually a small orange icon, as shown in Figure 8.21.

DO IT! Click on the orange RSS icon, as shown in Figure 8.21.

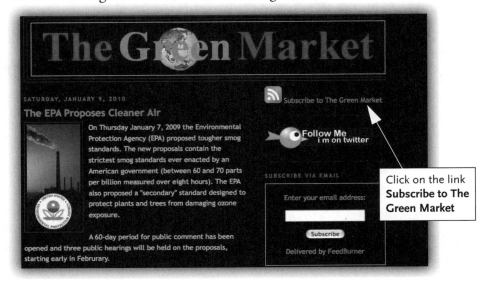

Figure 8.21—Subscribing to the Blog's RSS Feed

It is easy from here to subscribe to feeds by selecting **Google** from the readers that are provided.

DO IT! Click on **Google**, as shown in Figure 8.22.

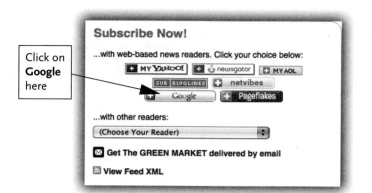

Figure 8.22—Selecting the RSS Reader You Want

After selecting **Google**, you'll see the familiar window prompting you to add the feed to Google Reader.

DO IT! Click on **Add to Google Reader**, as shown in Figure 8.23.

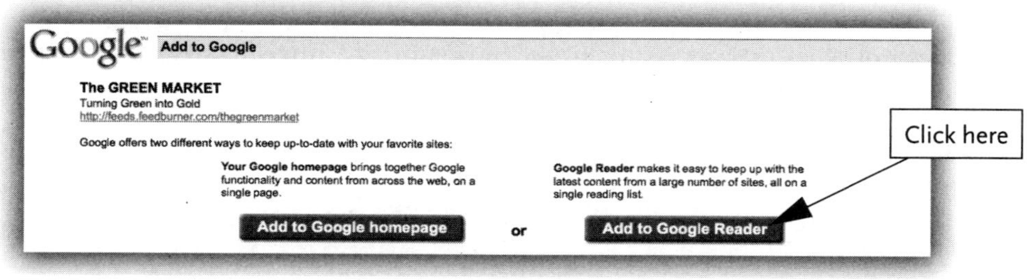

Figure 8.23—Adding the Blog's RSS Feed to Google Reader

If you are signed on to Google Reader, you'll immediately be taken to the reader with the latest feeds from the The Green Market. You can now create a new folder for the feeds by clicking on **Manage subscriptions**, then **New folder** from the **Add to a folder...** drop-down list, and naming the folder (in this case, we chose **Business**). If you forgot how to do this, follow the steps outlined in Activity 8.1.

2   Use FindBlogs.com to find a blog that focuses on the coffee business and add it to your RSS reader.

DO IT! Access FindBlogs.com by typing **http://www.findblogs.com** in the location bar.

DO IT! Type keywords **coffee shop** in the search form, as shown in Figure 8.24.

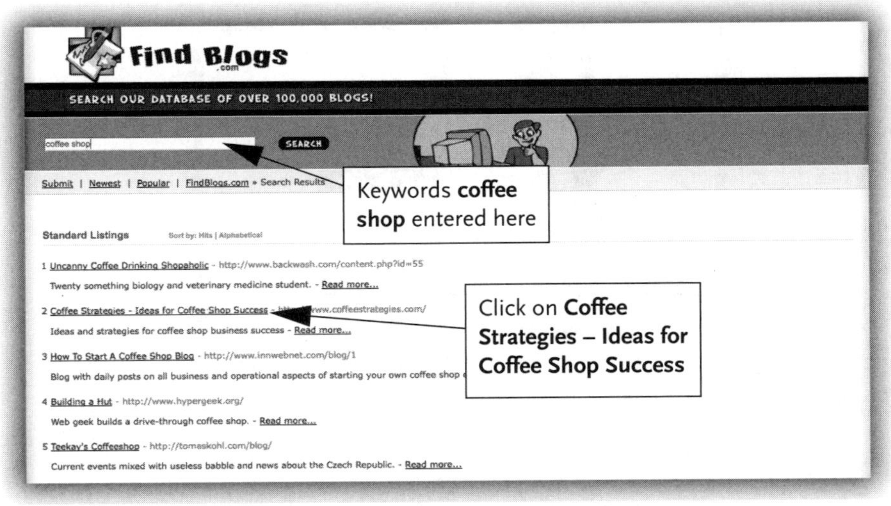

Figure 8.24—Blogs focusing on coffee shops in FindBlogs.com

From the list of blogs that are returned, the blog entitled **Coffee Strategies – Ideas for Coffee Shop Success** looks especially relevant and useful.

DO IT!   Click on the link **Coffee Strategies – Ideas for Coffee Shop Success**, as shown in Figure 8.24.

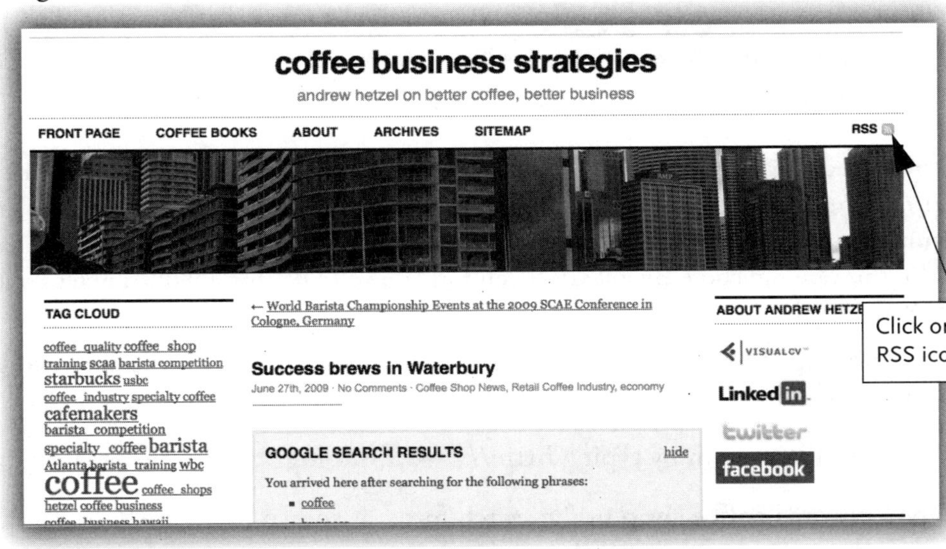

Figure 8.25—Accessing the RSS Feed for Coffee Business Strategies

Figure 8.25 shows the first page of this blog. To subscribe to its RSS feeds, you'll need to find the RSS icon. As shown in Figure 8.25, the icon is located in the upper right corner.

DO IT!   Click on the **RSS** icon as shown.

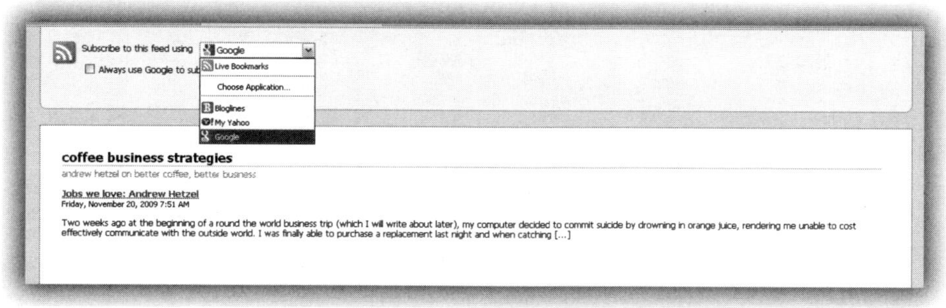

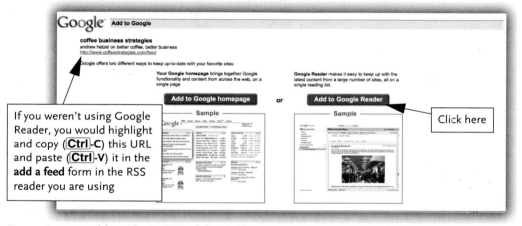

Figure 8.26—Selecting to Add Coffee Business Strategies to Google Reader

You will see a familiar-looking screen asking you which reader you want to use for this RSS feed.

DO IT! Select **Google** from the drop-down list, then click **Subscribe Now**.

Figure 8.27—Adding the RSS Feed for Coffee Business Strategies to Google Reader

If you weren't using Google Reader, you could copy and paste the feed URL into the RSS reader you are using, as shown in Figure 8.27.

One of the best ways to find blogs and other Web sites that you might want to follow is to check out blogs that are listed on a blog that you already read. Many bloggers refer to blogs that they follow as a *blogroll.* A blogroll is a collection of blogs and other Web sites that the blogger finds important and useful.

For example, note the blogroll in Figure 8.28. You can find this by scrolling down the first page of the Coffee Business Strategies blog.

DO IT! Click the Back button on your browser until you arrive at the home page for the Coffee Business Strategies blog. Scroll down until you find the blogroll along the right side of the page.

Figure 8.28—Blogroll from Coffee Busines Strategies

3   Subscribe to an RSS feed from several blogs on a particular topic.

For this part of the activity, we'll search Google's Blog Search for blog content on the coffee business.

DO IT!   Go to Google Blog Search at **http://blogsearch.google.com**.

DO IT!   Type **"coffee business"** in the search form and press **Enter**.

Figure 8.29—Searching Google's Blog Search for Blog Content

The results of this search are shown in Figure 8.29. If you'd like to subscribe to an RSS feed on this topic, it is easy to do so.

DO IT!   Click on **RSS**, as shown in Figure 8.29. Simply add the feed to your Google Reader. You will now receive blog articles on entries that refer to the coffee business whenever they are published.

END OF ACTIVITY 8.2

This activity showed how to find topical RSS feeds and add them to an RSS reader. We used Google Reader for this activity, but the highlighted steps will work much the same with any reader that you have chosen to use.

Summary

The Web, for many people, has become the preferred medium for accessing news. With content updated throughout the day, the Web provides on-demand coverage of current stories and archives of those from the past. Television networks, radio stations, newspapers, and magazines provide content updates along with audio and video clips. Searching for news has been facilitated by specialized news databases that are provided by major search engines such as Google and Yahoo! Several resources list newspapers and television and radio programs by locality in order to find local stories.

In addition to major network news, individuals and institutions publish news via blogs, Web pages that are frequently updated and focus on narrow audiences. There are also microblogging services, such as Twitter, that allow you find news as it's happening on a myriad of subjects. With hundreds of thousands of news sources available, it becomes difficult to track new developments without continually checking each resource throughout the day or week. With the advent of XML (Extensible Markup Language) technology, Web information can now be syndicated using RSS, or Really Simple Syndication. RSS makes it possible for you to set up a personal news aggregator, retrieving news feeds automatically to your desktop. In order to receive these feeds, or channels, you must have a newsreader configured. Newsreaders may be Web-based or downloaded to your computer. They may be free or require a fee. The major advantages of using RSS include the fact that you have control over which RSS feeds or channels you'd like to read, the news reader gives you a headline and description making it easy for you to scan the topics and decide which articles you'd like to read, and the hyperlinks provided will take you directly to the article you want.

Selected Terms Used in This Chapter

blog	news aggregator	XML (Extensible
blogroll	RSS	Markup Language)
microblog	syndication	

Review Questions

Multiple Choice

1. At Google News you can limit a search by
   a. title of source.
   b. date of the article.
   c. both a and b
   d. You can't limit a search.

2. Blogs differ from Web sites because
   a. they are more dynamic.
   b. they are authoritative resources.
   c. the author must know HTML to write one.
   d. all of the above
   e. none of the above

3. The best way to find a blog that focuses on a particular topic is to
   a. search through Google.
   b. search your school's Web site.
   c. search a directory such as Technorati's Blog Directory.
   d. both a and b
   e. none of the above

4. The term RSS stands for
   a. RDF Site Summary.
   b. Rich Site Summary.
   c. Really Simple Syndication.
   d. both a and b
   e. all of the above

5. Newsreaders allow you to receive
   a. e-zines.
   b. newspapers.
   c. broadcast news.
   d. both a and b
   e. all of the above

6. An example of a microblogging service is
   a. Google Reader
   b. Twitter
   c. Blogger
   d. MyYahoo!
   e. none of the above

7. An advantage of using RSS feeds is
   a. you can control what feeds you want to read.
   b. the hyperlinks included take you directly to the article.
   c. they are always authoritative information.
   d. both a and b
   e. both a and c

True / False

8. T   F   Local news stories are most easily found using one of the major search engines' news services.

9. T   F   Articles back to 1851 are available for free from the *New York Times* Web site.

10. T   F   It is important to verify the credentials of an author of a blog before using it as a source.

11. T   F   You may be able to access old news articles for free through your library's database subscriptions.

12. T   F   Search engines cannot search blogs.

13. T   F   It is impossible to search for Twitter feeds.

14. T   F   Google Reader is the only RSS reader available.

Fill in the Blanks

15. A frequently updated Web page that includes links to personal commentaries and opinions is known as a _____.

16. To limit a search in Google to only blog content you would add the term _____ _____ to your search expression.

17. A request made to a news database to be notified when a keyword appears in an article is called a _____.

18. You need to request permission to use a media file from the Web in order to abide by _____ laws.

19. A _____ is a site that creates a network of users who write short updates on just about anything they want to write about.

20. Periodicals that are only published online are known as _____.

Exercises and Projects

1. Suppose you are looking for news articles about the use of video games in education.
   a. Go to Google News at **http://news.google.com** and look for that subject. What search expression did you use? How many results did you find? Give the titles of the first three articles.
   b. Now go to Yahoo! News at **http://news.yahoo.com** and try the same search. Again, how did you formulate your search expression? How many results did you find here? Give the titles of the first three articles.
   c. Which news searching site did you prefer? Why?

2. Go to the Open Directory Project at **http://dmoz.org** and type **blogs** in the search form as we did in the chapter.
   a. Search for blogs on typewriters and see what you find. How many different categories were listed? How many sites were found?
   b. Choose one of the results and click on it. Describe what you find at the site.

3. Now go back to the main page of the Open Directory Project at **http://dmoz.org** and again type **blogs** into the search form.
   a. Choose a topic you are interested in (motorcycles, dance, antique furniture, whatever you'd like!) and search for it. Again, tell how many categories are found. How many sites?
   b. Choose two blogs from the list and describe what you find at each of them

4. Search on Google Blog Search for content contained in blogs on a topic. Travel is something that is often described in blogs. Try looking for information about travel in the country of Belize that is contained in a blog. Go to **http://blogsearch.google.com** to get started.
   a. How many results do you find?
   b. Go to three of the results, give the URLs, and describe what you find at each site.

5. Now let's try setting a news alert at Yahoo! Go to **http://news.yahoo.com** and click on **NewsAlerts** at the very bottom of the page.

    a. Set a news alert for computer viruses. Choose the option for **As they happen**. How many alerts did you receive in two days?

    b. Go to Google Alerts at **http://www.google.com/alerts?hl=en** and set a news alert for a topic of your choice. Choose **as-it-happens**. What topic did you choose? How many alerts did you receive in two days?

    c. Remember to go in and cancel your alerts if you want to!

6. Activity 8.1 in the chapter had you set up your own RSS reader by setting up an account with Google Reader. Let's add some content to your reader.

    a. Go to the RSS section at **http://news.yahoo.com**. Click on the orange RSS icon next to **Technology** Following the instructions in the chapter, add the feed to your reader.

    b. Check to make sure the feed is added. Now go to this new link listed on the left side of your page and describe what news is listed.

CHAPTER
9

Searching for Multimedia

There is an amazing amount of multimedia on the Web. If something can be digitized (put into some digital format) then it is likely to be available on the Web. We can access photos, still images, audio recordings, and video. This is available in a variety of organizational formats: individual items, specialized collections or databases, or as parts of a store.

Almost all of the music we listen to and almost all of the pictures and videos we take are in a digital format. We are familiar working with media in digital formats. The tools (mostly software) to copy from one format to another or one device to another are relatively common and not too hard to use. Combine all this media in digital format with the fact that anyone may put anything they'd like on the Web (technically speaking all parts of the Internet have equal access), and it is no surprise that we can find all sorts of information in a variety of media formats.

Being available and accessible on the Web doesn't guarantee that the information is reliable or that it is legal to use. Still, there is a good deal of very useful and significant multimedia information on the Web. The media is on a digital network so we can access it, save it, and distribute an exact copy of it to others. This makes some people nervous and raises some important questions for all of us to consider regarding the nature of copyright and its effects on our culture and society. Sticking with the theme we've established, we will look at ways to find information that can be useful to us and consider the implications of the ways we use it.

This chapter includes the following sections:
♦ Metadata and Copyright
♦ Searching for Audio and Video Files
♦ Searching for Podcasts
♦ Searching for Images
♦ Searching for Maps and Satellite Images

Metadata and Copyright

Before exploring how to search for multimedia, there are two issues to consider: metadata and copyright.

Metadata—the Difference in Searching

There is a fundamental difference in searching for non-text items compared to searching for text items. It is not in the techniques we use since we usually use text for our searches. When we search for non-text items we base our search on secondary information, often descriptive in nature. This secondary information that describes an item is called *metadata*.

Almost all of our search tools use text to match items in a database. This is entirely natural, especially since finding text-based items is what people have traditionally searched for when researching a topic. When we use text to search for an item in text format we are doing a direct or primary search in the same medium as we are looking for.

Imagine what it would be like if we could search for images using images. We could submit one image to the search engine and have it find a collection of images that are similar in one way or the other to the one we submit. Thinking through what it means for one image to be similar to another helps us understand what people have had to do to successfully use text to search for images. Would we consider one image similar to another if it only had the same colors? The same number of primary objects? In many cases, we'd like to have the search engine return items that had similar content, and being able to express that notion of similar content is the issue. If we have an image of red and black butterflies, is there software available that can determine that and find other images with red and black butterflies? What if it turned up images of red and black kites or boats with red and black sails?

What makes two audio files similar? The same audio frequencies, the same rhythm, or if one file is a comedy sketch should a similar audio file be a collection of jokes by the same person? How can software determine whether the contents of an audio file are humorous?

Attempting to derive characteristics or descriptive information directly from non-text files brings forth a number of interesting issues. Many of these are very difficult to deal with. Advances in pattern recognition software for images, visual analysis for video files, and speech recognition software for audio files will continue to make searching for this content much easier.

Because we have not developed the software that can quickly analyze and classify non-text items we rely on secondary, descriptive text associated with the item. You likely have heard about or thought about this issue before. For a file containing text, the name of the file, the date is was created, the date it was last modified, the size of the file, and the name of the site that hosts or publishes the file are all considered metadata. A list of key terms or words about the content is also metadata.

Some metadata is technical. For example, the bit sampling rate associated with an audio file; and the exposure information, the encoding process, and so on for pictures taken with digital cameras. The extension on a file name, such as **.jpg**, **.mp3**, **.wav**, or **.mov** is metadata too because it tells us the type of file in which the information is stored and that tells about the type of encoding or compression used.

Still, we use the same techniques for searching for text and non-text files, but in the case of non-text files we rely on text metadata in the form of titles, descriptions, and tags associated with non-text files. The issue here is that we are relying on information that someone provides us about the file's contents, not the contents of the file itself to help us locate it. Since these descriptions, titles, and tags do not follow strict rules, the coverage can be spotty or inaccurate. That is to be expected. What you think is funny may not give me much of a chuckle. On the other hand, it is reasonable to expect that you and I will use the tag 'butterfly' in pretty much the same way.

The collection of tools and techniques we've developed for finding text items such as including phrases in quotes and specifying appropriate key words will work for us then in finding non-text items. Sometimes we have to be more persistent and flexible because we are really searching through the metadata associated with the information. For example when searching for images using Google Image Search we can specify the size of the image to show, its type such as news, face, clip art, line drawing or photo, and the dominant color in the photo.

Copyright—the Law and the Practice

If you have come across some media on the Web that you like, what can you legally do with it? The term *legally* is important here, because for any item on the Web (a network) we know we *can* make an exact copy and save it on our computer or a memory card/stick attached to our computer.

All the media is on one platform—the Web. That has implications for how the media is distributed, how it is used, and how it is valued. Copies have little value because they are easily made. Consider Pandora, **http://pandora.com**, where we can legally listen to music anywhere on the Web. Another example is Lala, **http://lala.com**. There we can upload our music and listen to it through any Web connection. Because the media is available through one platform it is essentially in one format, in this case digital, and so it can be easily modified and different items can be combined.

The way the law in the U.S. is written, much of what we're likely to find on the Web is copyrighted material. Copyright does not have to be claimed or asserted on a Web site. Whenever a work such as text, audio, images, or video is given a form by being encoded as a file and then put on the Web, the person or entity that created it automatically holds the copyright. To be sure, there are exceptions such as items put into the public domain or items produced by employees of the U.S. Government. The holder of the copyright on an item has the exclusive right to

♦ make, sell, or distribute copies
♦ create new items based on the copyrighted item

These rights are arguably meant to provide some protection for the person who creates an item so that it is not misused or that any profits derived from the use, sale, or distribution go to the creator. These rights continue for many decades after the death of the original copyright holder. Some say that copyright laws that give exclusive rights for a long period of time is too restrictive and limits ways we share our culture.

You need to determine what the copyright restrictions are on an item before you make a copy or modify any media that you've found on the Web. This is true regardless of whether the site where you found the material contains any statements claiming copyright or how the material is used. If guidelines for using the material are present, follow them.

Most copyright statutes or conventions include a provision that makes it possible for individuals to copy portions of a document for short-term use. This is know as ***fair use***, and it is what makes it possible for people to legally write reviews about copyrighted work, and for people to include some copyrighted work in materials that they produce for academic or scholarly purposes.

Some people use Creative Commons, **http://creativecommons.org**, to set permissions for the ways their works may be used. This has advantages for both the producer and consumer. A producer can set permissions—either very strict, very lax, or somewhere in between—for reuse of her items. This is done online, once, and easily. A consumer readily finds the permissions associated with an item. For example, all of Wikipedia is under a Creative Commons license that allows for use if the use includes proper attribution and any item derived from the Wikipedia source is likewise sharable by others. This is an example of using copyright to put information into the hands of others for sharing, remixing, and reusing.

The site Copyright and Fair Use in the Classroom, on the Internet, and the World Wide Web, **http://www.umuc.edu/library/copy.shtml,** explains copyright issues and helps students and faculty determine if they can use information from the Internet. For guidance on dealing with copyright issues in commercial settings, see A Guide to Copyright Compliance for Business Professionals, **http://www.copyright.com/Services/CorporateGuide/index.htm**, produced by Copyright Clearance Center. In Chapter 10 we further discuss copyright issues and Creative Commons.

ACTIVITY
9.1   METADATA AND CREATIVE COMMONS

Overview

To make some of the ideas we've mentioned above more definite we'll take a look at a Web page available through Flickr, the photo and video sharing service. Ernest Ackermann took the photo we'll look at. It is available for anyone to view on Flickr, it has a Creative Commons license for copyright, and the Web page includes several tags and other items that serve as metadata.

The steps we'll follow are
1. View the page with URL **http://www.flickr.com/photos/eca/2755690098**.
2. Take note of the metadata with the photo.
3. Read the Creative Commons license for the photo.

Details

1   View the page with URL **http://www.flickr.com/photos/eca/2755690098**.

When you do that the Web page shown in Figure 9.1 appears.

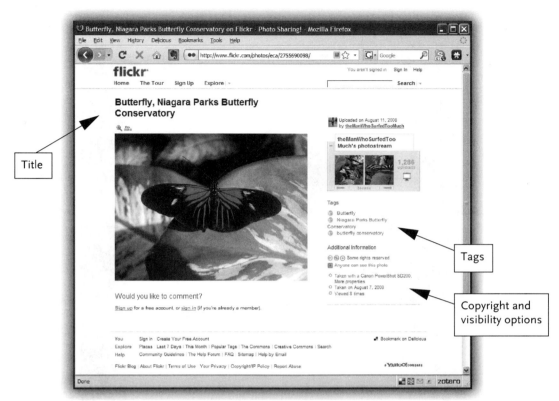

Figure 9.1—Image of Butterfly from Ackermann's Flickr Photos

2   Take note of the metadata with the photo.

Metadata appears in several forms on the Web page in Figure 9.1:

♦ The title

♦ The tags

♦ The information about the camera used, date the image was taken, and the number of views. These all appear below the copyright information.

In Flickr you can search on any of these types of metadata. For example, you can search for all publicly viewable images that have the tag "Niagara Parks Butterfly Conservatory."

Flickr makes it easy to apply a Creative Commons license to photos posted through their service. The three icons to the left of the link **Some rights reserved** indicate what rights are reserved or what can be done with the photo without asking further permission.

3   Read the Creative Commons license for the photo.

Click on the link **Some rights reserved** to see the details of the license for this photo. The rules for using the photo are in Figure 9.2.

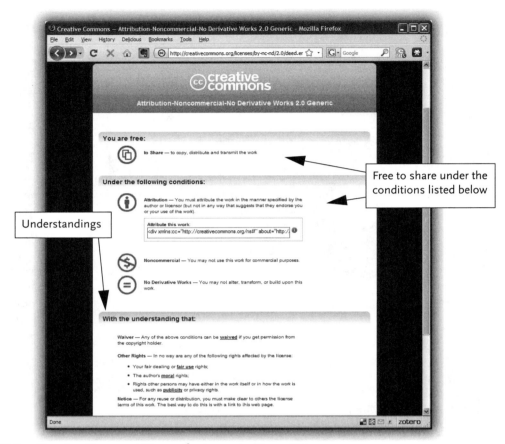

Figure 9.2—Creative Commons License for Image in Figure 9.1

Looking at the license in Figure 9.2 we see that Ackermann has given permission to anyone to copy or distribute the photo in Figure 9.1, provided that its use carries proper attribution, that the photo is not used for commercial purposes, and the image is not altered. Note also in the **With the understanding that:** section that Ackermann may waive any of the conditions and your fair use rights are not taken away by this license. If under this license you wanted to use this photo for commercial purposes, it may still be possible, but first contact the person who holds the copyright.

END OF ACTIVITY 9.1

Now we're going to take a look at the following sections of the chapter:
- Searching for Audio and Video Files
- Searching for Podcasts
- Searching for Images
- Searching for Maps and Satellite Images

Searching for Audio and Video Files

The number of audio and video offerings on the Web has skyrocketed in the past few years. The widespread availability of broadband connections has made it much easier to view video and listen to audio files.

In some cases you can download an audio or video file to save the files on your computer or other digital device such as an iPod or other MP3 player. Many audio and video files are available using **streaming media** technology. That means you listen to or view files without downloading the files to your computer.

Software Requirements

All modern computers have the necessary hardware—audio and graphics cards—to deal with the audio and video you'll find on the Web. You may need to download some software, plug-ins or a player, but most modern computers and browsers have the software already installed. If your computer has a player installed, accessing a file that requires it will activate it. If the required software is not on your computer, a dialog box may pop up with an option to download it. If you find a file not supported by your computer, there may be a link on the Web page to a free download of the required player. Some plug-ins are free of charge, and others require purchase. The following are some of the more popular plug-ins that you'll need in order to use multimedia files. They all have a version you can download and use at no charge.

- QuickTime, a player for video and some audio files, **http://www.apple.com/quicktime/download**
- RealPlayer, a player for most multimedia formats, **http://www.real.com/realplayer.html**
- Windows Media Player, a player for both audio and video files, **http://windowsmedia.com/download**
- Adobe Flash, a plug-in that allows interactive or animated Web pages, **http://get.adobe.com/flashplayer**
- Adobe Shockwave, similar to Flash, Shockwave creates rich graphics for multimedia like games and animations, **http://get.adobe.com/shockwave**
- iTunes, a player for audio, video, and podcasts, **http://www.apple.com/itunes/download**

Searching for Audio

Audio files, including music, radio shows, speeches, sound effects, podcasts, and others, are sometimes not found easily by using general search engines. The files may be embedded in Web pages. A good idea is to find them using specialized databases dedicated to audio. We will explore the more popular audio file sites and give you ways to find them. For the sites that stream their music it is best to have a high-speed connection. Streaming media doesn't work well with a dial-up connection.

Radio

- Radio-Locator, **http://www.radio-locator.com**

     This site includes searching capabilities to search by city, country, or call letters. Listening to radio stations is a way to keep up with news and local culture from different parts of the US or around the world. The radio stations often stream a live broadcast, so it is best to have a high-speed connection.

Music

There are many sites available where you can listen to or buy music. On some sites, such as lala. com, you can upload your own music and listen to it on the Internet at no charge. Some sites provide specialized collections that are typically of scholarly interest—like the Traditional Music and Spoken Word Catalog from the American Folklife Center, **http://lcweb2.loc.gov/diglib/ihas/ loc.afc.afc9999005.8209/default.html**.

At sites that specialize in popular culture music you search for and listen to music they provide, but a monthly subscription fee is usually required. Here is a list of a few of those sites.

- iTunes, **http://www.apple.com/itunes**

    iTunes is a very usable system that allows you to download music, podcasts, TV shows, and movies. It has had a major impact on the commercial distribution of music, taking full advantage of electronic commerce and Internet technology. You can buy individual songs or an entire album, and you can listen to a sample of a song at no charge. You can use it to play audio and video that is already on your computer. It is useful for getting access to podcasts, audio, and video that is part of iTunes U, which is geared to an academic or general audience. We discuss getting podcasts in a subsequent section. The software for iTunes may have to be downloaded and installed on your computer. Use the URL **http:// www.apple.com/itunes/download**.

- Pandora, **http://www.pandora.com**

    Pandora, a personalized Internet radio service, is a product of the Music Genome Project. You access it using a Web browser, and you need to register before using it. Streaming media technology allows you to hear music based on your preferences; you can say whether you like or dislike each piece. It is not a pick and play service—you type in an artist or a song and Pandora will play a song that is similar to what was asked for. Pandora provides links to Amazon.com or iTunes if you want to buy a particular song. Using Pandora you can create a personalized Internet radio station based on music similar to a specific artist or group. Figure 9.3 shows a personalized station based on the type of music played by the band A Place to Bury Strangers. At the time of this writing Pandora gives you 40 hours per month of listening at no charge. For more listening time and more features you need to set up a paid subscription. A similar service is last.fm, **http://www.last.fm**.

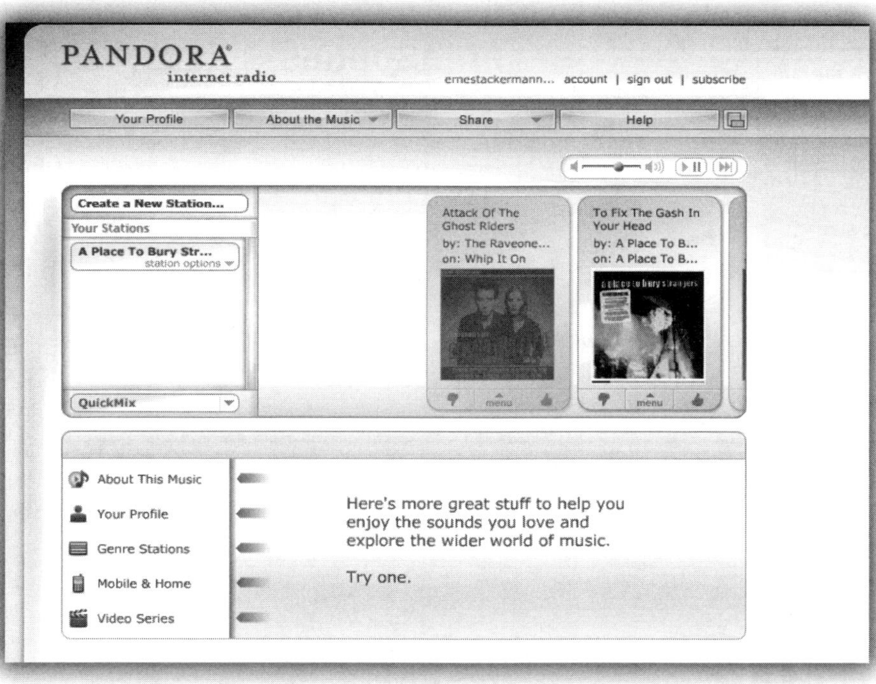

Figure 9.3—Pandora Internet Radio Station Created for "A Place to Bury Strangers"

♦ Yahoo! Music **http://new.music.yahoo.com**

Yahoo! Music allows users to stream music videos and songs for free, as well as download songs through subscription. Through Rhapsody, **http://www.rhapsody.com/ yahoo**, users can purchase monthly or yearly subscriptions and get access to millions of songs. Internet radio is also available through Yahoo! Music. Look for the link **Yahoo Music Worlwide** for a pop-up that gives links to other versions of this service specific to countries outside the US.

Sounds—All Sorts of Audio

To find sound effects, examples of musical instruments, and other audio samples, check out FindSounds, **http://www.findsounds.com**. You search by keyword to easily find sound effects. Figure 9.4 shows the results of searching the site using the phrase **rain forest**. You can also search for similar sounds using the "sounds-like" search button as shown in Figure 9.4.

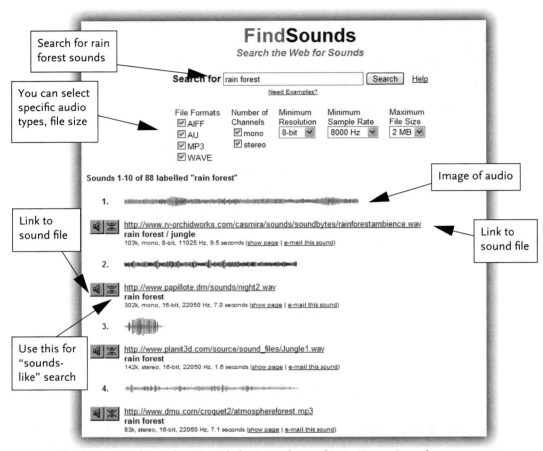

Figure 9.4—Using FindSounds to Search for Recordings of Rain Forest Sounds

Searching for Podcasts

Formed from the name of Apple's portable digital player, the iPod, and the word "broadcast," the term **podcast** refers to a digital recording that can be downloaded to a computer or some other digital device. Podcasts can be audio or video files, and all sorts of events can be made into podcasts. This includes audio language classes, university lectures, radio programs, interviews and speeches, audio books, and entertainment. Most of them are free. A wide variety of items are available as podcasts, in part because it is not too hard to learn how to produce a podcast and make it available on the Internet. Podcasts are distributed using RSS technology, so you can subscribe to them if they are part of a series.

To listen to a podcast all you need is an MP3 player on your computer or digital device. If it is a video podcast then you'll need to have some sort of media player installed to view it. These are all common on modern computers/devices, so it is no hassle. Many podcasts follow a regular publishing schedule, just as we expect from many media broadcasts. That way you can track the podcasts, select the ones to listen to, and usually see a brief summary of what a particular show or podcast is about. To subscribe to a podcast you need to download the necessary software. The software is called an aggregator or podcatcher. The two most popular of these are Juice and iTunes. The site Podcatcher Matrix provides a comparison of iTunes and Juice, see **http://www. podcatchermatrix.org/compare/itunes+juice**.

Juice, **http://juicereceiver.sourceforge.net/index.php**, is an open source project with versions available for Mac OS X and Windows, and the people at Juice are working on a version for Linux. iTunes is supported by Apple, the company that made the iPod the primary device for podcasts. The iTunes Store has an extensive, searchable collection of podcasts. It is relatively easy to locate, subscribe to, and play podcasts all in iTunes. Even though you use the iTunes store, there is no charge for most podcasts. As long as you have a media player on your computer/device then when you subscribe with Juice, the player plays the podcasts. We've used iTunes for some time and it is our default media player. When we installed and tried Juice, the podcasts we "caught" with Juice were automatically played by iTunes.

Both iTunes and Juice have ample documentation about how to use them. Part of the reason for their popularity is their ease of use.

When you "catch" a podcast you are subscribing to an RSS feed. That means you'll be giving a URL to the podcatcher or aggregator to represent the podcast. Then the aggregator contacts the site that hosts the feed, you get a list of episodes or podcasts to listen to and review, and the aggregator software keeps the list of podcasts up to date. For example, the URL for the podcast the NPR Business Story of the Day is **http://www.npr.org/rss/podcast.php?id=1095**.

Finding Podcasts

You'll find podcasts on most sites that deal in broadcasts. For example: NPR, BBC, and CNN each have a portion of their site dedicated to podcasts. If you already know who produced the podcast you want, just go to that site. If you like National Public Radio programs, for example, and want to see if there are any that are available as podcasts, go to **http://www.npr.org**. The NPR site lists podcasts by subject. You choose the one you want to subscribe to and add it to your podcatcher. If you want to download it to your MP3 player just follow the instructions for the podcatcher you are using. If you want to burn the file to a CD you can do that too.

The next places to look are search engines or search tools that specialize in podcasts. There are three types of tools:

♦ For the first type you search for a podcast and then use a player or aggregator to listen to it. The site gives you information about a podcast and provides the URL to subscribe to it. Then you add the URL to an aggregator to listen to the podcast. One good example is PodcastAlley, **http://www.podcastalley.com**. In Web 2.0 fashion the site lets registered users comment on and vote for the listed podcasts. If you are producing a podcast, you can also submit it to this site.

♦ The second type of Web site is one you use to search for a podcast and then listen to it through a media player built in to the Web site. The advantage here is that you can do this on any computer or device that has a browser and a connection to the Internet. You also can get the URL you'll need to subscribe to the podcast. Here is a list of two search tools that you can use through your browser. Each provides ways to search or browse a directory of podcasts.

  ♦ Podcast Pickle (Anjuna), **http://www.podcastpickle.com**. This has an easy-to-use interface.

  ♦ Podfeed.net, **http://www.podfeed.net**. This includes resources for doing your own podcasting.

◆ The third type is one that you have to download to your computer or digital device. Then you use it to search for and subscribe to podcasts. iTunes is the premier example of this type of service. After you install iTunes and register at the iTunes store you are ready to go. Start iTunes, click on **Store** in the menu bar of iTunes, then select **Search**, and then select **Podcasts** from the drop-down menu you see after clicking on **Power Search**. At that point you can search by category, title, author, or description. iTunes is really *the* place to go for individual and collections of podcasts. For example, iTunes U is a collection of over 100,000 offerings from a wide variety of universities, museums, and public broadcast networks. Take a look at An Introduction to iTunes U, **http://www.apple.com/education/guidedtours/itunesu.html**.

◆ACTIVITY◆
9.2 SEARCHING FOR A PODCAST

Overview

In this activity, we'll take a look at two of the types of tools you can use to search for podcasts. In each case, we'll search for podcasts that deal with the topic **small business**.

First, we'll use Podcast Pickle to find and listen to a podcast through our browser. Then we'll start iTunes and search for podcasts. We're assuming iTunes has been installed on the computer you're using. If not you can install iTunes; go to **http://www.apple.com/itunes/download** and follow the instructions.

Steps for Podcast Pickle
1. Access the home page for Podcast Pickle.
2. Find a podcast that deals with small business.
3. Listen to a podcast.
4. Subscribe to a podcast.

Steps for iTunes
1. Start iTunes and access the iTunes Store.
2. Find a podcast that deals with small business.
3. Listen to an episode.
4. Subscribe to a podcast.

Details

1 Access the home page for Podcast Pickle.

DO IT! Type **http://www.podcastpickle.com** in the location bar of your browser and press ⌷Enter⌷.

DO IT! When the home page appears enter **small business** in the search field and press ⌷Enter⌷.

Figure 9.5 shows the home page and the search term entered.

*Figure 9.5—Home Page for Podcast Pickle with Search Term **small business** Entered*

2   Find a podcast that deals with small business.

You will see a page listing several podcasts that deal with small business.

DO IT!   Double-click the podcast titled **Small Business Trends Radio**. There are lots of others to browse. When you double-click, a page similar to Figure 9.6 appears.

Figure 9.6—Listing of Episodes for the Podcast "Small Business Trends Radio"

3   Listen to a podcast.

DO IT!   Podcast Pickle includes a built-in player. Play an episode by clicking on the appropriate button as shown in Figure 9.6

4   Subscribe to a podcast.

DO IT!   Click on the iTunes icon to subscribe to the podcast in iTunes. Depending on the browser you're using, you can click on the RSS icon to subscribe to the podcast using other aggregators.

Using iTunes

1   Start iTunes and access the iTunes Store.

DO IT!   With iTunes installed, you start it by double-clicking on the iTunes icon on your desktop.

DO IT!   Click on **iTunes Store** from the menu of choices in iTunes.

DO IT!   Click on **Podcasts** to start searching for a podcast. By the way, do you notice the entry **iTunes U**? You can follow that sometime to check out all the great resources available there.

Figure 9.7—iTunes Store Start Page

2   Find a podcast that deals with small business.

Figure 9.8—Podcasts Pages in iTunes Store

DO IT!   Click on **Power Search**, as shown in Figure 9.8, to use that feature.

In this mode we'll specify the description as **small business** in the category titled **Business**.

DO IT!   Type **small business** in the description field and select the category **Business** as shown in Figure 9.9.

DO IT!   Click on **Search.** You'll see results similar to those in Figure 9.9.

*Figure 9.9—iTunes Store Power Search Results for **small business** in the Business Category*

3   Listen to an episode.

DO IT!   Click on a podcast to bring up a view that lists recent episodes. Select any one to listen to it through iTunes. Try the podcast **Wall Street Journal on Small Business**. It is popular and current.

4   Subscribe to a podcast.

DO IT!   Click on a **SUBSCRIBE** button as shown in Figure 9.9 to subscribe to any podcast.

Once you've subscribed to a podcast in iTunes, you can download episodes to your computer and listen on your iPod, any MP3 player, or directly from your computer. You can also burn the podcast onto a CD and listen that way.

—————————————————————————————————————**END OF ACTIVITY 9.2**

Searching for Video

Just like audio, video files are on the Web in streaming and downloadable formats. User-generated videos and commercially produced videos, such as television shows and films (either free or for a cost), are available through a variety of sites. Here is a list of a few of those sites.

◆ Blinkx, **http://www.blinkx.com**

Blinkx is a video search engine with several unique characteristics. It uses speech recognition and video analysis software to search the millions of videos available on the Web.

◆ Google Video, **http://video.google.com**

The Google Video database contains millions of videos that exist on the Web. Using Google Video, you can search for TV shows, movie clips, music videos, documentaries, and more. The database is comprised of videos that people have uploaded to Google's services, including YouTube, as well as videos from other sources.

♦ Hulu, **http://www.hulu.com**

Hulu is a free site that provides thousands of TV shows and films as streaming videos that contain short commercials.

♦ Internet Archive Moving Images, **http://www.archive.org/details/movies**

The Internet Archive keeps a permanent record of Web materials so historians, academics, and other researchers can access them. It also serves as a repository for moving images (video), audio files, texts, and software in the public domain or available for use through a creative commons license. There are over 200,000 videos in the moving images collection ranging from historical pieces such as the Kennedy-Nixon presidential debates to cartoons form the 1930s and 1940s.

♦ iTunes, **http://www.apple.com/itunes/download**

iTunes not only provides music, audiobooks, and podcasts, but also videos, including films and television shows. Some podcasts are video podcasts. There's lots of free stuff available as well as films and episodes of TV shows that can be rented or purchased.

♦ YouTube, **http://www.youtube.com**

YouTube is the leading video-sharing Web site. YouTube allows people to upload and share video clips on its Web site as well as through mobile devices, blogs, and email. With millions of videos available, you will find current events, historical events and videos on virtually anything that may interest you. YouTube, owned by Google, has partnerships with several content providers, including CBS and BBC. Register for your own account at YouTube, and you can comment on videos and easily share them. Once registered you'll be able to join the YouTube community.

Searching is straightforward; enter one or more keywords and press **Enter**. Remember that YouTube is owned by Google, so you are likely to see the benefits of that when you search. You can display results by relevance or by date of uploading.

Once you select an item, YouTube displays a list of related videos. These can be helpful in your search for appropriate material.

Searching for Images

Images, like information in other media, are available in general and specialized collections. It may be that there are many types of image collections and databases on the Web because people have been collecting images on specific topics long before the creation of the Internet. Furthermore, many of these image collections exist at academic or research institutions. For example, if you're looking for botanical images, simply do a search in a major search engine such as Google using the words **botany image database** and you'll find several collections including the CSU Stanislaus Botanical Image Database, **http://arnica.csustan.edu/botany**, and the Plant Image Collection, Biology Division, Smithsonian Institution, **http://botany.si.edu/PlantImages**. The Web site Digital Librarian: Images, **http://www.digital-librarian.com/images.html**, maintained by Margaret Vail Anderson, has a huge list of image collections.

Most of the major search engines have image databases, the largest collections provided by Yahoo!, **http://images.search.yahoo.com**, Google, **http://images.google.com**, and Bing, **http://**

www.bing.com/images. These search tools provide a way to search for images quite easily, but the search is usually on the metadata associated with each image. We recommend that you not stick with just one search engine when doing a comprehensive search—each one has a different database of images.

The search engines have different options when searching. For most you can specify filters or choices for the size of the image, the file type, and the predominant color. We'll demonstrate two variations of this. The first shows using more extensive filters with Yahoo! Image Search, and the second demonstrates searching for pictures that are similar to others, a service developed by Google Labs.

Yahoo! Images Search Filters

The major search engines provide options when searching for images—the size of the image, some colors represented, and so on. Yahoo! also includes filters related to Creative Commons licenses and the source of the images. Suppose you want to prepare a report or brochure that includes images of the mountain gorillas in Rwanda. Figure 9.9 below shows the Yahoo! Image Search page to use to find images that can be used commercially or those that can be used as the basis for other works. To get to that page follow these steps.

- Enter **http://images.yahoo.com** in the location bar of your Web browser. This takes you to the Yahoo! Image Search page.
- Click on the link **Options**, then choose **Advanced Search** next to the search field.
- Enter **rwanda mountain gorillas** in the search field, then scroll down to the **Creator Allow Reuse** section and select the options **Commercial Use** and **Remix, tweak, build upon**. At the bottom of the page, click on the Yahoo! **Search** button.

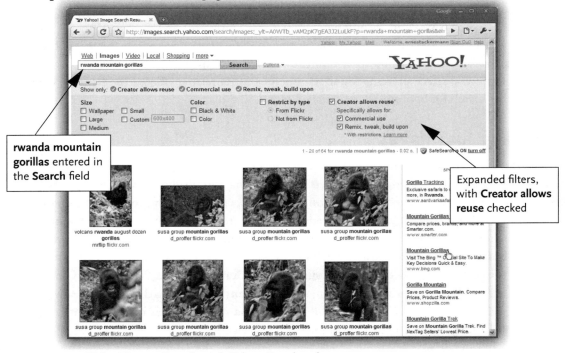

Figure 9.10—Yahoo! Image Search with Filters Displayed

The images you get here can be used for commercial use or remixed, according to Yahoo! Check on that by clicking on an image and reading the license information before you use an image. Try checking or unchecking some of the filter options to gain familiarity with their use and to see how they can be helpful to you.

Google Images—Find Similar Images Search

Google Labs, **http://www.googlelabs.com**, is the place where Google announces some software they've been working on but aren't ready to make the feature a full-fledged part of their offerings. One feature that used to be available only in Google Labs now incorporated into Google's Image Search is the Find Similar Images feature. Earlier we said we wished a service like this were available! We can try it out here. In this case, let's suppose we are looking for some pictures of a garden pond. Something that is not too large, a little rustic, and with rocks surrounding it. Similar images might be helpful here, since it might be difficult to describe what we like using text-based search techniques.

- ◆ Go to the home page for Google Images, **http://images.google.com**.
- ◆ Type in the keywords **garden pond** and click on **Search Images**. We show the results of that in Figure 9.11.
- ◆ See if there is a picture similar to what we had in mind and click on the link **Find similar images**. This brings up another page as shown in Figure 9.12.

*Figure 9.11—Google Images Search Using the Keywords **garden pond***

Click on **Find similar images** for any of the images with that option to see a page of images like the one selected. We chose the image labeled **Tall Trees Garden** as shown in Figure 9.11 above. Figure 9.12 shows the page of results.

Figure 9.12—Google Images Page of Results from Selection in Figure 9.11

As in the previous example, experiment with some of the features to see what is helpful to you. In addition to the special collections and the major search engines, here are a few other image databases that you might want to check out:

♦ Corbis, **http://pro.corbis.com**, has a large database of professionally produced images suitable for advertising. It has several useful filters and features that let you save a collection of images as well as look at other related images taken in the same photo session.

♦ Exalead Image Search, **http://www.exalead.com/search/image**, has a clean interface to searching, with several useful filters.

♦ Getty Images, **http://www.gettyimages.com**, one of the worldwide leaders of providing digital images and video. Many stock photos of celebrities and news events.

♦ Imagery, **http://elzr.com/imagery**, offers an improved interface to Google images.

♦ PicSearch, http:**//www.picsearch.com**, has a database of over three billion images and is family friendly by default.

♦ Pixsy, **http://www.pixsy.com**, searches photo-sharing sites and stock image sites, with several useful filters.

Searching Shared Image Databases

Flickr, **http://www.flickr.com**, is the most popular user-generated image database. After a simple registration process, you may upload photos in files on your computer/device to Flickr into what Flickr calls your photostream. The images can be shared with others or kept private. You can reserve all rights on your images, as in traditional copyright, or you can reserve some or no rights using a Creative Commons license. Flickr encourages a community built on images in several ways:

♦ facilitating Flickr groups based on certain types of images or topics,
♦ permitting comments on all public photos,

♦ by encouraging users to tag their images with information about subject, location, keywords, and so on.

The members of Flickr provide some of the metadata for each image. You can search for photos by descriptive information or by tags. Registration for a simple account is free. A yearly fee ($25 at the time of this writing) gives unlimited uploading and other features. Flickr is a Yahoo! company and registration is handled by Yahoo!.

Figures 9.1 and 9.2 show some of what you can expect at Flickr, but there is more!

Several substantial public collections of photographs and images have put their items in a section of the Flickr site titled The Commons, **http://www.flickr.com/commons**. Collections available include those of the Smithsonian Institution, the State Library of New South Wales, Bibliothèque de Toulouse, and many others. The Commons is searchable by description or by tags. Registered Flickr members are encouraged to tag the photos in The Commons.

Encouraging Creative Commons licenses, Flickr lets you search for images based on the type of reuse permitted by the Creative Commons license. Look at Figure 9.13 to see a portion of what is available at Flickr: Creative Commons, **http://www.flickr.com/creativecommons**.

Figure 9.13. Flickr: Creative Commons Page, http://www.flickr.com/creativecommons

Searching for Maps and Satellite Images

You've got the address for that party tonight, and you're picking up a friend to join in the fun. What about directions?

What does the street look like near that hotel at which you're hoping to make a reservation? You're going camping in Big Bend Park, Texas. What's the topography of the area?

What are the locations of the libraries in or around Fredericksburg, VA?

This spring you've got a trip planned to Florence, Italy. You know it has some wonderful art and architecture. What are others saying about the locations you might visit? Is there an annotated map of the city and its attractions?

These are just some questions you can answer by accessing some of the map and satellite image resources on the Web. Searching for locations using maps can be very exact. You can enter an address or the latitude and longitude of a location. You can also look for businesses or attractions by descriptive terms.

Map & Satellite Services Through Your Browser

Here are some map services you can use through your browser. They all have a zoom capability and you can pan across a map by moving the mouse cursor. Maps and directions can be printed or shared with others via email or URLs.

- MapQuest, **http://www.mapquest.com**, was one of the first map and directions services on the Web. You can view street maps (illustrations) or an aerial map (satellite image), and you can get driving directions between addresses.

- Bing Maps, **http://www.bing.com/maps**, is the latest incarnation of Microsoft's mapping and direction service. You can view street maps (road view), and two versions of satellite views called "Bird's eye" and "Aerial." Use the aerial view to check out the physical features of an area. Three-dimensional views are available after downloading and installing some additional software. For some browsers (Internet Explorer and FireFox only at the time of this writing). Bing includes a feature called "Collections" through which you can find travelogues and links to other resources about a location. Individuals can save directions or the locations of places in their own collections, and then make them public or private.

- Google Maps, **http://maps.google.com**, has been a leader in providing innovative and useful features. Like the map services above, it has several views: Traffic, Map, Satellite, and Terrain (a combination of the map and satellite view.) You can include links to videos, pictures, Wikipedia, or webcams for a given location. Google Maps also offers a feature called "Street View" for many locations. With this you can travel up and down a street for an address. This helps see the details of a neighborhood. When you get directions between two locations, you can click and drag portions of the directions to see about changing your route. This is great for considering a variety of possibilities for a trip. Directions and maps saved by individuals, as you expect, can be made public or private.

Stand-alone Map & Satellite Services

The two major services in this category are Google Earth, **http://earth.google.com**, and NASA World Wind, **http://worldwind.arc.nasa.gov**. Google Earth has many more options and features, so we'll concentrate on that. For a comparison of features read the Wikipedia article "Virtual globe," **http://en.wikipedia.org/wiki/Virtual_globe**.

Google Earth provides a virtual globe, a worldview that you can search by location or attraction or even through tours that you or others have put together. When you visit a location, it is as if you are viewing the location from space. You can change the viewing altitude or viewing angle.

Wikipedia articles, notes written by individuals, and photos annotate many locations. The default view is recent satellite images. Google Earth also includes some historical imagery, views of the ocean floor, and tours with audio and voice recording.

You download the software for Google Earth using the software available at Google Earth, **http://earth.google.com/download-earth.html**. Versions are available for Linux, Mac, or PC. There is also a single-user version available in case you do not have administrative rights on the computer you're using.

Going over all the features of Google Earth would take much more space than we have here. We will show one example here.

Figure 9.14 shows a view of Florence, Italy, near Michelangelo's statue of David. We got there by starting Google Earth and entering **david florence italy** as search terms. Some of the features are noted on Figure 9.14

Figure 9.14 Google Earth View of Florence, Italy Near Michaelangelo's David

You really need to use it to see its features and you should follow the tutorial, **http://earth. google.com/tour.html**, and spend some time at one of the items listed in the "Google Earth Gallery," **http://www.google.com/gadgets/directory?synd=earth&cat=featured&preview=on**.

Summary

There is a large amount of information available on the Web in the form of all sorts of multimedia—photos, images, audio, video, animations, charts—anything that can be put into a digital format. When we search for this information, because methods of searching text have been dealt with successfully, we often search through information that describes the items—metadata. When we access any of this media on the Web we are in the position of making an exact digital copy. Before using these items in other situations, we need to be aware of the copyright information associated with the items. With no copyright information available or if the message "All Rights Reserved" is present then all rights for distributions, use, or modification belong to the copyright holder. Some people use Creative Commons licenses for their works so that it is easier for their work to be used by others.

Modern computers contain the basic hardware to deal with audio and video. You may need to download and install a media player to play certain types of files. There are several specialized sites and search tools to access audio and video files. For all sorts of media some sites are scholarly in nature or contain collections of files that may be culturally or historically significant, and some sites allow you to search by example. There's also a growing collection of course lectures in audio and video formats, many of which can be accessed at iTunes U. Some sites focus on access to popular culture—radio broadcasts, popular music, pictures from the news and advertising, and TV shows and movies. In each medium we also find sites that feature user-contributed materials. Flickr allows for posting and sharing photos, and YouTube deals with video. Each facilitates a community among its registered users.

The advent of the iPod instigated podcasts—digital recordings that can be downloaded to a computer or other device. Using RSS technologies, these podcasts are readily available as individual episodes or through subscriptions. Podcasts can be accessed through the browser or through software installed on the listening device. iTunes is the most substantial and fully featured of the latter type with a rich collection of audio and video podcasts.

Access to maps and satellite images is as easy as any other type of media. Several map services that give directions, street and road maps, and satellite views of locations can be used through your browser. Software that lets you traverse the globe with two- and three-dimensional views will likely need to be installed on your computer. Google Earth is one of the more widely used of these with a rich collection of features and user-contributed information.

Selected Terms Used in This Chapter

fair use
metadata
podcast
streaming media

Review Questions

Multiple Choice

1. A place to find an podcasts and lectures that deal with fashion design is
   a. YouTube.
   b. iTunes U.
   c. flickr.com.
   d. lala.com.
   e. all of the above
   f. a and b only

2. The bit sampling rate is metadata that would be included for
   a. an audio file.
   b. an image in the collection at Bing.com.
   c. the items at FindSounds.com.
   d. an image at Creative Commons.
   e. all of the above
   f. a and c only

3. The name of some software you can use to listen to the podcasts you subcribe to is
   a. podcastalley.
   b. podcast aggregator .
   c. Flickr.
   d. iTunes.
   e. any of the above
   f. a and b only
   g. b and d only

4. You can view videos produced by both professionals and amateurs at
   a. YouTube.
   b. BlinkX.
   c. Hulu.
   d. Internet Archive.
   e. all of the above
   f. a and c only
   g. a, b, and d only

5. You can find images that can be used without charge and without writing for permission at
   a. Google images.
   b. Flickr.
   c. Corbis.
   d. Getty images.
   e. all of the above
   f. a and b only

6. If a work has a Creative Commons License then
   a. it is in the public domain.
   b. it can be used only by an individual.
   c. it may not be used for commercial purposes.
   d. it may be used for any purpose as long as the source is mentioned.
   e. all of the above
   f. none of the above

True or False

7. T F Copyright laws do not apply on the Internet.
8. T F It is not legal to play a copyrighted **.mp3** on your computer.
9. T F Searching for media files such as images is more difficult than searching for text files.

10. T   F   Pandora is a Web service you can use to share pictures.
11. T   F   When you use Flickr you can search for items that have Creative Copyright licenses.
12. T   F   iTunes can be used to find and play podcasts.
13. T   F   Podcasts are only done with audio.
14. T   F   Anyone can search youtube, but you have to login before you can post anything.

Completion

15. To follow _____ laws you need to request permission to use a media file from the Web, unless the file is labeled for reuse.
16. Use the site Flickr to search for _____ that are posted by the general public.
17. The secondary information that describes a media object is called _____.
18. The _____ _____ provision often included in copyright laws makes it possible for individuals to copy portions of a document or a media file for short-term use.
19. A _____ is a digital recording that can be downloaded to a computer or some other digital device.
20. One site that lists several podcasts that are offered by educational institutions is _____

Exercises and Projects

1. Images are a popular item to search for on the Web. Let's compare a search at Google's and Yahoo!'s image search sites.
    a. Using Google Images, **http://images.google.com**, search for images of the Washington Monument. How many do you find? Now do a search limiting the file type to **.jpg** files. How many images do you find now?
    b. Using Yahoo!'s image search, **http://search.yahoo.com/images**, perform the same search for the Washington Monument. How many images do you find if you search all the available sources? How many do you find if you limit the search to the Corbis.com collection?

2. iTunes is a great resource for podcasts and other audio files. Let's practice using iTunes.
    a. Open iTunes and click on **Podcasts**. At the bottom of the window, click on **Podcasts** in the iTunes Store. Browse the directory for podcasts that interest you. You can subscribe to the podcasts for free by clicking **SUBSCRIBE**.
    b. Next, click on **iTunes Store** and browse for audiobooks. In the left hand menu, you will see a list of types of media available for download. Click on **Audiobooks**. You can browse by most popular and genre.

3. Flickr is an exciting and popular image resource for photo sharing. Create a profile at Flickr. Upload a picture of your choice, such as a landscape or family photo. Then, join a group that relates to the photo. If it is a landscape, search for the area, such as Yellowstone or Rocky Mountains, join a related group, and upload the photo to the group's database.

4. Google Earth is a fascinating tool. Download the application, and use it to find your house, your high school, a capital of a foreign nation, and a remote island. Explore posted items from other users.

5. Use Google Maps to find your way around. Plan a walking trip around Washington, DC. Go to Google Maps and find the White House. Click on **Directions From Here** and enter the U.S. Capitol as your destination. Be sure to use the "Walking" option instead of "Driving."

6. YouTube can be very helpful in research. Let's say you are interested in the rebuilding of New Orleans after Hurricane Katrina. Go to YouTube and search for "Rebuilding New Orleans." Sort the search results by play count to see the most popular videos first.

7. Nine people were inaugurated as President of the United States during the time period from 1953 to 1993.
   a. Find the name and an image of each of these people. Include a URL for each image.
   b. Find an image, and the corresponding URL, of each of these people where the image may be legally reused without asking for permission.
   c. Find a video or film of the inauguration of each. Be sure to include the URL of the video.

CHAPTER
10

Working and Learning Together
by Sharing Information

In order to discuss how the Web enables people to work and learn together, we must understand the phenomenon of what is called Web 2.0. The online encyclopedia Wikipedia offers the following definition:

> The term "Web 2.0" refers to a perceived second generation of web development and design that aims to facilitate communication, secure information sharing, interoperability, and collaboration on the World Wide Web. Web 2.0 concepts have led to the development and evolution of web-based communities, hosted services, and applications, such as social-networking sites, video-sharing sites, wikis, blogs, and folksonomies. (http://en.wikipedia.org/wiki/Web_2.0)

Web 2.0 tools have enabled us to collaborate and learn from each other in ways that we have never done before. We can collaborate with people that we know, and with people that we have never met. These people may live in our community or on distant continents. We can work together for fun or for work and school projects. Web 2.0 has allowed people to publish information on the Web, contribute to community projects, provide input to governmental decisions, and more. We've gone from merely consuming Web information to publishing it, editing it, and collaborating about it. In this chapter we will show you several different types of collaborative tools: those for collaborative writing, document sharing, knowledge sharing and discussion tools, social networking sites, and mashups (ways that the user can add value to existing information by overlaying other information to make it more meaningful). We will also discuss the open-access movement and show you a few open-access repositories and how to search them. Finally, we will discuss the very important topic of copyright in this rapidly changing digital environment.

This chapter includes the following sections:
- ♦ Collaborative Web Sites
- ♦ Document Sharing
- ♦ Knowledge-sharing and Discussion Tools
- ♦ Social Networking

+ Mashups
+ Open Access Movement
+ Copyright in a Web 2.0 Environment

Collaborative Web Sites

When we speak of collaborative Web sites we are referring to sites that are written and edited by everyone who can access them. The most popular type of collaborative Web site is a ***wiki***. According to the online encyclopedia Wikipedia, a wiki . . .

> is a page or collection of Web pages designed to enable anyone who accesses it to contribute or modify content, using a simplified markup language. Wikis are often used to create collaborative websites and to power community websites. The collaborative encyclopedia Wikipedia is one of the best-known wikis. Wikis are used in business to provide intranet and Knowledge Management systems. Ward Cunningham, the developer of the first wiki software, WikiWikiWeb, originally described it as "the simplest online database that could possibly work."

Usually each wiki page has a subject, and the entire collection of pages within a wiki can be searched by keyword. We briefly covered searching Wikipedia in Chapter 5, "A Researcher's Toolkit." By contributing to a wiki you are adding your knowledge to the Web, which makes it a richer and more informative resource. In some wikis, editors need to register to obtain a login and password in order to edit it. In others, there is no such requirement. In Wikipedia, for example, most pages can be edited by anyone, but having an account makes it more likely that your contributions will not be deleted by someone else. Wikis can be private or public. They can be placed on an institution's intranet or be accessed on the World Wide Web. Private wikis are password protected and their administrators can allow others access.

Wiki Software Features

+ Most wikis allow you to set up RSS feeds that will alert you when changes have been made to particular pages or sections.
+ Most wikis allow you to see the history of page changes. This is useful when you'd like to go back and see what a page looked like before. The page history shows the name of the person who edited the page if they have a login name attached to the content update. It's also a way for people to republish information that may have been deleted inappropriately or incorrectly.
+ Some wiki software is WYSIWYG (what you see is what you get) enabled. This means that a person can add information easily without knowing any special markup language. Other wiki software has markup language that one has to learn. Usually if there is markup language the wiki will provide a user guide to help people.
+ Some wiki software allows you to tag the wiki pages with subject keywords. These keywords can sometimes appear in s.

Choosing Wiki Software

You can find many types of wiki software at WikiMatrix, **http://www.wikimatrix.org.** Some are hosted, while some require a download to your computer. WikiMatrix provides a "Wiki Choice Wizard" that helps you pick and compare software packages that have features that you need.

Searching for Wikis

There are several ways to search for publicly accessible wikis. You could do a search in a global search engine such as Google by adding the word **wiki** to the subject of the wiki you're looking for. Most of the wiki-hosting sites, such as Wikia at **http://www.wikia.com** and Wetpaint at **http://www.wetpaint.com**, allow you to search them by keyword. There is also a search engine called Wiki.com at **http://www.wiki.com** that indexes wikis from many platforms. For example, Figure 10.1 shows the results of searching Wiki.com for wikis on environmental issues. Note that we can limit the search to Wikipedia only.

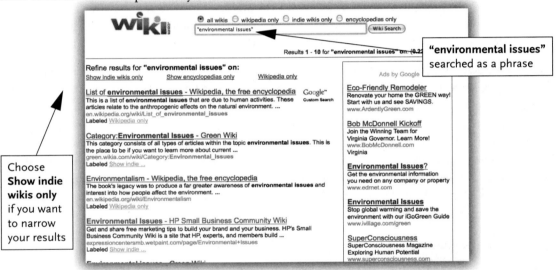

Figure 10.1—Searching Wiki.com for Environmental Issues in Wikis

Editing and Contributing to a Wiki

In Chapter 5 we discussed how to use the online encyclopedia Wikipedia to find information. Now we will explore how to contribute to Wikipedia. To help people learn how to use the wiki, Wikipedia has created a Sandbox. The Sandbox is a place where people can practice editing a wiki. Wikipedia also has a tutorial on this subject. Let's go to the tutorial and learn how to contribute to Wikipedia.

1. Go to the tutorial at **http://en.wikipedia.org/wiki/Wikipedia:Tutorial_(Editing)/ sandbox**. To avoid typing in this long URL, you could do the following: go to Google at **http://www.google.com** and type the following into the search form: **wikipedia sandbox tutorial.**

The Sandbox Tutorial should look like the picture in Figure 10.2.

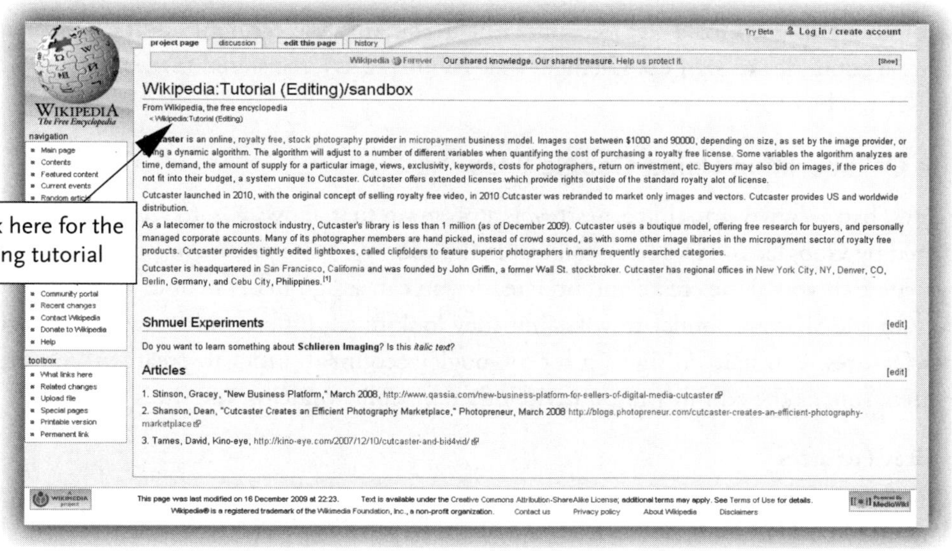

Figure 10.2—Wikipedia's Sandbox Tutorial

2.   To read about how to edit a wiki, click on **Wikipedia: Tutorial (Editing)**, as shown in Figure 10.2. The Web page that appears will introduce you to the tutorial. On the bottom of this page there is a sentence that reads "Try editing in the sandbox." Click **sandbox**.

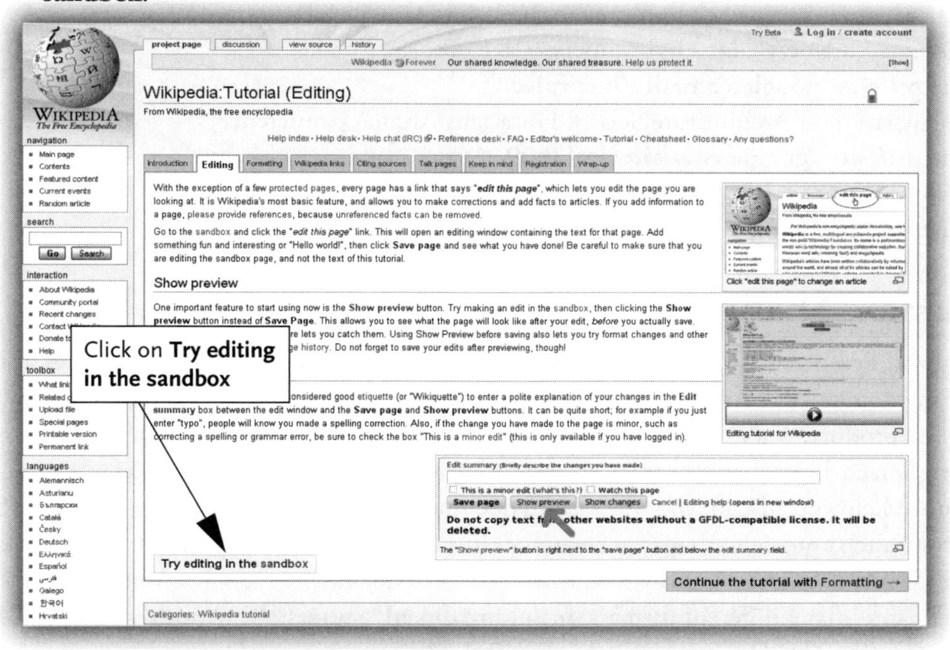

Figure 10.3—The Editing Portion of Wikipedia's Tutorial

Follow the tutorial by doing the activities asked of you. To begin, go to the Sandbox and click the **edit this page** link. Add some words of your choosing and then click on **Save page** at the bottom of the page. Continue to read through the tutorial and learn about the ways you can add information to a wiki. Remember to save your changes! In Wikipedia you can make changes to any article without signing up for a free account. But if you are serious about adding information to the wiki, it's a good idea to sign up. Changes that you make as a registered member are more likely to not be deleted by others.

Web Site Collaboration Using Google Sites

Google Sites, **http://www.google.com/sites**, is a program that allows you to create a Web site. The site is hosted by Google, and it is free. You can make your Web site private or public, you can set it up to be a site that you alone create and update, or you can assign many people to collaborate on it with you. Google Sites are similar to wikis but they look much different. It is easy to add graphics and other features. You have to sign up for a Google account in order to create a Web site using Google Sites. You, as the administrator, invite others to collaborate on the site.

Google Sites Features

- Provides a version history
- Easy to add tables, images, links, and so forth
- Can be private or public
- No cost up to 100Mb/site; unlimited pages per site
- Can subscribe to page changes
- Can insert logo and modify layout
- Is keyword searchable

Here are some examples of public Web sites using Google Sites:
- Integrated Knowledge Environments (IKE) Project Wiki,
  http://sites.google.com/site/ikeproject
- Association of Architecture School Librarians Annual Conference,
  https://sites.google.com/site/aasl2009
- An Almanac of Things for Learning,
  https://sites.google.com/site/thingstolearnwith/Home

Document Sharing

The major difference between collaborating on a wiki or other collaborative Web sites and using file sharing and collaborative editing/writing sites is that the wiki (or site using Google Sites) is a Web-based product, whereas file sharing sites allow you to work on files in several different formats, including spreadsheets, text documents, and slide presentations. For example, let's say you want a colleague to help you edit an Microsoft Word document, but your colleague doesn't have MS Word on his computer. You could share the document in a collaborative editing site such as Google Docs, give the person access to it, and you can work on the document together. You can also save the document into many different formats, including OpenDocument Text (**.odt**), Rich Text Format (**.rtf**), or even Portable Document Format (**.pdf**). In Google Docs, and other sharing sites, the only two requirements for writing and sharing documents are that you have a browser with a connection to the Internet. The phenomenon of using software that exists outside of your own computer is referred to as ***cloud computing***. Cloud computing is a growing trend that may impact how we use software in the future. There are several services that allow you to create or upload documents for sharing with others. We have listed some of them here:

- Google Docs, **http://docs.google.com**
- Microsoft Office Live Workspace, **http://workspace.officelive.com**
- SlideShare, **http://www.slideshare.net**
- Zoho, **http://www.zoho.com**

Now we will show you how easy it is create a document on one of these services and share it with others. We will showcase **Zoho Writer** for this brief activity.

1. Go to Zoho at **http://www.zoho.com** and set up an account. Once you have your account set up, click on Zoho Writer, as shown in Figure 10.4.

Figure 10.4—Choosing Zoho Writer at Zoho.com, http://www.zoho.com

2. Zoho will return with a document workspace that looks much like a typical word processing document. You have several choices at this point. If you'd like to upload a document from your computer to the workspace, simply click on **Import** as shown in Figure 10.5.

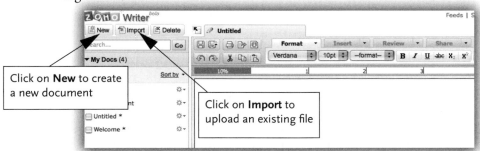

Figure 10.5—Zoho Writer's Workspace

You will be instructed to find the file on your computer to import. Figure 10.6 shows the dialog box that will appear. Note that you can also upload documents from the Web, or if you also use Google Docs you can import a document from that service as well. You must name your document as shown. Once you do this, the file will appear in your workspace for you to work on and share.

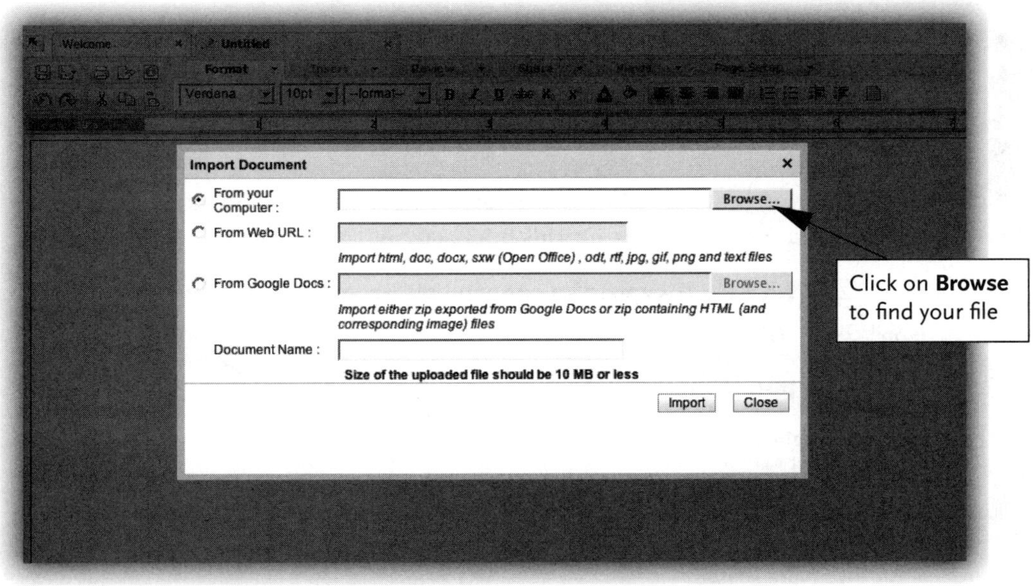

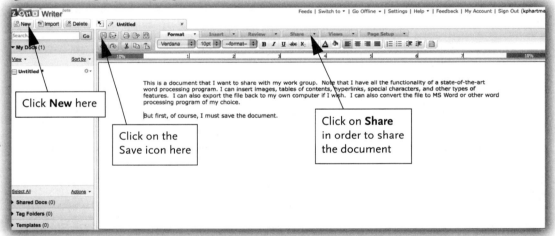

Figure 10.6—Importing a Document from Your Computer to Zoho Writer

Zoho Writer also allows you to create a new document. To do this, click on **New** as shown in Figure 10.7. Simply start typing your document in the workspace provided, as shown in Figure 10.7.

Figure 10.7—Text Typed in Zoho Writer's Workspace

To save the document, click on the Save icon, as shown in Figure 10.7. Name the file. Now you can share it with others. Click on **Share** as shown in Figure 10.7. Figure 10.8 shows the window that will pop up. You will now enter the email addresses of the people you want to share your document with. Note that you can choose whether people have read-only privileges or read/write privileges. Zoho also gives you the opportunity to formulate an invitation message that will be sent to the people you invite.

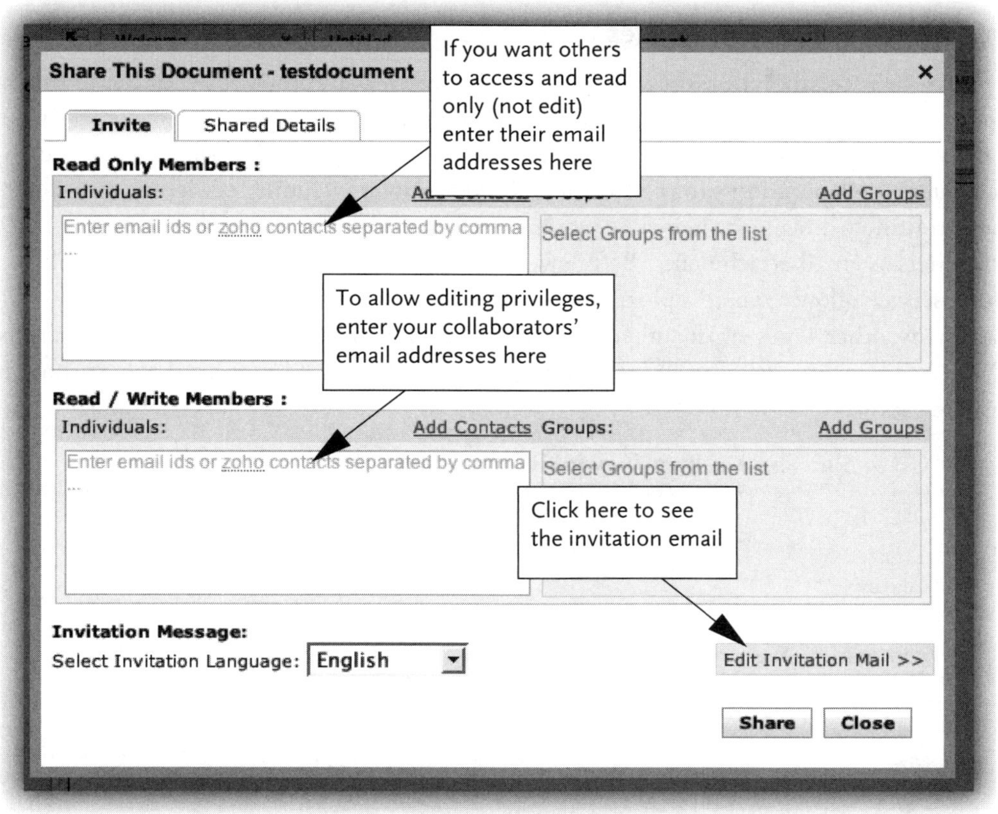

Figure 10.8—Sharing a Document with Others Using Zoho Writer

If you would like to view and/or edit the invitation email that goes to your collaborators, click on **Edit Invitation Email**, as shown in Figure 10.8.

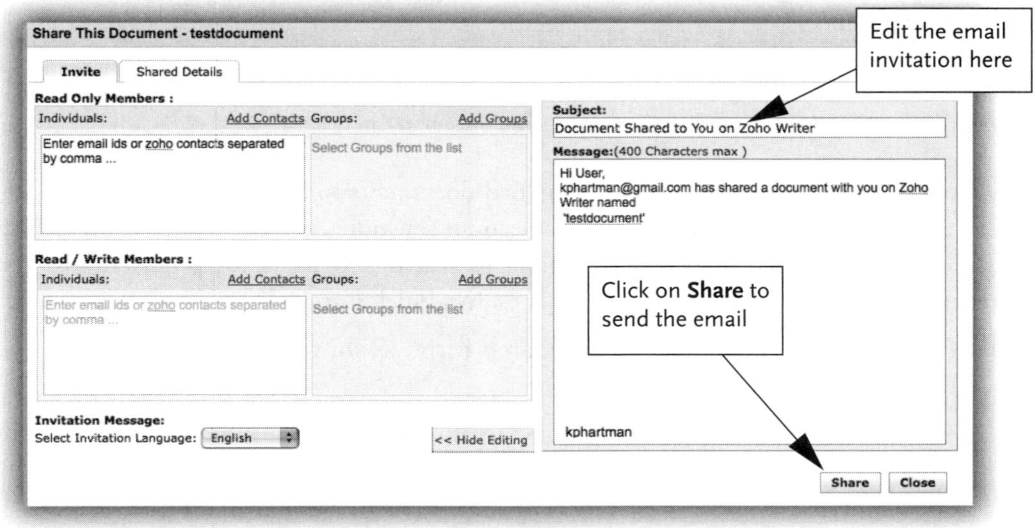

Figure 10.9—Editing the Invitation Email Message and Sharing the Document

Once you click on **Share**, as shown in Figure 10.9, your message will be sent, and the person will be able to access the document. Please note that the person will have to sign up for a Zoho account in order to work on the document.

Searching File Collaboration Sites

Many document collaboration sites, including Zoho, allow you to publish your file to the public. In Zoho, you have that choice when you choose the menu under **Share**. If you share your files with the world, then there is a way for folks to search for your file and learn from it. One popular and useful file-collaboration site is SlideShare. Many people, including conference presenters and teachers, routinely download their slide presentations to SlideShare rather than sending these huge files to others as email attachments. Before we get started showing how to search SlideShare, note that this service allows you to upload slides without creating an account. It also allows you to upload many other types of documents besides slide presentations, including spreadsheets and MS Word documents. You can share privately or publicly, just like Zoho. Let's see how useful SlideShare can be.

1. Go to SlideShare at **http://www.slideshare.net**.

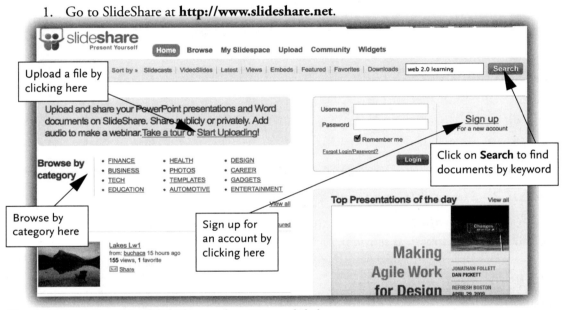

Figure 10.10—Searching SlideShare at http://www.slideshare.net

As shown in Figure 10.10, in order to upload documents to SlideShare, you can do a Quick Upload as a guest, or you can sign up for an account for more extended options and features. To search SlideShare, you don't need an account. To search SlideShare for presentations, you can browse categories or search using keywords. Let's do a quick search.

DO IT! Type in **web 2.0 learning** in the search form, as shown in Figure 10.10.

Figure 10.11 shows the results of the search. Note that the results are returned by relevance, but you can choose to have them displayed by how recent they are, or how many people have viewed or downloaded them. You can view the presentations by clicking on the title.

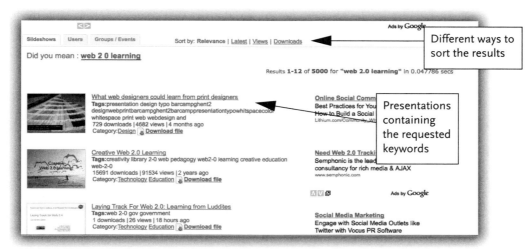

Figure 10.11—Results of Searching SlideShare

Note that SlideShare tells us how many times a file has been viewed and downloaded. You can also sort using these parameters, in addition to files that have been recently added.

Knowledge-sharing and Discussion Tools

There are several types of knowledge-sharing and discussion tools. We will categorize these tools into the following categories:

- Blogs
- Microblogging Tools
- Social Bookmarking
- Discussion Groups and Forums

Blogs

Blogs can be great tools to facilitate conversations, brainstorming, and topical discussions. Blogs are usually authored by one person or a team of people. The public can usually insert comments, which makes them excellent interactive tools. In Chapter 8, we discussed searching for information in blogs. Now we will focus on how you can create your own blogs.

There are several free blog services. We list a few of the more popular ones here:

- Blogger, **http://www.blogger.com**
- LiveJournal, **http://www.livejournal.com**
- WordPress, **http://wordpress.com**

ACTIVITY
10.1 CREATING YOUR OWN BLOG

Overview

For this short activity, we will create a blog using WordPress. This will be a brief overview outlining the major steps in getting started with blogging. There are many features of WordPress that we won't cover here. To learn more about the Word Press and its features see The Features You'll Love, **http://en.wordpress.com/features**.

There are essentially three steps in this activity:

1. Sign up for a WordPress blog.
2. Create a title for your blog.
3. Add a blog post.
4. Assign tags and a category for your post.

Let's get started!

Details

1   Sign up for a WordPress blog.

DO IT!   Go to WordPress at **http://wordpress.com**.

DO IT!   Click on **Sign up now**.

DO IT!   Create a username, password, and email address, as shown in Figure 10.12.

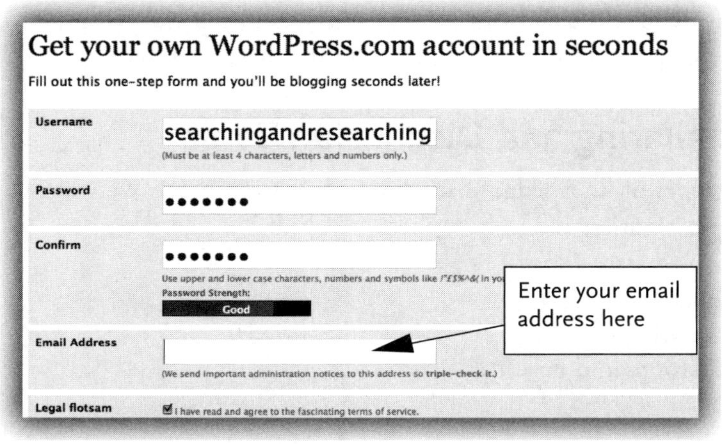

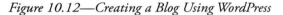

Figure 10.12—Creating a Blog Using WordPress

Note that your username will become the default title of your blog. You can change the title later. Follow the prompts on the screen to complete the registration process. Upon submitting this information, WordPress.com will email you with a confirmation message. You must respond to the confirmation within two days or your account will be canceled. Once your blog is confirmed, you can access it, create the blog title, and begin to add content.

2   Create a title for your blog.

DO IT!   After confirming your account by email, log back in to WordPress, then click on **My Dashboard** at the top of the screen. Scroll down and click on the **Settings** heading on the left side of the page. Click on **General**, then enter the title of your blog. We changed the title of our blog to be **Searching and Researching**. Under the title you can add a tagline.

3   Add a blog post.

DO IT!   Click on **New Post**, as shown in Figure 10.13.

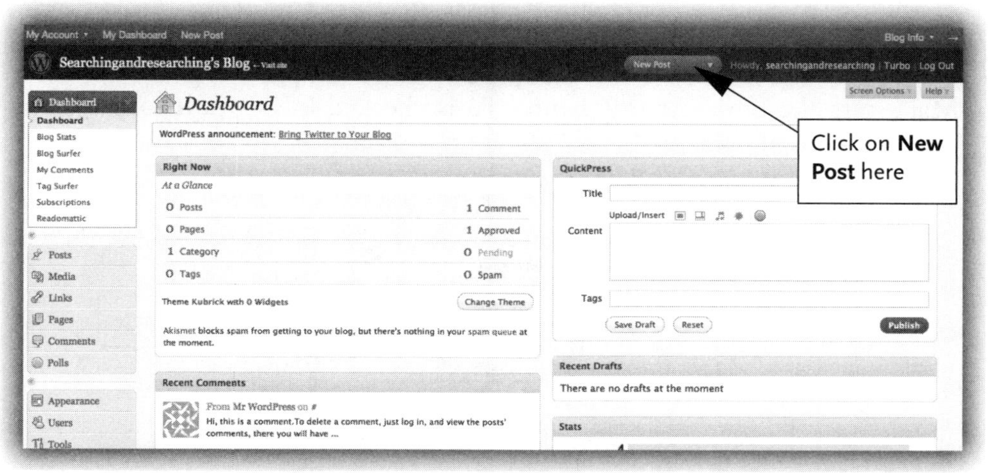

Figure 10.13—Adding a Post to Your Blog

DO IT! First you'll need to create a title for your post. In Figure 10.14 we typed in **Need some input for Chapter 10**.

DO IT! Add the content of your post in the space provided.

Notice that you can save this post as a draft or you can publish it immediately.

4 Assign tags and a category for your post. Assigning tags and putting your posts in categories will help you and others with navigating the content of your site as it grows.

DO IT! In the **Categories** section, click on **+ Add New Category**. We are naming our first category **Chapter 10**.

DO IT! To add a tag to your post, click on **Add**, as shown in Figure 10.14. Type in the tag that best describes the content of your post.

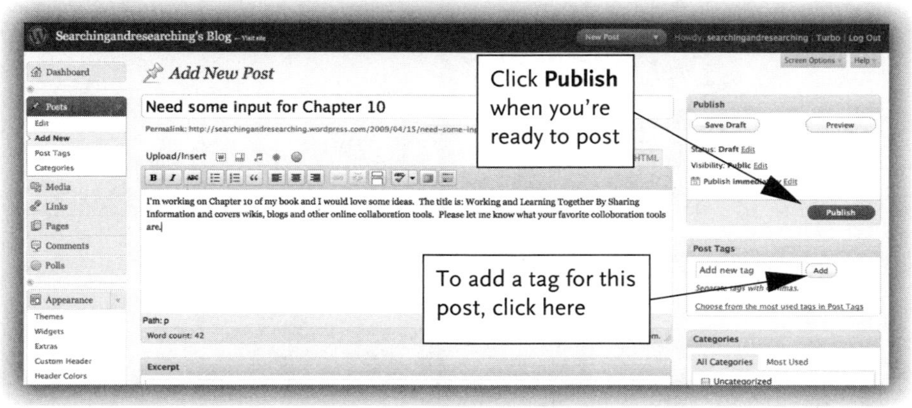

Figure 10.14—Adding a Post to Your Blog Using WordPress

For this post, we used the word **collaboration**. Figure 10.15 shows this tag typed in. To add another tag, click on **Add**, as shown. You might want to add the tag **blogs** as well.

DO IT! Make sure the box next to Chapter 10 is checked in the **Category** section, then click on **Add**.

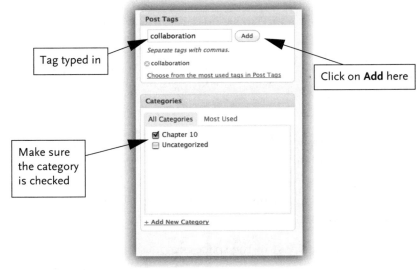

Figure 10.15—Adding a Tag to Your Post

DO IT! When you're ready to publish your post, click on **Publish**, as shown in Figure 10.14.

Note you can make your posting private if you wish.

DO IT! To publish, click on **Update Post**, as shown in Figure 10.16.

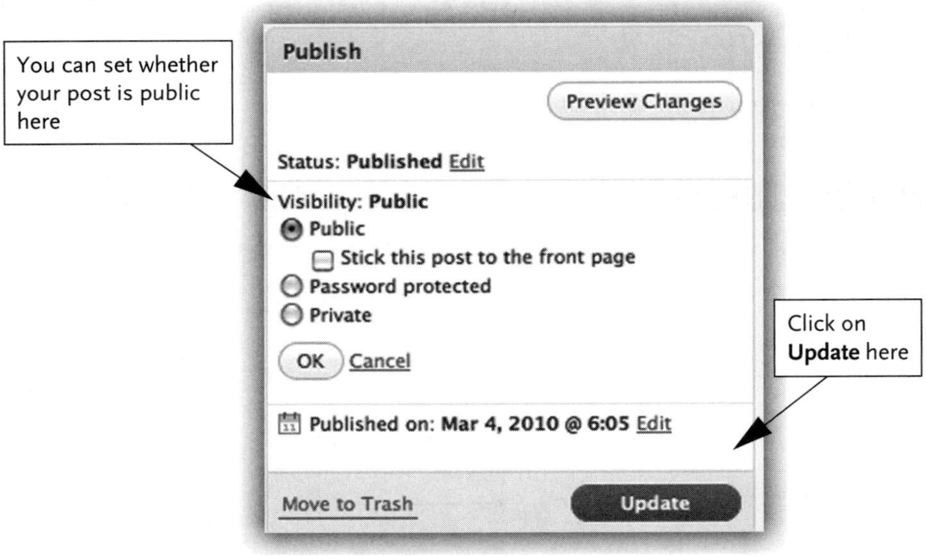

Figure 10.16—Publishing a Post in WordPress; Figure 10.17 shows the result of our first posting

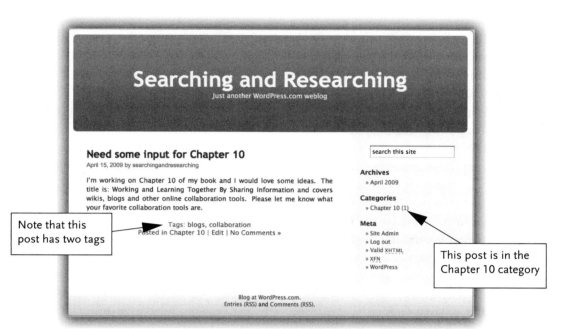

Figure 10.17—A Post Published on the Blog "Searching and Researching" Using WordPress.com

--**END OF ACTIVITY 10.1**

That's all there is to it! Starting a blog is a fairly easy and straightforward task. Now we'll talk about knowledge-sharing and discussion tools: Microblogging.

Microblogging Tools

Microblogging is a type of blogging that allows you to publish brief updates that are viewed by anyone or by people that you choose. These messages can be submitted and received by others via their cell phones, on the Web, email, and more. While a microblog post is different from a traditional blog post in that it is much smaller (typically 140–200 characters), its purpose is similar to that of a regular blog. Microbloggers post comments on topics that can range from very simple, such as what you are doing at a particular time, to purposeful topics such as commenting on a professional conference session, or a book you have read or a product that you have used. Microblogs can be useful when you want to report on a fast-breaking local news story that may help others make decisions. For example, if you just viewed an accident or experienced a train breakdown, you could blog about it so others could perhaps avoid that area of town or route in their travels. Many libraries use microblogging to announce new books or upcoming programs. The goal of microblogging is to gain a group of followers who read your updates.

Here is a list of the most popular microblogging sites:

♦ Jaiku **http://www.jaiku.com**

   Jaiku, originally developed by Google, is now an open-source service. You can connect with others through the Web, SMS (short messaging service) via your mobile phone, or via IM (instant messaging) services. You can add comments to others' postings and create separate conversations, called channels. By using a channel, multiple people can post to a stream of messages related to the same topic. Original posts must be under 140 characters, but comments made my others can total up to 2000 characters.

♦ identi.ca **http://identi.ca**

Identi.ca is also an open-source microblogging service. It supports the 140-character limit on posting length. It also allows people who use other microblogging services to send messages to it. It supports tagging of posts with hashmarks (#) to help you organize your messages. You can use these tags for people or for notices. This is an effective way to keep track of a conversation. The most popular tags are represented by a tag cloud. The tags' size indicates their popularity and how recent they are.

♦ Twitter **http://www.twitter.com**

Twitter is currently the most popular microblogging service. It supports messages of up to 140 characters sent to and from your mobile phone as SMS, Web browser, or an IM application. It also allows you to attach hashmarks to topics that you want to be easily searched for or followed. Twitter doesn't allow users to leave threaded comments on postings, as Jaiku does.

All of these services have many other features that we don't have room to discuss here. We suggest that you sign up for one of these services and explore it for yourself. To help you understand the process, we will show you brief step-by-step instructions for getting started with Twitter.

We will cover the following:

1.   How to sign up for Twitter.
2.   How to find people and other entities to follow.
3.   How to write your own update.

1   Go to Twitter, at **http://www.twitter.com**. Your screen should look like the one in Figure 10.18.

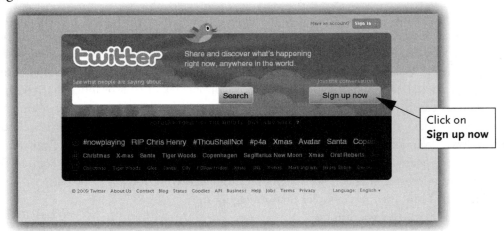

Figure 10.18—Signing Up for Twitter at http://www.twitter.com

Choose a username, password, and other information, as shown in Figures 10.19.

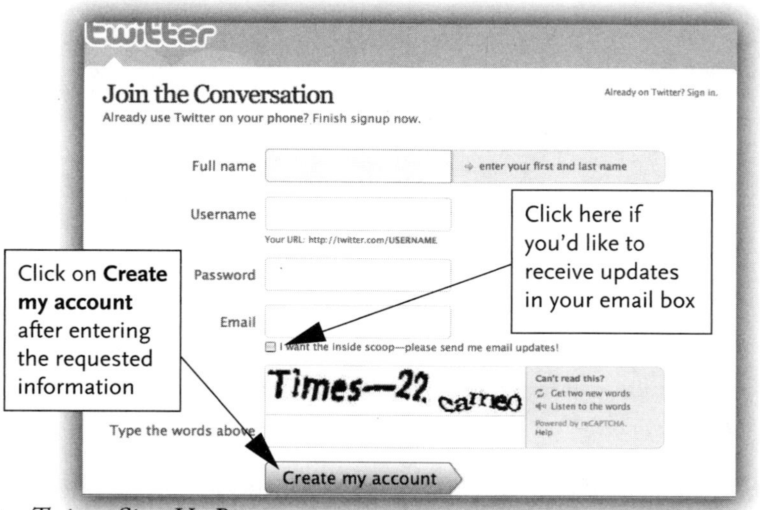

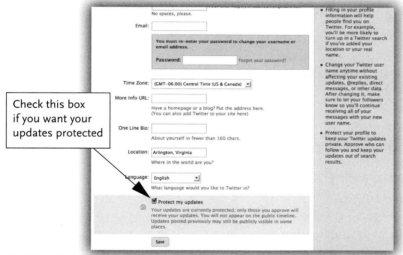

Figure 10.19—Twitter Sign Up Page

After creating your account, you can go to **Settings** and protect your updates if you wish. If you don't protect your updates, anyone in the world can read what you write or "follow you" without getting your permission.

Figure 10.20—Twitter's Settings Page—How to Protect Your Updates

2 Finding people and organizations that you want to "follow" is relatively easy. Simply click on **Find People** and search for the name. We searched for our favorite magazine, *The New Yorker*, as shown in Figure 10.21. Several publications, government agencies, media outlets, and companies have Twitter feeds. If we want to follow *The New Yorker*, in other words, receive its updates, we simply click on **Follow**.

Figure 10.21—How to Follow the New Yorker in Twitter

Figure 10.22 shows an update from *The New Yorker*. It consists of a short statement with a URL to click on for more information.

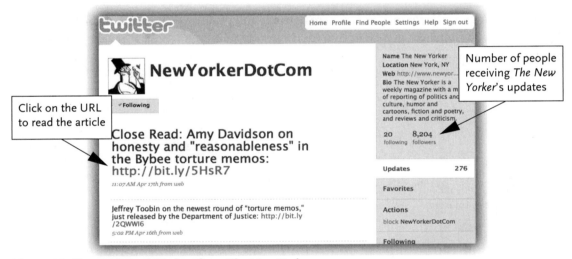

Figure 10.22—A Typical Update from The New Yorker

3   To create your own updates, you must first decide what you want to write. Let's say you found an interesting article that you want to share. We found an article by Clay Shirky, entitled "Ontology is Overrated: Categories, Links, and Tags." The URL of the article is **http://www.shirky.com/writings/ontology_overrated.html**. One limiting factor of Twitter is your posting must be 140 characters or fewer. When your update contains a long URL, you could conceivably use up half of your post with the URL. There are services that take URLs, shorten them, and give you a new unique URL to use instead. One such service is TinyURL, **http://www.tinyurl. com**. Figures 10.23 and 10.24 show how we entered the URL of Shirky's article and were given a new, much shorter URL to use instead.

Figure 10.23—Entering a URL to Shorten in TinyURL.com

After clicking on **Make TinyURL**, as shown in Figure 10.23, a new URL is created immediately, as shown in Figure 10.24.

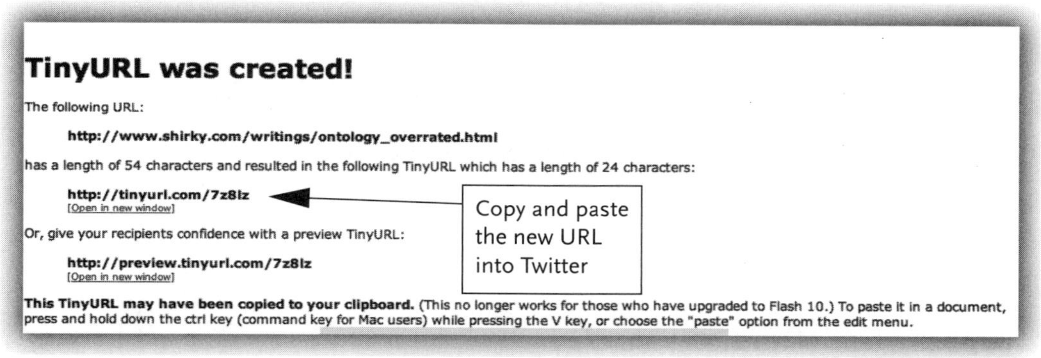

Figure 10.24—New URL Created by TinyURL.com

After you copy the URL that TinyURL created, simply paste it (press **Ctrl** + **V**) into the form in Twitter. Figure 10.25 shows how our "tweet" appears. Simply click on **update** and you've made your first "tweet"!

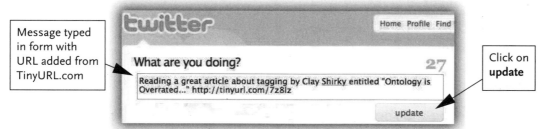

Figure 10.25—Entering an Update, or a "Tweet" in Twitter

Social Bookmarking

Social bookmarking is a method for people to store, organize, search, and manage bookmarks of Web pages on the Internet by using subject headings, or tags, to help manage them. We discussed social bookmarking tools in Chapter 4 in the context of using them to help you organize Web sites that you've found useful for your private needs. To contribute your sites to the rest of the Internet community, you would follow the same instructions outlined there, but make your account public instead of private. You can share your sites with everyone, or you can share them with specified people or groups.

Searching social bookmarking sites such as Delicious, **http://www.delicious.com**, can be a very good way to find important Web sites that others have found useful. If someone has gone to the trouble of bookmarking a site, you can be pretty sure that the site is particularly relevant, especially if others that have similar research interests as you reviewed the sites. For example, you can search Delicious quite easily. Let's say we were looking for information on the open access movement. By searching Delicious, we can find Web sites that others have found particularly useful. Figure 10.26 shows the results of a Delicious search for sites containing the phrase **open access**. The number shown on the right of each site is how many people bookmarked the site.

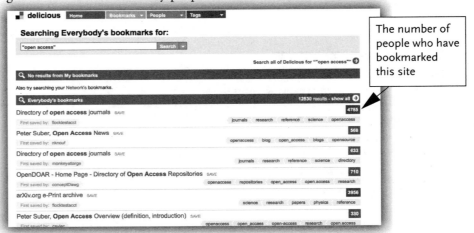

*Figure 10.26—Searching Delicious for Web Sites Tagged **open access***

There are many social bookmarking sites other than Delicious. We have listed a few of the more popular ones here:

- Connotea, **http://www.connotea.org**
- Digg, **http://digg.com**
- Diigo, **http://www.diigo.com**
- StumbleUpon, **http://www.stumbleupon.com**

Discussion Groups and Forums

There are tens of thousands of discussion groups and forums on the Web. For example, if you search on **discussion groups forums** on Google, you'll retrieve over 50 million Web pages! There are discussion boards discussing health issues, consumer products, science, politics—you name it, there is probably a discussion group or forum on that topic. There are several ways to find discussions. If you were interested in reading discussions on arthritis or another health issue, for example, you could do a general search in a search engine using the keywords **health discussion board** or **health discussion group**. An example of a health discussion group portal that results from both of these searches is **Health Message Boards at WebMD.** A screenshot of that portal is shown in Figure 10.27.

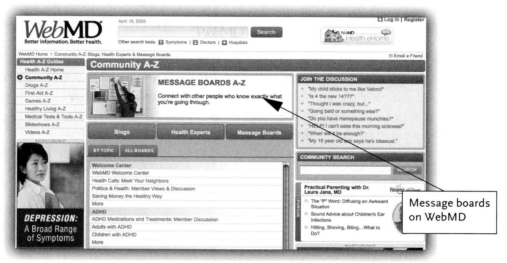

Figure 10.27 —Message Boards on WebMD, at http://www.webmd.com/community

There are other ways to find group discussions, message boards, and forums. We describe a few of the more popular resources below.

- Google Groups, **http://groups.google.com**
    - A free service where groups of people have discussions about common interests. It contains an archive of Usenet newsgroup postings dating back to 1981.
    - You can search existing conversations, join an existing group, or create your own group.
    - You don't need to create a Google account to enjoy many of the useful features of Google Groups, such as reading posts in public groups; searching for groups, posts, or authors; and posting to or joining unrestricted groups via email.
    - Activities that require a Google account include creating and managing your own Google Group, posting to groups via the Web, creating pages and uploading files, and subscribing to Usenet newsgroups.
- Omgili, **http://www.omgili.com**
    - Omgili is a search engine that focuses on Web sites that contain debates, forums, discussion groups, personal experiences, questions and their answers, and more.
    - It covers over 100,000 boards, forums, and other discussion-related resources
- BoardReader, **http://www.boardreader.com**
    - BoardReader was founded in 2000 by engineers and students at the University of Michigan.
    - It allows you to search multiple message boards simultaneously.

Social Networking

Social networking has encouraged new ways to communicate and share information. Social networking is an extremely popular way for people to build online communities to share interests and activities. Millions of people around the world participate in these networks. The most popular social networking site in the United States is Facebook, **http://www.facebook.com**. Another is MySpace, **http://www.myspace.com**. LinkedIn, **http://www.linkedin.com,** is another popular network which provides professional people advantages such as new job leads, networking on work issues, and more. There are also social networking platforms used within the workplace, on company's intranets; for example, Yammer, **http://www.yammer.com**. All of these networking sites are similar in that the individual joining creates a profile. This profile can include varying information, depending on the service. In order to be linked to other people, or to be connected as "friends" the person must verify that the person requesting the connection is truly a "friend." Most social networks allow users to create special groups focusing on special interests. These sites also allow the user to create privacy settings that control who is able to see the user's profile.

Special Interest Social Networking Sites

In addition to these general social networking sites, there are growing number of sites that focus on specific interests. We describe a few of these below:

- LibraryThing, **http://www.librarything.com**
  - LibraryThing allows users to network by sharing books and reviews of those books. You can link yourself with others who own the same books, and learn about books from others who have the same reading interests as you. LibraryThing is free for book collections of 200 or fewer.
- Graduate Junction, **http://www.graduatejunction.net**
  - Graduate Junction was created to connect people in academic communities working on graduate degrees. It's useful to connect with others who are working on the same, or similar research projects.
- Ravelry, **https://www.ravelry.com**
  - Ravelry is a site for knitters, crocheters, designers, spinners, and dyers. It's a place for these people to discuss yarn, tools, pattern information, and get ideas and inspiration from others.
- ResearchGate, **http://www.researchgate.net**
  - ResearchGate is a social networking tool for scientific researchers. It's a way to connect with researchers and collaborate on new discoveries.

Mashups

A *mashup* is a Web page or application that combines information from two or more sources. It combines one set of data with other data to make the original data more meaningful. Mashups are considered an example of Web 2.0 technology because they are result of people participating and manipulating free Web information and making the information richer and more meaningful to others.

An example of a mashup is the map shown in Figure 10.28 found in the "Rivers of the World" mashup, **http://www.rapidmonkey.com**. Click on **Rivers of the World** and choose **Rivers of**

South Africa. Scroll down until you see **Limpopo River**. When we clicked on the balloon, we were able to access a lot of information about this river, including a link to the Wikipedia article that discusses it.

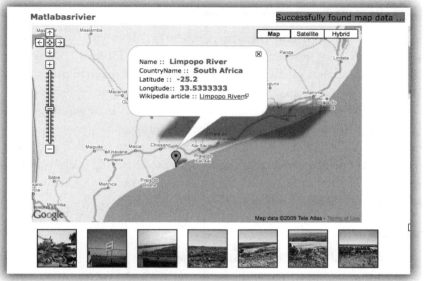

Figure 10.28—Results of Browsing the Rivers of the World Mashup for the Limpopo River at Rapidmonkey.com

Other examples of mashups are:

- HousingMaps, **http://www.housingmaps.com**
    - This site mashes up data from Craigslist (an online classified ad service) and Google Maps.
- GovTrack.us: Tracking the U.S. Congress, **http://govtrack.us**
    - The information on this site is taken from official U.S. government sites such as THOMAS, the official site that documents legislation status, run by the Library of Congress, Project Vote Smart, the U.S. Census Bureau, and many others.
- Fortune100 Best Companies to Work For, **http://www.mibazaar.com/fortune/fortune100.html**
    - This site mashes up a Google map with data from **money.cnn.com** to show where the best companies to work for are located, with other related information.

To find more mashups, see the Programmable Web, **http://programmableweb.com**.

Open Access Movement

According to the Budapest Open Access Initiative, **http://www.soros.org/openaccess/read.shtml,** *open access* can be defined as information that is freely available on the public Internet, and permits users . . .

> . . . to read, download, copy, distribute, print, search, or link to the full text of these articles, crawl them for indexing, pass them as data to software, or use them for any other lawful purpose, without financial, legal, or technical barriers

other than those inseparable from gaining access to the Internet itself. The only constraint on reproduction and distribution, and the only role for copyright in this domain, should be to give authors control over the integrity of their work and the right to be properly acknowledged and cited.

A growing number of academic researchers, scientists, librarians, and others are involved in this movement of making research freely available on the Internet. In the past, most peer-reviewed academic research was solely published in journals that required purchase. Now there are thousands of peer-reviewed academic journals freely available. Digital repositories are another type of information that is rapidly becoming available to the public. These repositories are most often from universities, foundations, research institutes, and other types of organizations. They consist of historical archives, including photographs, datasets, unpublished research, and so forth. As more of these formerly print-only resources are digitized, they are becoming freely available to the public on the Internet. Luckily, there are directories and portals that make it easier for researchers to find these resources. We will list a few of them here.

Open Access Journals

- African Journals Online (AJOL), **http://www.ajol.info**
  AJOL covers over 340 peer-reviewed journals from 25 African countries. These journals cover the full range of academic disciplines, emphasizing health, education, agriculture, science and technology, the environment, and arts and culture.
- Directory of Open Access Journals (DOAJ), **http://www.doaj.org**
  DOAJ offers free, full-text scientific and scholarly peer-reviewed journals. As of the time of this writing, the DOAJ contains over 4,000 journal titles and over 250,000 articles.
- Electronic Journals Library,
  http://rzblx1.uni-regensburg.de/ezeit/index.phtml?lang=en
  Provided by the University Library of Regensburg (Germany), the Electronic Journals Library contains over 43,000 titles, of which over 20,000 journals can be read free of charge.
- Highwire Press (Stanford University), **http://highwire.stanford.edu/lists/freeart.dtl**
  Highwire Press facilitates access to almost two million full-text scholarly articles on medical/biomedical topics.
- Public Library of Science (PLoS), **http://www.plos.org**
  PLoS consists of seven biomedical peer-reviewed research journals. Researchers are urged to submit their articles to this open access database.

Open Access Repositories

- Directory of Open Access Repositories (OpenDOAR), **http://www.opendoar.org**
  OpenDOAR is a directory of thousands of institutional and subject-based archives and repositories from universities and other worldwide organizations.
- AIster, **http://www.oaister.org**
  AIster is a portal to worldwide open archive collections. It includes over 20 million records from 1108 institutions worldwide.
- Registry of Open Access Repositories (ROAR), **http://roar.eprints.org**

ROAR is a place where institutions can record details about their digital repositories, including what software they are using to hold the archives, subject matter of the archives, and more.

Open Courseware

The growth of increased access to academic research has coincided with the trend, starting with the Massachusetts Institute of Technology's Open Courseware program in 2002, of universities posting their course materials for free use by the public. These programs provide free, searchable access to course materials for educators, students, and self-directed learners. The following are some open courseware programs:

- Columbia University, **http://ci.columbia.edu/ci**
- Massachusetts Institute of Technology's MIT Open Courseware, **http://ocw.mit.edu/OcwWeb/web/home/home/index.htm**
- Carnegie-Mellon University's Open Learning Initiative, **http://www.cmu.edu/oli/index.shtml**

For more open courseware, a list is provided by the Online Education Database, **http://oedb.org/library/features/236-open-courseware-collections#OCC**.

If you would like to read more about open access, Peter Suber's blog, Open Access News, **http://www.earlham.edu/~peters/fos/fosblog.html**, is a great resource.

Copyright in a Web 2.0 Environment

Much of what you find on the Web and Internet can be saved in a file on your computer, which makes it easy to share and distribute information to others. Exchanging information was one of the main reasons the Internet began, and it is a desirable activity, but there is a drawback. Free access to information makes it difficult to control unauthorized distribution of anything that's available. Anyone with a Web browser can make an exact digital copy of information. This sometimes is illegal.

Only the owners of information can grant the right to copy or duplicate materials. This is called the ***copyright***. Some documents on the Internet contain a statement asserting the copyright and giving permission for distributing the document in an electronic form, provided it isn't sold or made part of some commercial product. For example, here's a quote from **http://ibiblio.org/expo/vatican.exhibit/exhibit/About.html** describing limitations on the use of the materials in the exhibit "Rome Reborn" offered by the Library of Congress:

> The text and images in the Online Exhibit ROME REBORN: THE VATICAN LIBRARY AND RENAISSANCE CULTURE are for the personal use of students, scholars, and the public. Any commercial use or publication of them is strictly prohibited.

Regardless of whether a Web page is accompanied by a statement asserting copyright, it is still protected by the copyright laws of the United States, the Universal Copyright Convention, or the Berne Union. Most copyright conventions or statutes include a provision that makes it possible for individuals to copy portions of a document for short-term use. This is known as ***fair use***. If information is obtainable on the Internet and there is no charge to access the information, it often can be shared in an electronic form. That certainly doesn't mean you can copy images or documents and make them available on the Internet, make copies and share them in a printed form, or distribute them to several people using email attachments. Quite naturally, many people who create or provide material available on the Internet expect to get credit and/or be paid for their work.

Remember that anything available in electronic form on the Internet or World Wide Web is a copyrighted work, and you need to treat it in the same way as a book, journal article, artwork, play, video, or a piece of recorded music. Just because something is available on the Web doesn't mean that you may copy it. You are allowed to copy the material for personal use, but in almost every case, you cannot use it for commercial purposes without written permission from the copyright holder.

Creative Commons

One alternative to traditional copyright is *Creative Commons*. Creative Commons was developed by a non-profit organization of the same name. As we stated above, most works are protected by copyright, which grants specific rights regarding its use. Creative Commons allows for the copyright owner to license his or her work with varying levels of rights. Authors, artists, scientists, and other creators can mark their work with the freedoms they want it to have. For example, a copyright owner can decide to allow the public to copy and distribute the work and create derivative works, as long as the user cites the work properly and doesn't use it for commercial purposes. The way it works is that the copyright owner consults the Creative Commons Web site, **http://creativecommons.org** and answers questions regarding what level of rights he or she wants to give to others. The copyright owner can insert a hyperlink on his work, which will take the user to the copyright guidelines for that particular work. You can also search Creative Commons for works that authors have agreed can be used for commercial purposes or for works that can be modified or adapted into new creations.

The following are two examples of Web sites using Creative Commons licenses. The first, shown in Figure 10.29, is from TEDTalks, a collection of videos provided by TED (Technology, Entertainment, Design), **http://www.ted.com/talks**. The second is from the White House Web site, **http://www.whitehouse.gov**.

Are TEDTalks copyrighted?
Yes. TEDTalks are distributed under a **Creative Commons (CC) license.** This doesn't replace copyright – which remains undivided with TED Conferences LLC – but it makes the terms more flexible. Anyone is free to download the videos from TED.com; share them with friends; republish or embed them on their website or blog. But this use must be made within the terms of the CC license "Attribution – NonCommercial – NonDerivative."

Click here to read the details of the license

Figure 10.29—The Link to TEDTalk's Creative Commons License Information (http://www.ted.com/pages/view/id/195)

Clicking on **Creative Commons (CC) license**, as shown in Figure 10.29, takes you to the Creative Commons Web site. This is where the details of the TED.com license are available, as shown in Figure 10.30. TED.com has given permission to share the work only if it is attributed and is for noncommercial purposes. You may not alter or transform the work.

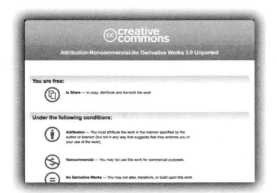

Figure 10.30—Creative Commons License for TED Talks

The second example is from the White House Web site, **http://www.whitehouse.gov**. If you click on the CC (Creative Commons) logo, as shown in Figure 10.31, you will find the details of copyright license chosen by Whitehouse.gov.

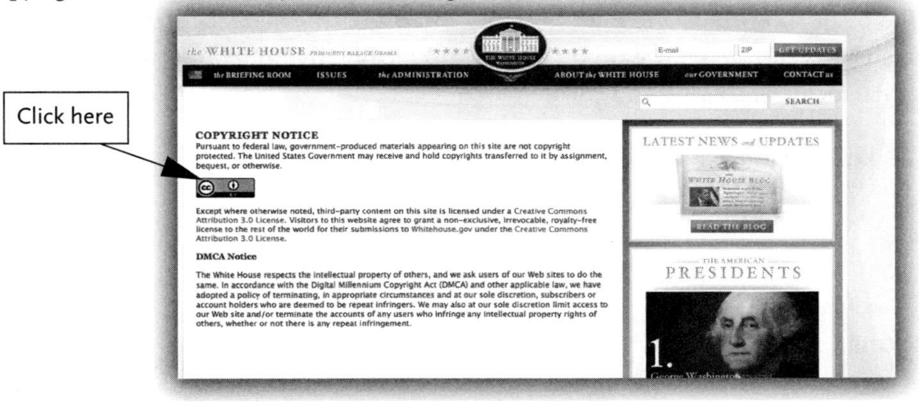

Figure 10.31—Whitehouse.gov's Link to Creative Commons License Information

If you click on the **CC** icon, as shown in Figure 10.31, you'll be taken to the Creative Commons license information for this site, as shown in Figure 10.32. Note that the Whitehouse.gov has given permission to share and adapt the work but you must attribute the work properly.

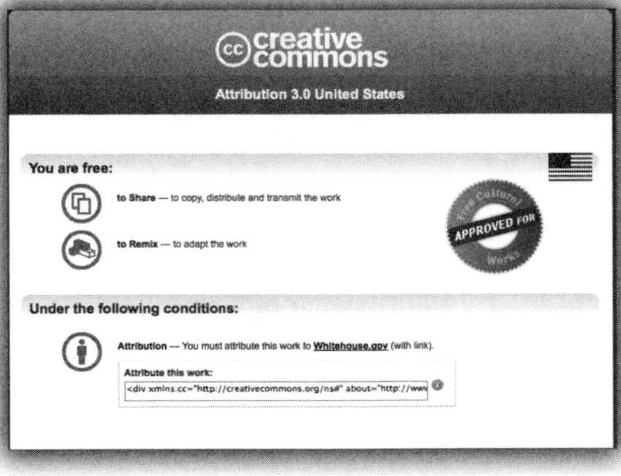

Figure 10.32—Creative Commons License Information for Whitehouse.gov

If you would like to read more about copyright in general and specifically in a digital environment, the following Web sites may be useful:

♦ Copyright and Fair Use (Stanford University), **http://fairuse.stanford.edu**
♦ Copyright and Intellectual Property Rights (University of California, Berkeley), **http://sunsite.berkeley.edu/Copyright**
♦ Copyright Website (Digital section), **http://www.benedict.com/digital/Digital.aspx**
♦ Digital Copyright, by the Center for Democracy and Technology, **http://www.cdt.org/copyright**

Summary

This chapter focused on Web tools that make it easier for people to share information, collaborate on its discovery, edit this information in group environments, transform it into richer forms, and how to protect authors' creative expression. Web 2.0 tools such as wikis, blogs, social bookmarking and networking, and mashups have all made the Web a more dynamic and rapidly changing environment. The open access movement has revolutionized the way many academic researchers publish their research. As the Web moves to become more collaborative and open, we're sure to see many new tools that facilitate sharing and collaboration.

Selected Terms Used in This Chapter

cloud computing	fair use	open access
copyright	mashup	social networking
Creative Commons	microblogging	wiki

Review Questions

Multiple Choice

1. Document sharing sites such as Zoho and Google Docs differ from wikis in that they
   a. are always private.
   b. allow you to work on files in different formats.
   c. require the download of special software.
   d. are not freely accessible.
2. The major advantage of a file collaboration site such as SlideShare is
   a. authors can share their work without sending their files to others via email.
   b. others can learn from an author's work.
   c. the files can be used without attribution.
   d. a and b
   e. none of the above
3. A microblog posts differs from a regular blog post in that
   a. it is much smaller (140–200 characters).
   b. it includes a URL directing the reader to another Web site.
   c. it is not posted immediately.
   d. none of the above

4. TinyURL is a tool that
   a. automatically embeds URLs in Web sites.
   b. shortens URLs to use in blog and microblog postings.
   c. makes it easier to create temporary Web sites.
   d. none of the above
5. Social bookmarking is a way
   a. to find Web sites that others have found useful.
   b. to organize your personal favorite Web sites.
   c. to meet others that have similar research interests.
   d. all of the above

True or False

6. T F Cloud computing is the phenomenon of using software that exists outside one's own computer.
7. T F Creating a blog requires downloading software to your computer.
8. T F Twitter is currently the most popular microblogging tool.
9. T F Twitter profiles must be public.
10. T F Creative Commons is a service that the copyright holder must pay for.

Completion

11. _____ is a popular way for people to build online communities to share interests.
12. A _____ is a Web page or application that combines information from two or more sources.
13. _____ is information that is freely available on the public Internet.
14. _____ allows a copyright holder to license his or her work with varying levels of rights.
15. A _____ is a page or collection of Web pages designed to enable anyone who accesses it to contribute or modify content.

Exercises and Activities

1. Go to Wikimatrix at **http://www.wikimatrix.org**, use the Choice Wizard to locate wiki software with the following attributes: page history availability, WYSISYG (what you see is what you get) functionality, professional support availability, and English language. The wiki should be hosted by someone else. How many wikis meet these requirements?
2. Sign up for a Google account and create a small Web site using Google Sites. Invite a classmate to co-edit the site with you.
3. Sign up for an account with Zoho Writer, **http://www.zoho.com**. Create a new document and share it with a colleague.
4. Search for a recent article about the open access movement. Sign up for Twitter and post a tweet about the article, and include a link to the article's URL. If your tweet goes over 140 characters, use TinyURL.com to make the URL shorter.

5. Search Omgili, **http://www.omgili.com**, for a forum on the topic of post-traumatic stress disorder.

6. Search LibraryThing, **http://www.librarything.com**, for the book titled *Kartography* by Kamila Shamsie. How many people with LibraryThing accounts have this book in their personal libraries?

7. Go to the Programmable Web, **http://programmableweb.com**. Find two U.S. government–related mashup projects and describe each of them.

8. Go to OpenDOAR, **http://www.opendoar.org,** and see if any institutions in your state have a digital repository related to philosophy and religion. If there are none in your state, find another state that has one on this topic.

Privacy and Security
on the Internet and the Web

I t's easy to get excited about using the Internet and the World Wide Web. They're vivacious, interesting, and important places to work, learn, do business, and just have fun. The World Wide Web always seems to have something new. You find not only new resources, but better services and programs, making the Web and the Internet easier to use and more powerful. There's also a great deal of diversity; different cultures, nations, and outlooks are represented on the Web. All these things make for an exciting environment, but we also need to consider the effect of the Internet on our lives, our communities, and society as its use becomes more widespread.

The Internet and the World Wide Web have grown rapidly from a research project into part of the infrastructure of daily life that involves over a billion people worldwide. Much of the Internet's usefulness comes from the fact that users and service providers depend on each other and need to support each other. Hopefully, that sort of sharing and respect will continue. Your behavior, your expectations of others, and your activities will make the difference. There are also genuine concerns about privacy and security on the Internet. You'll see that some of the reasons for a lack of privacy and security are based on the nature of the technology that makes up the Internet. In some cases there are ways you can use technology to give more privacy and security. Regardless of the technology there are matters of law, ethics, and human behavior that also come into play.

Privacy

Your initial response might be that you expect the same protection of your privacy on the Internet as you have in your other dealings in society. In some situations you will find your privacy determined by existing laws and modes of behavior.

When you sign up or register with some services (such as an email provider or a social networking site) you often have to give some information about yourself. Sometimes this is only your name and email address, but some services ask for a mailing address, phone number, zip code, your age, your income, and so on. There are two things to consider here. First, is the service worth the cost of giving information about yourself, and just as important, what will be done with the information? Are you giving away your privacy? Check on these issues before you give information about yourself.

Social networks such as Facebook make it easy for you to connect with your friends. They also expose some of your comments to all the friends of a friend of yours. These connections can be used to create a profile of an individual, by putting together information about their friends. An old adage is "You are known by the company you keep," and it is relatively easy to see the types of people you are connected with on the Internet. This isn't stopping us from using the Web and social networking sites, but we do need to remember that we are sacrificing some of our privacy by participating in these social networking sites.

Who owns your email? If you use an email service, Internet services, or a computer network that's provided for by your employer, then your employer may monitor all of that. Several courts in the U.S. have ruled that an employer that provides an email service may monitor, read, or save an employee's email. The same holds true for monitoring the use of the Web or other Internet services, or for use of a network. In fact, an employer may do this without notifying the person being monitored. That's not a good way to develop a working relationship, but it is legal. On the other hand, if you are a student (and not an employee) at a college or university your email privacy is protected by law as mentioned below.

You need to become familiar with the policies and rules of operations (if they exist) for the organization(s) that provide you with any of the several Internet services. Some measure of privacy can be provided for email and other communication on the Internet, but you need to know that absolute privacy isn't guaranteed by the technology or the law.

Email Privacy

When you send a message by email, the message is separated into packets and the packets are sent out over the Internet. The number of packets depends on the size of the message, since each packet on a particular network has a standard size. Each message has the Internet address of the sender (your address) and the address of the recipient. Packets from a single message may take different routes to the destination, or may take different routes at different times. This works well for the Internet and for you. Since packets are generally sent through the best path, depending on the traffic load on the Internet, the path doesn't depend on certain systems being in operation, and all you have to give is the address of the destination.

The packets making up an email message may pass through several different systems before reaching their destination. This means there may be some places between you and the destination where the packets could be intercepted and examined. If you're using a computer system shared by others or if the system at the destination is shared by others, there is usually someone (a system administrator) capable of examining all the messages. So, in the absence of codes of ethics or without the protection of law, email could be very public. Needless to say, you shouldn't be reading someone else's email. Most system administrators adopt a code of ethics under which they will not examine email unless they feel it's important to support the system(s) they administer. The truth of the matter is they are generally too busy to bother reading other people's mail. But, as we noted above, if you're using an email system provided by your employer then it is legal for your employer to monitor your email.

Electronic Communications Privacy Act

One example of a law to ensure the privacy of email is the Electronic Communications Privacy Act (ECPA) passed in 1986 by Congress. It prohibits anyone from intentionally intercepting, using, and/or disclosing email messages without the sender's permission. The ECPA was passed to protect individuals from having their private messages accessed by government officers or others without legal permission. That bill extended the protections that existed for voice communications to non-voice communications conveyed through wires or over the airwaves. You can, of course, give your permission for someone to access your email. However, according to the ECPA, law enforcement officials or others cannot access your email in stored form (on a disk or tape) without a warrant, and electronic transmission of your email can't be intercepted or "tapped" without a court order. The ECPA does allow a system administrator to access users' email on a computer system if it's necessary for the operation or security of the system. The ECPA then gives the system administrator the responsibility to allow no access to email passing within or through a system without a court order or warrant. She can and indeed should refuse any requests to examine email unless the proper legal steps are followed.

Other laws, for example the "PATRIOT Act" of 2001, have amended the ECPA to make it easier for court or law enforcement officials to intercept and monitor email and other electronic communications. In fact, according to investigative reporter James Bamford, the National Security Agency is constructing two massive data-storage facilities, one in Utah and another in San Antonio, Texas. The Texas location is reported to be nearly the size of the Alamodome; the Utah construction will be two million square feet. There is every reason to believe that full-scale email storage, if not surveillance, will be in practice in the very near future, if it is not already underway.

Encryption

When you send a message by email it's often transmitted in the same form you typed it. Even though it may be unethical or illegal for someone else to read it, the message is in a form that's easy to read. This is similar to sending a message written on a postcard through the postal service. One way to avoid this is to use encryption to put a message into an unreadable form. The characters in the message can be changed by substitution or scrambling, usually based on some secret code. The message can't be read unless the code and method of encryption are known. The code is called a key. Many messages are encoded by a method called public key encryption. If you encrypt a message and send it on to someone, that person has to know the key to decode your message. If the key is also sent by email, it might be easy to intercept the key and decode the encrypted message.

With public key encryption there are two keys, one public and the other private. The public key needs to be known. To send a message to a friend, you use her or his public key to encrypt the message. Your friend then uses her or his private key to decode the message after receiving it.

Suppose you want to send an encrypted message to your friend Milo. He tells you his public key; in fact, there's no harm if he tells everybody. You write the message and then encrypt it using Milo's public key. He receives the message and then uses his private key to decode it. It doesn't matter who sent the message to Milo as long as it was encrypted with his public key. Also, even if the message is intercepted, it can't be read without knowing Milo's private key. It's up to him to keep that secret. Likewise, if he wanted to respond, he would use your public key to encrypt the message. You would use your private key to decode it.

You can obtain a version of public key encryption software called PGP, for Pretty Good Privacy. It's freely available to individuals and may be purchased for commercial use. There are some licensing restrictions on the use of the commercial versions in the United States and Canada. Furthermore, U.S. State Department regulations prohibit the export of some versions of this program to other countries. In fact, current restrictions in the United States prohibit the export of most encryption methods, while other countries allow the export of encryption methods and algorithms. Some people feel strongly that these policies should be changed for the sake of sharing information and for the sake of allowing common encryption of sensitive and business messages, but others don't agree.

To read more about PGP, take a look at one or more of these:

◆ How PGP Works, **http://www.pgpi.org/doc/pgpintro**.
◆ Where to Get PGP (Pretty Good Privacy), **http://www.cryptography.org/getpgp.htm**.

One issue that needs to be resolved is whether it should be possible for law enforcement or other government officials to decode encrypted messages. Some argue that because of the need to detect criminal action or in the interests of national security, the means to decode any messages should be available to the appropriate authorities. Others argue that individuals have the right to privacy in their communications. In the United States, and other countries, there have been cases of government-approved surveillance and interception of email regardless of laws protecting privacy. These have been carried out in the name of national security.

Here's a list of some extensive resources for information about electronic privacy:

◆ 6.805/STS085: Readings on Encryption and National Security, **http://groups.csail.mit.edu/mac/classes/6.805/readings-crypto.html**.
◆ 6.805/STS085: Readings on Privacy Implications of Computer Networks, **http://groups.csail.mit.edu/mac/classes/6.805/readings-privacy.html**.
◆ EPIC Online Guide to Privacy Resources, **http://epic.org/privacy/privacy_resources_faq.html**.

Privacy on the Web

It's easy to get the impression that we're browsing the Web and using Internet services in an anonymous manner. But that's not the case. Every time you visit a Web site some information about your computer system is transmitted to the server. When you fill out a form the information you provide is passed to a server. Some Web sites track the activities of users through the use of cookies, information that's passed from the computer that's using a Web browser to a Web server. You also need to be aware of the risks involved with giving out personal information through email, chat groups, and forms. Since it may be difficult to know with whom you are communicating, you especially need to be careful about disclosing personal information. Children especially need to know about and be informed of the risks and dangers involved in using the Internet.

What Happens When You Go to a Web Site—What the Server Knows

When you go to a Web site, either by clicking on a hyperlink or by typing in a URL in the location field, your browser (the client program) sends a request to a Web server. This request includes the IP address of your computer system, the URL of the file or Web page you've requested, the time the request was made, and whether the request was successful. If you clicked on a hyperlink from a

Web page, the URL of the Web page is also passed to the server. All of this information is kept in log files on the server. It's possible to have the log files analyzed and track all access to a Web server.

The Trail Left on Your Computer

We've seen that each server keeps log files to identify requests for Web pages. So in that sense you leave a trail of your activities on each of the Web servers that you contact. There's also a trail of your activities kept on the computer you use to access the Web. Recently accessed Web pages and a list of the URLs accessed are kept in the cache—a folder or directory that contains recently viewed Web pages, images, and other resources—and the history list. If you're using a computer to access the Web in a public place, such as a lab or library, then it's possible for someone to check on your activities.

Cache

Most Web browsers keep copies of recently accessed Web pages, images, and other files. Firefox and other browsers call this the cache; Microsoft Internet Explorer calls these "temporary Internet files." When you return to a Web page you've visited recently, the browser first checks to see if it's available in the cache and retrieves it from your computer rather than retrieving it from a remote site. It's much faster to retrieve a Web page from the cache rather than from a remote site. This is convenient, but it also leaves a record of your activities. It is possible to clear the cache or remove the temporary files.

If you're using Firefox on a PC, click on **Tools** in the menu bar, select **Options**, select **Advanced**, then click on the tab **Network** to work with the cache. If you are using Firefox on a Mac, Click on **Firefox** in the menu bar, select **Preferences**, then click on **Advanced** and then select **Network**.

History List

The Web browser keeps a record of the path you've taken to get to the current location. To see the path and select a site from it, click on **History** in the menu bar. The browser also keeps a list of all the Web pages visited recently in the history list. This list is kept around for a time period specified in days. You can set the number of days an item may be kept on the list. You can also delete the files from the history list. To set options for the history list, select **Options** (or **Preferences** if you are using a Mac) as above and then select **Privacy**.

Cookies

A cookie is information that's passed to a Web server by the Web browser program. In the early days of Web browsers, Netscape developed the terms and methods for working with cookies. A Web server requests and/or writes a cookie to your computer only if you access a Web page that contains the commands to do that.

Cookies are sometimes viewed as an invasion of privacy, but they are useful to you in some cases. Suppose you want to visit a site frequently that requires you to give a password or a site that you can customize to match your preferences. The protocol HTTP is used when you visit a Web site. When a Web page is requested, a connection is made between the client and the server, the server delivers a Web page, and the connection is terminated once the page has been transmitted. If you visit a site again, the server, through HTTP, has no information about a previous visit. Cookies can be used to keep track of your password or keep track of some preferences you've set for every visit to that site. That way you don't have to enter the information each time you visit.

To get more information and the latest news about cookies visit Cookie Central, **http://www. cookiecentral.com**.

Private Browsing

Modern browsers give you the option of turning off the cache, the history list, and cookies by switching to a "private browsing" mode. This way you can use a browser without it keeping track of what you have been using it for. This doesn't stop all forms of monitoring your use of the Internet. Server requests are still tracked, someone can still look over your shoulder as you type, and the packets that get sent across the Internet to and from your computer can still be traced.

There are tools available to give you completely anonymous use of a browser, with packets going to a secure proxy service that handles them so that the possibility of tracking is minimized. Some add-ons to Firefox for this purpose are "FoxyProxy," "TorButton," and "BetterPrivacy." The Web site Free Anonymous Surfing, Free Anonymous Proxies, **http://www.thefreecountry.com/security/ anonymous.shtml**, is a good source for information about using your browser anonymously.

Spyware, Adware, Hijacked Web Browsers

Some programs that you use on your computer include code that sends information from your system to another one on the Internet. This code can be used to report your Web activity, such as which sites you visit. That is perfectly legal in the U.S. and it can be done without your knowledge, even though most people wouldn't choose to allow that type of activity if they were given a choice. That type of software is called spyware or adware. The included code is often used for marketing purposes, and in that way it's similar to including advertisements with a program or Web site. The same techniques can be used to keep track of all your keystrokes, thus recording and transmitting user names and passwords (that may be illegal!), or it can be used to involve your computer system in some distributed computing effort. In some cases the options or preferences on your browser may be changed—such as changing the URL for your home page—by visiting a Web site designed to do just that. Scary stuff!

You can learn more about this topic by reading the Wikipedia entry "Spyware," **http:// en.wikipedia.org/wiki/Spyware**. More importantly, you'll want to install a program that will detect and remove spyware. There are several good ones available, and like antivirus software they need to be regularly updated. One of the most highly recommended ones is SpyBot - S&D. It is distributed with no required fee, but if you find it useful make a donation to support the software. The URL to download SpyBot is **http://www.safer-networking.org/en/download/index.html**.

Computer and Network Security

When you use a computer system connected to the Internet, you're able to reach a rich variety of sites and information. By the same token, any system connected to the Internet can be reached in some manner by any of the other computer systems connected to the Internet. Partaking of the material on the Internet also means that you have to be concerned about the security of your computer system and other systems. The reason for the concern about your system is obvious—you don't want unauthorized persons accessing your information or information belonging to others who share your system. You want to protect your system from malicious or unintentional actions that could destroy stored information or halt your system. You don't want others masquerading as you. You need to be concerned about the security of other systems so you can have some faith in the information you retrieve from those systems, and so you can conduct some business transactions. A lack of security results in damage, theft, and what may be worse in some cases, a lack of confidence or trust.

Maintaining security becomes more important as we use the Internet for commercial transactions or transmitting sensitive data. There is always the chance that new services introduced to the Internet won't be completely tested for security flaws or that security problems will be discovered. While it's exciting to be at the cutting edge, there's some virtue in not adopting the latest service or the latest version of software until it has been around for a while. This gives the Internet community a chance to discover problems. Several agencies are dedicated to finding, publicizing, and dealing with security problems. One site that does this is maintained by the U.S. Department of Energy.

Use your Web browser to access the Computer Security Division: Computer Security Resource Center (CSRC) of the National Institute of Standards and Technology by using the URL **http://csrc.nist.gov/index.html**.

You don't need to be paranoid about security, but you do need to be aware of anything that seems suspicious. Report any suspicious activity or changes to your directory or files to your system administrator. The system administrator can often take actions to track down a possible break in security. Be suspicious if you're asked for your password at unusual times. You should be asked for it only when you log in. Never give your password to anyone. If a program changes its behavior in terms of requiring more information from you than it did before, it could be an unauthorized user replaced the original program with another. This is called a Trojan horse, because of the similarity of the program to the classic Greek tale. What appears to be benign could hide some malicious actions or threats.

Passwords

If you have to log on to a computer system that is connected to the Internet, then one of your primary defenses against intrusion is your password.

To choose a password that will be difficult to guess, follow these guidelines:

◆ Choose a password that's at least six characters long. You'll also want to use a password that contains upper- and lowercase letters and some nonalphabetic characters. Additionally, the password shouldn't represent a word, and it shouldn't be something that's easy to identify with you such as a phone number, room number, birth date, or license number. Some bad choices are Skippy, 3451234a, or gloria4me. Better choices might be All452on, jmr!pmQ7, or sHo$7otg. Naturally, you have to choose something you'll remember.

◆ Never write down your password; doing that makes it easy to find.

Persons who try to gain unauthorized access to a system are called crackers. A cracker will, by some means, get a copy of the password file for a system containing the names of all the users along with their passwords. (In some cases the permissions on a password file are set so anyone can read it. This is necessary for certain programs to run. Fortunately, the passwords are encrypted.) A cracker who gets a copy of a password file will run a program that attempts to guess the encrypted passwords. If a password is an encrypted version of a word, a word in reverse order, or a word with one numeral or punctuation mark, it is not too difficult for the program to decipher it. If a cracker has one password on a system, she can gain access to that login name and from there possibly go to other portions of the system.

♦ In addition to creating a good password, you also need to change it regularly.

Firewalls

Because connecting a network to the Internet allows access to that network, system administrators and other persons concerned with network security are very concerned about making that connection. One device or part of a network that can help enhance security is called a firewall. A firewall can be a separate computer, a router, or some other network device that allows certain packets into a network. (Remember that all information is passed throughout the Internet as packets.) By using a firewall and configuring it correctly, only certain types of Internet services can be allowed through to the network. Organizations with firewalls often place their Web, FTP, and other servers on one part of their network and put a firewall system between those servers and the rest of the network. The firewall restricts access to the protected internal network by letting through only packets associated with certain protocols. Email can still be delivered and sometimes Telnet to the internal network is allowed. If you are on the protected portion of the network, behind the firewall, then you can access Internet and Web sites on the Internet, but they may not be able to gain direct access to you. Firewalls also perform logging and auditing functions so that if security is breached, the source of the problem may be determined. You can find out more about firewalls at the site Internet Firewalls: Frequently Asked Questions, **http://www.interhack.net/pubs/fwfaq**.

If you have a high-speed connection to the Internet in your home, through a cable modem, DSL, or satellite connection you should consider installing a personal firewall whether you have set up a network or not. That high-speed connection is always (unless the power is off) connected to the Internet, and so your home computer or network is a possible target for others who look for systems they can use for other purposes or systems from which they can steal information. Microsoft offers some good advice about installing and using a firewall at home. It's available at Microsoft Online Safety, **http://www.microsoft.com/protect/default.aspx**.

Viruses and Worms

One type of program that causes problems for Internet users is called a virus. A virus doesn't necessarily copy your data or attempt to use your system. However, it can make it difficult or impossible to use your system. A virus is a piece of code or instructions that attaches itself to existing programs. Just like a biological virus, a computer virus can't run or exist on its own, but must be part of an executing program. When these programs are run, the added instructions are also executed. Sometimes the virus does nothing more than announce its presence; in other cases the virus erases files from your disk. A virus moves from system to system by being part of an executable program. A worm is a program that replicates itself by spreading from one computer on a network to another, usually making many copies of itself. That way it steals resources from the host system, slowing it down or doing other damage. Viruses and worms are spread as part of some program that when executed on your computer infects your computer system and possibly others on your network. These are often spread through programs that are attachments to email. Sometimes they are disguised as images, word processing documents, or spreadsheets. In any case,

- **DO NOT CLICK ON AN ATTACHMENT TO AN EMAIL UNLESS YOU ARE EXPECTING THE ATTACHMENT,**
- **EVEN IF YOU KNOW THE PERSON WHOSE EMAIL ADDRESS WAS USED TO SEND AN ATTACHMENT.**

Some viruses or worms, once they infect a computer system, send forged mail with malicious attachments from addresses in the address book of an infected computer to other addresses in the address book. So, never click on or open an attachment unless you know what it is. Seems simple, doesn't it? Still, that is the most common way that viruses are spread.

It is absolutely necessary that you have some antivirus software installed on your computer system. Use that software to scan your system for viruses, and to scan incoming mail and programs you load onto your system for known viruses. Once you have the antivirus software, it is important to keep it up to date, so new viruses are detected before they infect your computer system.

Getting documents and images from other sites on the Internet won't bring a virus to your system. A virus comes only from running programs on your system. Viruses can exist in executable programs and also have been found in word-processing documents that contain portions of code called macros.

For more information on viruses, check the hyperlinks at Virus Bulletin: Independent Malware Advice, **http://www.virusbtn.com/index**.

Other Concerns

There are lots of other things to be concerned about when we think about security on a computer and a network. If you engage in peer-to-peer networks, you are likely exchanging files with another computer system. That is similar to the activity in a client-server situation, such as the relationship between a Web browser (the client) and a Web server, but in that situation files are sent from the server to the client. In a peer-to-peer relationship files are exchanged both ways, so that you not only open your system to receive files, but you also allow other computer systems to copy files from your system. Without appropriate controls private files can be copied from your computer, and malicious programs can be installed there. If you use an IM (instant messaging) program, you may be allowing people to send you files or accept files form you as part of a peer-to-peer relationship.

You will want to limit that activity to times when you explicitly permit it. Just as in the physical world, the virtual world of the Internet is filled with scams that attempt to swindle people out of money, and hoaxes that try to trick people into accepting spyware and viruses. Microsoft does not distribute security patches via email. Don't click on an attachment that claims to be one. Banks, credit card companies, EBay, PayPal, and other commercial or financial organizations don't send email asking you to verify or update your account by providing detailed information involving your bank account number, credit card number, and user names and passwords. Even if it looks like the URL they ask you to click on is legitimate, don't fall for those scams. You need to be aware that people use the Internet to trick others, and be careful in your dealings.

Giving Out Information About Yourself and Your Family

There are a number of situations in which you may be asked or tempted to give out personal information. These can range from being asked to fill out a form to download some software or sign up for a service on the Web to being asked for your address or phone number through email or a chat group. Any information you put into a form will be passed to a Web server and find its way into a database. Disclosing your street address to a business sometimes results in your receiving junk mail, and disclosing your email address may result in your getting unsolicited junk email, or spam as it's called. You can't be sure how the information will be used or marketed unless the organization gathering the data makes some explicit guarantees. We hear about and come across situations of fraudulent practices and schemes that swindle money from unsuspecting individuals in our daily lives, and we're just as likely to come across those types of situations when we're using the Internet. It's relatively easy to create an Internet or Web presence that makes an individual, a company, or an organization appear to be legitimate and trustworthy. Because of this we need to be all the more skeptical and cautious when conducting personal or commercial dealings on the Internet.

More dangerous situations can arise when we develop a relationship with someone through email or a chat group. These can arise because when we're communicating with someone on the Internet most of the communication is through text. We don't get to hear the person's voice or see them. We may see a picture, they may tell us about themselves, but we may never know with whom we are communicating. For example, I may be involved in a long series of email messages or have several conversations in a chat room with a person who claims to be my age and gender. The person may even send me a photograph. It could be that the person is totally misrepresenting their true self. So we need to be very careful about giving out any personal information, and we certainly wouldn't make arrangements to meet the person without having the meeting take place in a public location and without taking other precautions.

Children particularly need to discuss these issues with their parents, and they need to understand clearly stated rules about not giving out any personal information or telling someone where they go to school or play.

The Web site NetSmartz, **http://www.netsmartz.org**, is a good place to find information about Internet safety issues for children, teens, and parents.

Common sense tells us not to give out personal information, home phone numbers, or home addresses to people we don't know. We're likely not to do that in our daily lives when we don't know the person who is asking for the information, and it is just as important to apply the same rules when we're using the Internet or the World Wide Web.

The Internet and the World Wide Web give us lots of opportunities for learning, recreation, and communication. With the Internet and the Web becoming more significant parts of our lives, paying attention to situations that affect our security and privacy becomes more important. We don't need to be rude or unfriendly, but we do need to be careful, safe, and secure.

glossary

404 error A response code or error transmitted by a Web server to a client when a requested Web page or file is not present on the server.

acceptable use policy Within the context of the Internet, a policy that states the proper or acceptable uses of a computer network.

address bar The pane in the browser window of Mozilla Firefox that holds the current document's URL. You can type a URL in this box and press Enter to access a Web page. *See also* location field.

all-in-one search tool A tool that provides search forms for several search engines and directories all in one site. The tool also provides hyperlinks, which allow you to go to the services directly.

annotated directory Often referred to as a virtual library, this type of directory has brief summaries, descriptions, ratings, or reviews attached to Web pages and subject guides.

annotation A brief summary or description of a Web page or of any work listed in a database.

asynchronous communication Communication where the sender and receiver don't participate at the same time, for example, email or voicemail.

attachment A file that is sent as part of an email message but that is not part of the main message. Usually images, programs, or word-processing files are sent as attachments, because most email programs allow only plain text in the body of a message.

avatar An icon, image, or figure that you can use to represent yourself in a chat room.

bibliographic database An online database that includes citations that describe and identify titles, dates, authors, and other parts of written works. It doesn't contain the full text of the information itself. Some bibliographic databases are annotated, which means there is a brief summary of each work listed.

blog A Web site that is updated frequently with new information about a particular subject or range of subjects. Entries can be provided by the site owner, taken from other Web sites or outside sources, or contributed by users. Content is displayed in reverse chronological order, and comments from readers are often encouraged. While most blogs are text-based, there are also blogs that focus on music, art, video and audio.

blogroll A list of blogs that a blog writer, or blogger, recommends to others.

bookmark A hyperlink that is saved in the bookmark list, a file that you can access with your browser. You can use bookmarks to keep track of favorite or important sites and to return there whenever you are using your browser. *See also* favorite.

Boolean logic Search expressions that use Boolean operators (AND, OR, and NOT) in the search expression. Especially helpful in multifaceted or specific topics, Boolean operators help expand or narrow the scope of your search. A search for rivers OR lakes returns all documents with both words or either word in them. A search for rivers AND lakes returns documents with both words in them. A search for rivers AND lakes NOT swamps returns only documents that mention both rivers and lakes but omits those that also mention swamps.

browsing The process of going from one hyperlink to another on the World Wide Web. You can browse indiscriminately, or you can do structured browsing, using a hierarchical subject list in a directory.

cache A portion of memory (either in RAM or on a disk) set aside to hold the items retrieved most recently. For a Web browser, this refers to recent Web pages and images. The cache is used so that items may be retrieved more quickly without going back to the Internet. A browser can be set so that, in case an item hasn't changed, it will retrieve the item from the cache.

certificate authority A company that guarantees the identity of the holder of a digital certificate. A certificate is attached to a message or Web page and can be used to guarantee the authenticity of information.

chat room A conference or forum that allows two or more people to converse with each other at the same time by taking turns typing messages.

client/server The interaction between a system that requests information (the client) and another system that provides it (the server). The browser is the client, and a computer at the site that provides the information is the server.

cloud computing The phenomenon of storing information on servers outside of your own computer and using Internet-based software to access and manage it.

commercial database A database that requires you to pay a subscription cost before accessing it. *See also* proprietary database.

Communications Decency Act of 1996 Legislation approved by Congress that made it a criminal offense to include potentially indecent or offensive material on the Internet. The U.S. Supreme Court ruled in June of 1997 that this act abridged the freedom of speech that is protected by the First Amendment, and the act was ruled unconstitutional.

conferencing A conferencing system generally uses text, audio, and video for holding group meetings and uses protocols that allow for these means of synchronous communication on the Internet.

content area The part of a Web browser window that contains the current Web page; it contains images, text, or hyperlinks.

cookie A relatively small piece of information that is initially placed on a client's computer by a Web server. Once a cookie is present, the same Web server may read or rewrite the cookie. A Web server requests or writes a cookie to your computer only if you access a Web page that contains the commands to do that. Cookies are used to store information such as your login name and password or information about what portions of a Web site were visited on your computer. Sometimes viewed as an invasion of privacy, cookies are useful to you in some cases. Cookies can be used to keep track of your password or keep track of some preferences you've set for every visit to that site. You can set preferences in your browser to accept or reject cookies.

copyright The right to copy or duplicate material such as images, music, and written works. Only the owners of the information can grant this right. Regardless of whether information on the Internet or a Web page is accompanied by a statement asserting copyright, it is still protected by the copyright laws of the United States, the Universal Copyright Convention, or the Berne Union.

data transfer rate   The speed at which a circuit or communications line can transfer information, usually measured in bits per second (bps).

default setting   The configuration a search engine uses unless you override the setting by specifying another configuration. For example, in most search engines, the Boolean operator OR is the assumed relationship between two words unless you type AND between the words.

delimited format   A format often used to store tables of data. The data fields are separated by commas, tabs, semicolons, or some other delimiter. Spreadsheet programs usually include the facilities to import data that is in delimited format.

digital certificate   A device that is used to encrypt and decrypt information, and to guarantee the identity of the sender and the authenticity of the information.

directory   A topical list of Internet resources, arranged hierarchically. Directories are meant to be browsed, but they can also be searched. Directories differ from search engines in one major way—the human element involved in collecting and updating the information.

directory database   A database that provides brief descriptive information about people, businesses, places, and other facts.

discussion group   A group that discusses a single topic via email messages. An individual subscribes to or joins a discussion group electronically, and all messages sent to the group are distributed to the members by email.

domain name   The Internet name for a network or computer system. The name consists of a sequence of characters separated by periods, such as **www.mwc.edu**. The domain name is often the first part of a URL following **://**. For example, the domain name in the URL **http://sunsite. unc.edu/herbmed/culiherb.html is sunsite.unc.edu**.

download   To transfer or copy a file from another computer (the remote computer) to the computer you're using (the local computer). This term is often applied to the process of retrieving a file from a software library or FTP archive.

duplicate detection   An output feature of some search engines and meta-search tools that automatically filters out of your search results any URLs that are duplicated elsewhere in the results.

ECPA (Electronic Communications Privacy Act)   The U.S. law that prevents U.S. investigative agencies from intercepting or reading email messages without first obtaining a warrant.

electronic mail (email)   A basic Internet service that allows users to exchange messages electronically.

email discussion group   *See* discussion group.

emoticon   A symbol that can be typed using one or more characters to foster more expressive and efficient communication. For example, :-) and :) are used to represent a grin or smile. These are also used to denote that a sentence is to be interpreted as a joke.

encryption   A procedure to convert a file or message from its original form to one that can only be read by the intended recipient.

fair use   A provision in most copyright conventions or statutes that makes it possible for individuals to copy portions of a document or other piece of work for short-term use.

FAQ (frequently asked questions)   A list of commonly asked questions and answers on a specific topic. A FAQ is often associated with Usenet newsgroups, but several search tools also include a FAQ file. This, and online help, is usually the first place you should look to find answers.

favorite   A hyperlink that is saved in the favorites list. You can use favorites to keep track of useful or important sites and to return there whenever you are using your browser. *See also* bookmark.

field   Part of a Web page or bibliographic record that is designated for a particular kind of data or text.

field searching   A strategy in which you limit a search to a particular field. In a search engine, you might search only the URL field. In a library catalog, you could search for items by author, title, subject, call number, or any other data element that was designated as a field. By narrowing the scope of searchable items, field searching helps to eliminate the chance of retrieving irrelevant information.

file name extension   The end of a file name in some operating systems where the name of a file ends with a period followed by (usually) two to four letters. The extension is used to associate an application program with the file. For example, the file containing this glossary is named glossary. doc. The file name extension is .doc. Clicking on the name of the file automatically opens the file with the Microsoft Word word-processing software.

filter   Software that filters out certain Web sites from the results of a search.

firewall   A security device or system, usually a combination of hardware and software meant to protect a local network from intruders from the Internet.

flame   An email message or article in a Usenet newsgroup that's meant to insult someone or provoke controversy. This term is also applied to messages which contain strong criticism of or disagreement with a previous message or article.

folksonomy   Words and phrases that users attach to Web resources. These words or phrases are chosen freely by individuals rather than using a controlled vocabulary invented by someone else.

frame   Some Web pages are divided into rectangular regions called frames. Each frame has its own scroll bar, and in fact, each frame represents an individual Web page.

freeware   A software program that's available for use without any charge. This doesn't mean the program isn't copyrighted. Usually, the originator retains the copyright. Anyone can use it, but the program can't be legally sold or distributed without permission.

frequently asked questions (FAQ) *See* FAQ.

FTP (File Transfer Protocol) A means of transferring or sharing files across the Internet from one computer system to another.

full-text database   A database that contains the full text of the information it describes.

full-text indexing   A search engine feature in which every word, significant or insignificant, is indexed and retrievable through a search.

group address   The address to use to send email to each member of a discussion group, interest group, listserv list, or mailing list.

hidden Internet   *See* invisible Web.

hierarchy   A list of subjects in a directory. The subjects are organized in successive ranks with the broadest listed first and with more specific aspects or subdivisions listed below.

high precision/high recall   A phenomenon that occurs during a search when you retrieve all the relevant documents in the database and retrieve no unwanted ones.

high precision/low recall   A phenomenon that occurs when a search yields a small set of hits. Although each one may be very relevant to the search topic, some relevant documents will be missed.

history list   A list of Internet sites, services, and resources that have been accessed through a Web browser during recent sessions.

home page   The first screen or page of a site accessible through a Web browser.

HTML (Hypertext Markup Language)   The format used for writing documents to be viewed with a Web browser. Items in the document can be text, images, sounds, or links to other HTML documents, sites, services, and resources on the Web.

HTTP (Hypertext Transfer Protocol)   The standard protocol that World Wide Web servers and clients use to communicate.

hyperlink   A word, phrase, image, or region of an image that is often highlighted or colored differently and that can be selected as part of a WWW page. Each hyperlink represents another Web page; a location in the current Web page; an image, audio, video, or multimedia file; or some other resource on the World Wide Web. When the hyperlink is selected, it activates the resource that it represents.

hypermedia   An extension to hypertext that includes images, audio, and other media.

hypertext   A way of viewing or working with a document in text format that allows you to follow cross-references to other Web resources. By clicking on an embedded hyperlink, the user can choose her own path through the hypertext material.

implied Boolean operator   The characters + and -, which can be used to require or prohibit a word or phrase as part of a search expression. The + acts somewhat like AND, and the - acts as NOT would in a Boolean expression. For example, the Boolean expression rivers AND lakes NOT swamps may be expressed as +rivers +lakes -swamps.

interest group   Group discussion and sharing of information about a single topic carried out via email.

Internet   The collection of networks throughout the world that agree to communicate using specific telecommunication protocols, the most basic being Internet Protocol (IP) and Transmission Control Protocol (TCP), and the services supplied by those networks.

Internet domain name   The Internet name for a network or computer system. The name consists of a sequence of characters separated by periods, such as www.mwc.edu. The domain name is

often the first part of the URL that follows ://. For example, the domain name in the URL http://
www.ckp.edu/technical/reference/swftp.html is www.ckp.edu.

invisible Web Information that is not accessible via search engines. Also referred to as the hidden
Internet.

IP (Internet Protocol) The basic protocol used for the Internet. Information is put into a single
packet, containing the addresses of the sender and the recipient, and then sent out. The receiving
system removes the information from the packet.

IP address An Internet address in numeric form. It consists of four numerals, each in the range of
0 through 255, separated by periods. An example is 192.65.245.76. Each computer connected to
the Internet has an IP address assigned to it. The IP address is sometimes used for authentication.

ISP (Internet service provider) A usually commercial service that provides access to the Internet.
Fees often depend on the amount of time and the maximum possible speed, in bits per second,
of access to the Internet.

JavaScript A programming language used exclusively within Web pages. The statements in the
language are made part of a source file to enable some interactive features such as mouse clicks
and input to forms. JavaScript is not based on or part of Java.

keyword A descriptive or significant word in a Web document.

keyword searching A feature in which the search engine or computer program searches for every
occurrence of a particular word in the database, regardless of where it may appear.

LCSH (Library of Congress subject headings) A list of standardized subject headings that
are used to index materials by the Library of Congress. The subject headings are arranged in
alphabetical order by the broadest headings, with more precise headings listed under them. Most
academic library catalogs are searchable by subject heading as well as by keyword.

library catalog A searchable database of a library's holdings.

limiting by date A search tool feature that allows you to limit search results to pages that were
indexed after, before, or between certain dates.

link *See* hyperlink.

location field The pane on the browser window that holds the current document's URL.

low precision/high recall A phenomenon that occurs during a search when you retrieve a large
set of results, including many unwanted documents.

lurking Reading the email or articles in a discussion group, blog, or other collaborative Web site
without contributing or posting messages.

mailing list *See* discussion group.

mashup A Web page or application that combines information from two or more sources. A
mashup combines one set of data with other data to make the original data more meaningful.

menu bar The sequence of pulldown menus across the top of the Web browser window. All
browser commands are embedded in the menu bar.

meta-search tool A tool that allows you to search either more than one search engine or directory simultaneously or a list of search tools that can be accessed from that site. These two major types of meta-search tools are called parallel search tools and all-in-one search tools.

meta-tag A keyword inserted in the meta-tag portion of the HTML source document by the Web page author. If Web pages don't have much text, meta-tags help them come up in a keyword search.

metadata Secondary information that describes an item.

microblog A site that creates a network of users who write short updates (usually around 140 characters) on just about anything they want to write about. The most popular microblogging service is Twitter.

modifying search results Changing an initial search expression to obtain more relevant results. This can involve narrowing the results by field, limiting by date, adding keywords, subtracting keywords, and so forth.

natural language searching The capability of entering a search expression in the form of a question or statement.

navigation toolbar Often referred to as the command toolbar, this toolbar contains a sequence of icons or items that represent frequently used commands for navigation and other purposes, such as printing the current Web page.

nested Boolean logic The use of parentheses in Boolean search expressions. For example, the nested expression ((rivers OR lakes) AND canoeing) NOT camping will first find resources that contain either the words rivers or lakes and the term canoeing, but not resources that contain the term camping.

OPAC (Online Public Access Catalog) An electronic catalog of a library's holdings, usually searchable by author, title, subject, keyword, and call number. Thousands of OPACs from libraries all over the world are available on the World Wide Web.

open access Information that is freely available on the Internet without financial, legal, or technical barriers.

parallel search tool A search tool or service that takes one search expression, submits it to several search services, and returns selected results from each. This is an example of a meta-search tool.

phrase searching A search feature supported by most search engines that allows you to search for words that usually appear next to each other. It is possibly the most important search feature.

plug-in An application software that's used along with a Web browser to view or display certain types of files as part of a Web page. Shockwave from Macromedia is a plug-in that allows the browser to display interactive multimedia.

podcast Formed from the name of Apple's portable digital player, the iPod, and the word "broadcast," the term podcast refers to a digital recording that can be downloaded to a computer or some other digital device.

proprietary database A privately owned database that isn't available to the public and that is usually password protected. Universities, businesses, and research institutes are the institutions most likely to subscribe to this kind of database and make it available to their employees and students.

protocol   A set of rules for exchanging information between networks or computer systems. The rules specify the format and the content of the information and the procedures to follow during the exchange.

proximity searching   A search feature that makes it possible to search for words that are near each other in a document.

public key encryption   An encryption method that involves the use of two codes or keys. The two keys, one called the private key and the other called the public key, are assigned to an individual. Using the public key anyone can encrypt a message or file that can only be decrypted or decoded by the use of the corresponding private key.

reference work   A resource used to quickly find answers to questions. Traditionally thought of as being in the form of books (such as dictionaries, encyclopedias, quotation directories, manuals, guides, atlases, bibliographies, and indexes), a reference source on the World Wide Web closely resembles its print counterpart. A reference work doesn't necessarily contain hyperlinks to other resources, although it will often have hyperlinks within the document itself.

relevance   A measure of how closely a database entry matches a search request. Most search tools on the Web return results based on relevance. The specific algorithm for computing relevance varies from one service to another, but it's often based on the number of times terms in the search expression appear in the document and whether they appear in the appropriate fields.

relevancy ranking   A ranking of items retrieved from a database. The ranking is based on the relevancy score that a search engine has assigned.

results per page   A feature of some search engines that allows you to designate the number of results listed per page. Search engines usually list 10 results per page.

robot   *See* spider.

router   A device (hardware) that transfers information between networks.

RSS Really simple syndication, RDF Site Summary, or Rich Site Summary   RSS is an XML, or Extensible Markup Language based format for distributing and aggregating Web content.

RSS newsreader   Software that allows you to receive, within one page, news and other sources in XML-based formats, using RSS technology.

scroll bar   The rectangular area on the right side of the window that allows you to move up or down in the open document. You move by clicking and dragging it or clicking on the arrows at the bottom and the top of the bar.

search engine   A collection of programs that gather information from the Web (see spider), index it, and put it in a database so it can be searched. The search engine takes the keywords or phrases you enter, searches the database for words that match the search expression, and returns them to you. The results are hyperlinks to sources that have descriptions, titles, or contents matching the search expression.

search expression   The keywords and syntax that you enter in a search form. With this expression, you ask a search tool to seek relevant documents in a particular way.

search form   The rectangular pane or oblong box that appears on the home pages of most search engines and directories. In this space, you enter a search expression.

search tool   *See* directory and search engine.

shareware   Software that you are allowed to download and try for a specified period free of charge. If you continue to use the program after that time, you are expected to pay a usually modest fee to continue using the product legally.

social bookmarking services   A method for people to store, organize, search and manage bookmarks of Web resources by using subject headings, or tags, to help manage them.

social networking   A popular way for people to build online communities to communicate and share information and interests.

spam   Unwanted and unsolicited email. The electronic equivalent of paper junk mail.

special library   A library that focuses on the interests inherent in the institution it serves. Libraries in hospitals, corporations, associations, museums, and other types of institutions are all special libraries. In many cases, they are not open to the public. A special library's collection may be narrow in scope, but it will have depth within the specialty it covers.

specialized database   A self-contained index that is searchable and available on the Web. Items in specialized databases are often not accessible through a keyword search in a search engine.

spider   A computer program that travels the Internet to locate such resources as Web documents, FTP archives, and Gopher documents. It indexes the documents in a database, which is then searched using a search engine (such as AltaVista or Excite). A spider can also be referred to as a robot or wanderer. Each search engine uses a spider to build its database.

status bar   The bar or rectangular region at the bottom of the browser window that displays information regarding the transfer of a Web document to the browser. When the mouse moves over a hyperlink, the status bar shows the hyperlink's URL. When a Web page is requested, the status bar gives information about contacting and receiving information from a server. During transmission, the status bar displays a percentage that reflects how much of the document has been transferred. The status bar also indicates whether transmissions are occurring in a secure manner.

stemming   *See* truncation.

stop word   A word that an indexing program doesn't index. Stop words usually include articles (a, an, and the) and other common words.

streaming media   The method of displaying or playing media such as sound or video as it is being transmitted across the Internet rather than retrieving the entire file before displaying it.

subcategory   A subject category that is more narrowly focused than the broader subject category above it in a hierarchy.

subject catalog   *See* directory.

subject category   A division in a hierarchical subject classification system in a Web directory. You click on the subject category that is likely to contain either the Web pages you want or other subject categories that are more specific.

subject guide   A collection of URLs on a particular topic. Most easily found listed in virtual libraries, they are also referred to as meta-pages.

synchronous communication   Communication where the participants participate at the same time. Chat is an example of synchronous communication.

syndication   Making information on a Web site available as an RSS feed so that it can be distributed easily to other sites, such as RSS newsreaders.

syntax   The rules governing the construction of search expressions in search engines and directories.

tag cloud   A visual depiction of user-generated tags.

TCP/IP (Transmission Control Protocol/Internet Protocol)   A collection of protocols used to provide the basis for Internet and World Wide Web services.

text file   A file containing characters in a plain human-readable format. There are no formatting commands such as underlining or displaying characters in boldface or different fonts. It is also called an ASCII file.

toolbar   The sequence of icons below the menu bar. Clicking on a toolbar icon executes a command or causes an action.

top-level category   One of several main subjects in the top of a hierarchy in a directory's list of subjects.

truncation   The phenomenon in which you cut off the end of a word when creating a search expression. When given such a request, a search engine will look for all possible endings to the word, in addition to the root word itself.

unified search interface   A meta-search tool that allow you to use several search engines simultaneously.

upload   Transfer a file from the computer system being used to a remote system.

URL (Uniform Resource Locator)   A way of describing the location of an item (document, service, or resource) on the Internet and specifying the means by which to access that item.

virtual community   A collection of individuals who form a bond through electronic communication.

virus   A program or executable code that must be part of another executing program. Usually viruses change the configuration or cause havoc with a computer system. The viruses are hidden within some useful or standard program.

Web browser   A program used to access the Internet services and resources available through the World Wide Web.

Web hosting service   A commercial service (in most cases) that provides a Web server to host a Web site. Fees often depend on the amount of disk space available, monthly traffic measured in bytes, and types of services that are provided.

Web page   The information available and displayed by a Web browser as the result of opening a local file or opening a location (URL). The contents and format of the Web page are specified using HTML.

Web server   A computer that is running the software and has the Internet connections so that it can satisfy HTTP requests from clients. In other words, it is a properly configured computer system that makes it possible to make Web pages available on the Internet.

white page service   A Web search service that helps locate email or street addresses for individuals. Similar services for businesses and government agencies are called yellow page services.

wiki   A page or a collection of Web pages designed to enable anyone who accesses it to contribute or modify content using a simplified markup language.

wildcard   A character that stands in for another character or group of characters. Most search tools use an asterisk for this function. Although the wildcard is most often used in truncation, it can also be used in the middle of words (for example, wom*n).

World Wide Web   The collection of different services and resources available on the Internet and accessible through a Web browser.

XML   Extensible Markup Language is a standard text format for structured documents and data on the Web. XML uses a tag system similar to HTML but where HTML's tags describe how content will be displayed, XML tags define the data in the tagged elements, making information sharing easier.

yellow page services   Web-based business address and telephone directories.

index